Walking the Talk

Building a Culture for Success

Carolyn Taylor

RANDOM HOUSE
BUSINESS BOOKS

Published by Random House Business Books in 2005

5 7 9 10 8 6

First published in the United Kingdom by
Random House Business Books in 2005

Random House Business Books
The Random House Group Limited
20 Vauxhall Bridge Road, London, SW1V 2SA

Random House Australia (Pty) Limited
20 Alfred Street, Milsons Point, Sydney,
New South Wales 2061, Australia

Random House New Zealand Limited
18 Poland Road, Glenfield
Auckland 10, New Zealand

Random House (Pty) Limited
Isle of Houghton, Corner of Boundary Road & Carse O'Gowrie,
Houghton 2198, South Africa

Random House Publishers India Private Limited
301 World Trade Tower, Hotel Intercontinental Grand Complex,
Barakhamba Lane, New Delhi 110 001, India

The Random House Group Limited Reg. No. 954009

www.randomhouse.co.uk

businessbooks@randomhouse.co.uk

A CIP catalogue record for this book is available from the British Library

Papers used by Random House are natural, recyclable products made from
wood grown in sustainable forests. The manufacturing processes conform to
the environmental regulations of the country of origin

ISBN 9781844138074 (from January 2007)
ISBN 1844138070

Typeset by SX Composing DTP, Rayleigh, Essex
Printed and bound in Great Britain by
Mackays of Chatham Plc, Chatham, Kent

*To Sam, Louise and Josie and the culture
we have built in our family*

Praise for *Walking the Talk*

'*Walking the Talk* is the first guide that translates the assertion to the actual, to take actual experience and distil the lessons, to take the opportunity for great leadership and give it form. It is a book for the time and gives a door through which all leaders need to step. I recommend it highly – it is readable, human, full of insight and distils Carolyn's wealth of experience and that of others who have worked with her'

Ann Sherry, CEO, Westpac New Zealand

'Culture is the very essence of good leadership in a modern corporation. Culture flows from the top down and from the bottom up. Culture is a circular, living, pulsing, unifying, rhythm within an organisation that ignites employee passion, enthusiasm, pride, dedication, commitment, engagement and a sense of belonging and worth – which results in extraordinary performance and achievement. Carolyn Taylor is a remarkable visionary who has, in this book, explained what culture really is, and what it can do, and the steps needed, to grow and foster it'

Jim Kennedy, non-Executive Director, Qantas

'In this distillation of twenty years of insight and wisdom, Carolyn Taylor shows practicing managers that they can achieve what many aspire to . . . to fundamentally change the culture of their organisation. The task is daunting, but through a wonderful mix of blueprints, analogies and business examples, Carolyn shows what is possible. Packed with energy, enthusiasm and a "can do" attitude, *Walking the Talk* transforms the dream of change into an every day reality. A must read for any manager embarking on the journey of cultural change'

Professor Lynda Gratton, London Business School,
(www.lyndagratton.com)

'Brilliant and very timely. A detailed and practical roadmap for developing sustainable work environments. Carolyn's extensive experience in cultural change makes her book a must read for all CEOs and aspiring leaders'

Daniel Petre, author of *What Matters – Success and Work/Life Balance* **and the bestselling *Father Time***

'I recently read Carolyn Taylor's book *Walking the Talk* and found myself feeling quite excited. The book is a must for all Human Resources executives involved in culture change (or wanting to learn about it) as well as senior line executives whose companies are embarking on culture change. I'd highly recommend the book for practitioners who are just starting out but equally for those with more experience. It's the definitive "how to"'

Rilla Moore, Executive General Manager, HR, Stockland

'An excellent resource for leaders, organisational members and consultants who want to challenge and develop their own understanding of this increasingly important organisational and societal phenomena. Carolyn Taylor's book *Walking the Talk* is a valuable contribution to one of the most critical yet difficult issues that confront all managers and leaders'

Roger Collins, Australian Graduate School of Management

'Having worked successfully on leadership development, top team building and culture change with Carolyn's support and witnessed first hand the depth and breadth of her knowledge of these topics I have no doubt this book will become the benchmark reference in the field'

Ray Greenshields, Managing Director, Barclays Wealth Solutions

'As a new CEO for a major public corporation I was faced with an organisation that had a culture where the workforce felt alienated after years of restructuring and downsizing. Carolyn Taylor offered practical methods and frameworks aimed at recapturing our staff's loyalty and commitment. She convinced the executive that people and culture must be addressed strategically and measured. Carolyn walks the talk and I am proud to say that at SA Water our leaders do too. People now comment on the positive feel they get when visiting our workplaces. I recommend this book to anyone seeking to crack the culture change dilemma'

Anne Howe, CEO, SA Water Corporation

'This book brings clarity to what for many organisations is a dilemma. How to understand culture and change it, to achieve sustainable improvement'

Ross Pinney, CEO, National Australia Group, Europe

'There are few ways to get practical advice on how to analyse and change organisational culture. Most information on the subject is interesting in theory however this book is based on experience and results, with a large dose of the reality. It provides a practical guide to one of the most elusive drivers of shareholder value and I have experienced the power of its process first hand'

David Willis, CEO, Halifax Bank of Scotland, Australia

'*Walking the Talk* provides valuable insights to directors and executives as to causes of poor performance they might not have considered, and how to address them'

Trelawny Williams, Director of Corporate Finance, Fidelity Investments, London

Contents

Acknowledgements

THIS book is the result of twenty years of work by teams in my organisation. We have developed our thinking on what drives culture and how to advise others to build the culture they want. When we started building our models, there was very little other work available in the business community. My colleagues and I spent many hours pooling the data we were collecting from our many clients, our observations of what makes some leaders able to build cultures that deliver the results they want and others to get no further than mouthing the words and building the slogans. From this we drew our conclusions about what it actually meant to walk the talk, and how long the leaders' shadow really is.

The extraordinary thing I have found about our people is how much they care about clients – the people who work in the organisations who employ our services. To be effective, we have to *believe* that cultures can change, and that leaders can make a difference. This faith in the better side of human nature made our consultants go beyond the call of duty in their efforts to find the lever which will enable each client to effect change. In the process, precious insights are gained which gradually form patterns and conclusions. My role in this book has been to crystallise those patterns and to draw them into a framework which will make sense of this most mysterious of management disciplines: managing and building culture. For all those long hours round our boardroom table, all of the insights, reports, workshops, coaching, I want to thank all of our teams, present and past.

I am grateful to Fred Kofman, Andy Freire and my partners in Axialent, the organisation I joined recently, for stretching my thinking again and helping me realise that finishing this book freed my mind to embrace a whole new set of knowledge. David Sherbon had faith in me when I was unknown in the market, and set up Corporate Vision with me at the very beginning. Thanks to Pete Mildenhall for the many years we had working together, for encouraging me to keep stretching and for his wonderful way of observing what makes people tick. Ashley Levinson for his wise business counsel over many years. I am indebted to Cathy Glass, Liana di Stefano, Liza Spence, Tanya Gebbie for your help in building the models used in this book. Amanda Rudd wrote the beautiful proposal for the publishers, and persuaded me it was time well spent to present the idea for the book in its best possible light. As the book was drawing to a close, she checked all of my references, and helped ensure we credited ideas from their correct source. My assistant Bronwyn Kyriazis was the first to read and correct the manuscript and to encourage me to build in more stories. Laura Barber created all of the diagrams. Rilla Moore read the book from the perspective of an HR professional, and Rosemary Kirkby gave me stories from one of the exciting pioneers of culture in Australia, Lend Lease. John Wright, recently retired CEO of Clydesdale and Yorkshire Banks, thank you for your unswerving support, both as a client and an advocate. Ann Sherry, CEO of Westpac in New Zealand, thank you for introducing me to the Random House team, and for your continual support and friendship. At Random House, thanks to Clare Smith, Tiffany Stansfield and Rina Gill in London, Margie Seale in Australia and Michael Moynahan in New Zealand.

I have always been a keen learner, particularly the kind of learning that is transformational in nature, and resulted in my changing my view of myself and the world, in a fashion that helped me shift gear in my life. Three people have been teachers of this kind for me – Walter Bellin, Robert Kiyosaki and my early spiritual teacher, Gururaj. Thank you.

A special thanks to Gordon Cairns, Bob Barbour and the team at Lion Nathan for allowing me to showcase their cultural achievements in Chapter 15, for giving their time to help pull that chapter together. Participating in their courageous and determined effort to turn their culture around has been a highlight of my career.

My most important acknowledgements go to the people who you will hear described in many guises throughout this book: The leaders of organisations in the United Kingdom, Australia, New Zealand, Asia and the US with whom I have had the privilege of working during my career. I have always considered it an act of great trust to allow me to work with you, with your teams, and in your organisations. It has always felt an honour to be invited in, and even more so to work with you as individual leaders, give you my trademark 'brutally frank' feedback, and offer advice as to how to change yourselves, influence your people and change your cultures. You have allowed me to place you in situations which I know you sometimes found uncomfortable, and participated in them because you had faith that I had the best interests of your organisations at heart, and would not let you down. Thank you for that. I have left you un-named in this book, for reasons I explain in the introduction, but I hope you enjoy playing the game of 'spot the leader'!

There is an element of faith required to be successful at using culture as a key plank of a business strategy, and I acknowledge those who have taken this most personal of strategies to achieve the performance their business demands. The rewards are considerable, the competitive advantage almost impossible to replicate, but undoubtedly it asks more of a leader than some of the more traditional paths. I acknowledge every leader who takes it on.

About Axialent

THE ideas and practices in this book now form part of the services offered by the consulting group Axialent. I joined Axialent because, more than any consulting company I had seen, they had the capability to facilitate executives changing their behaviour and 'walking their talk'. I've always felt this was the key, and it has been exciting to learn from my new partners new ways of achieving this goal.

At Axialent we offer:

- Leadership development for managers
- Training and advice on how to lead a culture change
- Coaching on walking the talk and leading through values
- Culture assessments to test the alignment of culture to strategy

Axialent has offices in the US, Latin America and Europe, and undertakes assignments all over the world.

For more information, please contact me at carolyn@axialent.com or visit our website www.axialent.com

Introduction

THE PROMISE OF THIS BOOK

THIS is a 'how-to' book. It will take you step-by-step from the decision to take on culture as a strategic imperative, to how the process should unfold over a three to five year period, and what should be included during each phase. It will show you how to tackle the most challenging aspects: How to change yourself and how to change other people. It puts meat around the bones of the phrase 'Walking the Talk' by actually showing you how this is done.

In doing so, it creates a blueprint. You can use this blueprint as a starting point for designing and managing your own unique path, with you in the driver's seat. You will no longer be in that awkward situation of knowing that culture is important, but not knowing how to manage it, so either bluffing your way through, or rejecting it as 'too soft and fluffy for us'.

Many of you will have already undertaken work on your culture. This book, which lays out the process in a sequential manner, will enable you to review what you have achieved, map out your next step, and identify factors along the way, which may be contributing to difficulties you are having achieving the traction you seek.

Recently, high profile successes and failures – GE and Enron are examples – have been attributed to culture. It has now been well documented that there is a strong relationship between culture and performance. The benefits of a great culture include being in a position to delight customers and staff, increase accountability, innovation, speed of response and rigour. A great culture will make extraordinary performers out of people previously tagged as mediocre.

All this translates to increased revenue or reduced cost if you are an organisation driven to financial performance. Or to improved performance and effectiveness if you are a government body or sports group. The high profile that culture now has in the press makes it challenging for any manager to admit to not knowing how to build the right culture. Yet it has only been on the management agenda since the mid-1990s.

My passion for this work goes beyond the immediate benefits it delivers to organisations and their stakeholders. I would be doing this just for the pleasure of the journey itself, and for the increased life satisfaction learning to walk the talk has delivered to me personally, and to those I have influenced.

The discipline of culture change has taken a long time to be taken seriously in the business community because those who love the opportunity to add value to people have not always been clear enough in proving the links to performance. In the last few years this imbalance has been addressed. Culture and HR are no longer activities that are performed on the sidelines. They are the way business is done. The business community has now woken up to the fact that culture matters, but many do not know exactly what has to be done to turn around an ailing culture, or to ensure that your culture enables, rather than restricts, your growth. This book is for people who have reached this point. It provides a practical guide to how to lead a cultural journey that delivers satisfactory outcomes. In my experience very few people actually know how to do this.

You can influence culture from many positions in an organisation. Some of you will be in the top job, ostensibly in the best position to lead culture, but not knowing how to be sure your message is getting down far and fast enough. Others will be in an HR role, expected, because of your people-orientation, to provide the tools to drive culture, but being aware that so many of them are outside of your control. Many will be leaders at every level of organisations, wanting to support your people by providing the best environment for them to succeed, and feeling frustrated by the broader culture around you, and how difficult it is to influence it. Some may be outside the operations of the organisation, a Board member, a supplier, a customer or an owner, concerned that the culture may be putting the organisation's performance at risk, but unsure of what questions will answer your concerns. And you may be a motivated employee observing how much opportunity is being missed by the way the organisation is managed. This book is for all of you.

Most literature available on culture is written from the perspective of the journey's end, looking backwards. An organisation has achieved great cultural outcomes, and those involved describe how they did it. From the end, looking back, it looks like a straight line. Let me assure you that from the beginning looking forward – a position I expect many of you are at now – it looks like a big fog, and the process is one of taking a step at a time, pausing to get your bearings, and launching forward again. In fact many leaders I know would confess that it looks like a big fog through a great deal of the process, and suggest that it is only when history is being written that the full picture becomes clear. Throughout the course of my career, I've sat beside leaders during their journey, and I know the range of experiences leaders have. Inevitably there is an element of trial and error. Not every step moves you in the right direction, but over a period of time you can look back and see that you have come a long way. This book will provide the whole range of steps you could take, a map of a typical journey, so that you are making choices from within a logical framework. Many of you will already be some way down a cultural path. You will be able to map the pieces of work you have completed against the framework in this book, and see opportunities where you can gain more traction.

The process has a logical sequence. Logical does not mean easy. It is straightforward in that there is method to it, a set of steps and a dozen or so levers that need to be pulled, consistently, over time.

I will lay these out to enable you to see a step-by-step route, leading to a pre-determined outcome. Of course it will not quite work out that way, because you will be dealing with people's emotions and this is never a linear process. However, having a handbook to refer to, will help you back on course at times when you feel you are swimming in treacle.

It's difficult because one of the levers to change culture is you yourself. Another is your senior management team. It is a process of walking the talk. Culture, as I will explain, is created and sustained by human beings – their values, needs, aspirations, fears and behaviours. Once you understand how these come together to create your culture, and what levers are available to you to build the culture you need, you will be in a stronger position to lead this process. And whilst it is easy to blame the senior management team for many things (this seems to apply whether or not you are a member of that team) it is a whole other ball game devising a strategy to change their behaviour. We'll come to that.

MY EXPERIENCE IN CULTURE

I have been working in this field for twenty years. The organisation I founded, Corporate Vision, and Axialent, the firm I joined recently, provide advice on how to change culture, and works alongside clients over a period of time to help them through the steps I will describe here. I have seen some spectacular culture changes, some complete non-events, and some sad declines. I have also led our organisation through many transitions.

When we started our company in the early-1980s, culture wasn't a term used in organisations at all. Hardly anybody had a set of values. We studied culture as a result of getting frustrated with the level of impact we were able to have with our clients. We did good team-building work, and leadership development work, but realised there was a force at work stronger than the team or individual leader. Culture.

People we knew in one organisation would move to another one and start behaving differently. Individuals whose values and natural style we had grown to know would display quite different characteristics in their new organisation. Powerful leaders able to make decisions which changed the course of their organisations seemed helpless in the face of culture.

From our broad experience, we developed our approach to culture, and spent the next fifteen years helping leaders build the culture they wanted. The more work we did, the clearer it became how culture impacts performance, and what a huge opportunity it presents to companies looking for another edge, a boost to their growth, a competitive advantage, a way of serving customers better.

If you are reading this book, you must have had these thoughts too. You know, almost instinctively, that culture is important. You can see how much your culture costs your organisation in terms of delays, frustrations, avoidance, risk and duplications. You know how stressful and debilitating it is for you personally, and you've seen good colleagues leave out of sheer frustration and despair.

HOW TO APPROACH THIS JOURNEY

There are a couple of ways of thinking which will really help you get going. They are by no means the whole leadership picture, but without them you will struggle.

The Balcony and the Dance: Observer and Participant

You are a member of your culture. You participate in it every day. Yet you also intend to influence it. To achieve this you must be able to both participate, and observe your own participation. Ronald Heifetz and Martin Linsky, in their book *Leadership On The Line* (Heifetz & Linsky, 2002), refer to this as being both on the balcony and on the dance floor. To move in the dance and to watch the dance from the balcony at the same time is a skill you will have to develop. Most of us play one role more easily than the other. To be an effective cultural leader you must do both.

When you observe cause and effect, and notice the patterns of behaviour that make up your culture, while simultaneously being immersed in it, you can experiment with introducing new influences and watching their impact. At the same time you are walking your talk. You are right there on the dance floor participating, and every step you take either supports or contradicts your words about culture.

The leadership responsibility

This is as much about you as an individual as it is about your organisation. If you intend to take any position of leadership on culture you will have to become a role model of what you are seeking to create. This will require change. The leadership characteristics which have propelled you to the current position in your career, or which worked for you in your last organisation, will almost certainly not be enough to lead this next journey. The willingness to learn is a crucial mind-set for culture.

> *For things to change first I must change*

You will need to take responsibility for others' responses to you, rather than blaming them for their lack of vision. The judges as to whether you are walking the talk will be other people.

Consider the balcony/dance floor analogy, and what it means to take personal responsibility, as you read this book. This analogy will help you personalise it, and that is essential for walking the talk.

SUMMARY

When you have read this book, you will:

- Know whether culture change is really a path you and your organisation should be moving down
- Understand the choices you must make to focus your efforts
- Dispel the myths about culture, and learn straightforward techniques to use in their place
- Know the sequence of steps you need to take, how long it will

take, the type of investment and return you can expect
- Know what your leadership role looks like, and what it means to walk the talk

OK, let's go.

Section 1

PREPARING FOR THE JOURNEY

THE first section of this book provides you with the tools you need to build the framework for your cultural process. It covers what you need to do, and know, in order to ensure that you are well prepared, well trained, and well equipped. It is my hope that this section will ensure that you do not run off down the culture path and then lose interest part way through. Many organisations have had this occur, and it makes it much more difficult for those who follow to pick up the pieces again, because employees are, quite naturally, somewhat cynical.

The culture journey is a long one, it requires considerable investment of both time and emotional energy, and is not something to be undertaken in a hurry as a knee jerk response to remarks from analysts or the media.

You need a common understanding of what culture really is, how it works, and what creates, sustains and changes it. You need a conceptual framework which links culture to the other drivers of your business – vision, values, behaviours, strategy, and performance.

You need an understanding of the process itself, how long it is likely to take to deliver results, what level of investment will be required and what will be required of you personally.

You need a detailed description of what your end-goal looks like. What kind of culture do you want, and how does this link to your business strategy? What is the business case for undertaking this work?

You need an objective analysis of the current state of play. What is your culture like now, and what impact is it having on your business performance? Why is it the way it is? What is driving it to be that way? What would cause it to change?

Once you have all of this information, you need to know how to test the level of commitment from key players to this path. How much buy-in must you have before you start, and how can you tell when you have reached this level?

The first section of this book guides you through these preparatory stages. The middle section shows you how to build and implement a Culture Development Plan. The final section focuses on particular cultural circumstances and how to address them.

Demystifying Culture

WHAT IS CULTURE?

ULTURE is what is created from the messages that are received about how people are expected to behave. Cultures develop in any community of people who spend time together and who are bound together through shared goals, beliefs, routines, needs or values. Cultures exist in nations, corporations, sporting clubs, schools, families, religious communities, professions and social groups.

Humans are tribal animals; we are hard-wired to fit in with our tribe. We read the signals about what it takes to fit in, and we adapt our behaviour accordingly. This is a survival strategy. If we cannot do this, we either leave the tribe, or the tribe ejects us. As we adapt to fit in with our new tribe, we in turn reinforce these tribal norms, or accepted behaviours, and thus reinforce the culture.

The process is supported by peer pressure. Existing tribe members work together to ensure that the new member does not rock the boat, and thus expose weaknesses in individual members.

Behavioural norms evolve over long periods of time, and are influenced by many factors including the values or beliefs which brought the community together in the first place; the nature of the activity carried out by the group; past and present leaders and heroes; historical events, successes and traumas; physical and geographical conditions; the demands and behaviour of external parties – customers, owners, enemies; and many others.

5

I have observed cultures which lift people to operate at the highest level of their intellectual and emotional potential, where the group really does exceed the sum of its parts and individuals seem to become 'better people'; contributing more, whilst simultaneously supporting the success of their colleagues. Such groups deliver extraordinary results from ordinary people. I have seen others which turn fairly normal and well-meaning individuals into selfish, political, backstabbing monsters.

Behavioural norms become subconscious, they remain long after their original purpose disappears, and eventually may not be particularly useful in relation to the goals the community is seeking to achieve. This is often the case in organisations. Because established behaviour influences the behaviour of new members, cultures perpetuate themselves. They require extraordinarily strong and focussed leadership and/or a co-ordinated effort from a group of influential members, to change quickly.

While behavioural norms may be subconscious amongst existing members, new members notice them most acutely, but, if they are to survive, quickly adapt to the prevailing culture. Where members may be aware of the cultural tendencies, they rarely understand enough about their source, nor have sufficient confidence, power and determination to cause change. Holding one's own behaviour on a course which is at odds with that of one's community requires great resilience and self-belief. In the scheme of things, in a work setting, and assuming the required behaviour does not go beyond a certain personal point of integrity, most people adapt to the norm. If you are used to a culture in which everyone speaks their mind in meetings, and you arrive in a new organisation where the norm is not to do so, over time you are likely to speak up less frequently. You get tired of being the only one to object. You find colleagues use you and your outspokenness to further their own ends. Your voice becomes less credible, and you build a reputation for negativity. At this point, most people adapt, or leave.

Cultures are maintained through the messages that are sent and received about what behaviour is expected. These come from many sources, and most of these are non-verbal. An early myth to dispel is that an organisation's culture has very much at all to do with the values statement, which appears in the Annual Report. Unless the organisation has worked very actively on living its values over a period of time, the statement will be one of intent. A very fine intent, and a good thing to have, but it almost certainly does not describe the culture as it is.

To get a sense of how messages are picked up, imagine a child born, let's say in Italy. By the time this child is five years old, he is unmistakably Italian in his gestures, his expectations, his expressions, how he treats others, how he treats food, what he thinks about his home, his possessions. How did that occur? Somehow, along the way, this child picked up signals about how to be, and these signals were different from those picked up by, for example, an English child. This process is beautifully described in a book called *An Italian Education* by Tim Parks, (Parks, 1995), written by an Englishman about watching his son, born in Italy to his Italian wife, evolving into an Italian.

So culture is about messages sent. These messages demonstrate what is valued, what is important, what people do around here to fit in, to be accepted, and to be rewarded.

They come from three broad areas:

- *Behaviours* – The behaviour of others, especially those who appear to be important
- *Symbols* – observable events, artefacts and decisions to which people attribute meaning
- *Systems* – mechanisms for managing people and tasks

Two things to remember from this:

- Culture is about *messages* – culture management is about message management. If you can find, and change, enough of the sources of these messages, you will change the culture
- Culture is about what is *really* valued – demonstrated through

what people do, rather than what they say. When the 'walk' and the 'talk' do not line up, it is the 'walk' that shapes the culture

HOW VALUES DRIVE CULTURE

Your cultural work will give you new insight into how organisations tick. Above all, it will teach you to see your world in terms of cause and effect. As a leader of a cultural journey, you will learn to operate on the balcony and the dance floor simultaneously, to observe what is happening and see both:

• The underlying value-set that is driving what is occurring
• How others are interpreting this action

To lead culture change you will need to know how values actually work. And how they play out through the behaviours, symbols and systems of your organisation.

What Are Values?

When you work with culture, you need to be very clear on what is meant by the word 'value' because you will be using it a lot. Logically, the word 'value' describes exactly what a value is. It is *what we value*. What is important to us? As a society, we value 'integrity' because we see that people who operate from a sense of integrity are likely to take actions which benefit the larger whole. On closer examination, these values contain an ingredient which puts the whole ahead of, or at least alongside, the good of the individual.

But here's the tricky bit. Through our behaviour we show that we actually place value on a different set of attributes. We say we value honesty, but we also value being liked, and through our behaviour we hold back from telling the truth if we feel it will make us unpopular – thus the verb 'value', which ultimately guides our actions, and has come to mean 'that which is important to us'. It encompasses a much wider set of attributes than those normally described as 'values'.

This is not an argument in semantics. It lies at the heart of the challenge leaders face in influencing culture. Culture is the manifestation of what is really valued. If an organisation values being nice to each other more than they value honesty, their culture will reflect this, and it will play out, for example, in the way performance reviews are conducted. We can sit here and argue that honesty is a higher order value than being nice, but this is just talk. The walk shows that being nice is more important.

Working with this dilemma for many years, I have found it most useful to use the word 'value' to embrace a broader set of attributes than would normally be the case. This line of thinking results in two types of 'values'. The first set will be familiar to you. They are characteristics that enrich and benefit the whole, and which most organisations would like to value.

Enriching Values
- Performance
- Customer focus
- Teamwork
- Integrity
- Honesty
- Meritocracy
- Discipline
- Safety
- Innovation
- Doing what we say we will
- Environmental awareness
- Developing our people
- Cost containment
- Growth
- Service
- Caring for others
- Relationships

- Risk management
- Pursuit of excellence
- Continuous improvement
- Fun
- Loyalty
- Balance

This list is inspiring in terms of its ambition. It describes our desire to set standards around what is and is not acceptable. It develops a framework for how we should behave. These values usually benefit others as well as us, and are thus **Enriching Values**.

To understand the whole picture, however, we have to create another list. Another set of things that we value, that are important to us. These are not talked about as values, and yet we do value them. I will call them **Selfish Values**.

Selfish Values
- Money
- Status
- Independence
- Staying out of trouble
- Avoiding conflict
- Power
- Winning over others
- Looking good
- Keeping everyone on side
- Popularity
- Control
- Being right

This second list of values are more self-serving than the first. They are a set of attributes that do not always play to the greater good. However, they play a large part in organisational life. If we observe the behaviour of others, we will see it being influenced by attributes from both lists. When others look at us, they see the same. When leaders are accused of not walking the talk, it is usually because their behaviour is driven more by the second set, the selfish values, than the first. Their behaviour is demonstrating that they actually value being popular, for example, more than being honest.

The first list benefits me, but also others. The second benefits me but potentially at the expense of others. Your organisation's desired values will undoubtedly be drawn from the first list. But to understand how your organisation ticks, you have to understand how both sets play out to create the culture that currently drives behaviour in your organisation. Many cultures demonstrate (through the 'walk') that the second list is more important than the first.

I struggle to decide on which list to place profit, and believe it can belong on either. Contributing to the good of the organisation as a whole, rather than simply one's own personal gain, is a values-based approach. However, for some organisations, profit has become the only real value, and can therefore be self-serving, especially for those who gain personally from its achievement. A question to consider is:

> *What would your organisation* not *be prepared to do in the name of profit?*

The answer will give you an insight into the role of values in your organisation. If profit is the only driver, an organisation becomes self-serving, to the detriment of its other stakeholders. As you work more with values, you will find they are not just a means to an end (i.e. to profit), but an end in themselves. If honesty and fairness to customers is truly at the top of your values hierarchy, you will act in this manner even if it costs you profit. Organisations who act in this way are seen as trustworthy, a precious commodity and one which will probably lead to profit, but it is not with this end in sight that a truly values-driven organisation acts honourably. They do it because it is the right thing to do.

The societies within which our organisations operate have tended, in recent years, to lean more strongly towards materialism and being 'me-centred'. This makes our work on culture more difficult, because employees come to our organisations influenced by the values of the broader society. The differences between these two sets of values are well explained by Tim Kasser in his book *The High Price of Materialism*, (Kasser, 2002).

Without good leadership, it seems that as communities, we drop too easily to the lowest common denominator, and put our own selfish needs ahead of the group's. There is a point when almost everyone does this. Not many of us would be willing to die to uphold our values, although many have over the years. But the speed with which this occurs is the determinant of the quality of a culture.

Individuals may say they hold certain values, but their behaviour shows otherwise.

David has spent a lifetime forging independence as one of his driving values. He works in the IT industry, and started out on the sales side, where independence was encouraged as long as you delivered the numbers. He likes to be in control, and this is best achieved by keeping separate. He displays this in his personal life as well as at work. He believes that his area is held back by the broader organisation, and he likes to keep them as separate as possible. He has been a strong performer but there is an organisational cost to the lack of collaboration between his area and the others. He says he believes in teamwork, but observation suggests that this really refers to the team of which he is the leader. The organisation has adopted teamwork as one of its values. David is on a knife-edge with regard to whether he is going to be able to make the change. Last time I saw him I sensed he had not yet realised how perilous his position was. He had succeeded despite his style, and his organisation is at a point where this is not enough. He will have to do a lot of work on his internal beliefs and values to reach a point where he is able to continue to engage across the organisation with his peers. He still fundamentally believes that working with others slows him down. Unless he changes some of his own internal values, when under pressure he will revert to his habit of independence.

The Values Hierarchy

An industrial organisation has both Safety and Performance as organisational values. Both are enriching values – one the concern for the individual employee, the other the return to shareholders. What decision will a plant manager make when an individual flags a safety concern to the production line, especially during a week when production volumes are already behind target? What level of risk is he prepared to bear on both fronts? How he makes the call will depend on how clear his organisation has been about how these two values are to be balanced, as well as his own personal value-set in these areas.

Situations like this are values dilemmas. They force us to balance one value with another, and make choices and decisions. We actually have to develop a hierarchy of values. They all matter to us, but when it comes down to it, some matter more than others.

A challenge that you will have in your culture work is discovering true values that organisations display, and individuals hold. Most people either do not know what their values are, or hold a view that is not played out through their day-to-day decisions and behaviour. Do you know somebody who says they value health, but practices unhealthy habits? Who says they value their family, but acts in ways that are detrimental to their well-being? Enough said.

Listen very carefully to what is actually valued in your company. This will usually be different from what it aspires to value. Later in the book I will show you how to adjust the hierarchy of values so that the ones you aspire to move higher up the ladder, displacing the less beneficial values.

I understood the values hierarchy in a personal sense some years ago thanks to an experience with my in-laws. My father-in-law had recently been diagnosed with cancer, and the whole family had come together at his house for Easter weekend. Whilst nobody said anything, we all knew it could be the last time we were all together. Les was going into hospital the following week, and the prognosis was not good. My in-laws are an extremely sports-oriented family. Sport is valued very highly. In my family this was not the case, and my values have been influenced by this. There was an important game on during the evening that we were all together. So, naturally enough (at least from their perspective) everyone sat and watched the game, plates on laps. At half-time, between analyses by the commentators, Les turned around, said in two minutes how much he loved and appreciated us all, and then the second half commenced and we all turned back to the screen.

Now, my values hierarchy says that watching sport on television is not the most important thing to be doing on such a significant evening. I would place talking to each other, around a dinner table, at the top. But for my in-laws, sport was the shared value, and it brought them together. Different hierarchy of values.

In passing I should say that when I tell this story, some people ask me which game it was. As if that mattered! So I guess my values hierarchy is way out of whack with many of my colleagues' and clients'!

How to Know What is Really Valued?
There is one quick way to see what is really valued:

- Look at how the organisation spends its time and its money
- Or, for an individual, the chequebook and the diary

All of us would agree that the values on the enriching list are indispensable. We believe they are important to the well-being of our customers, owners and ourselves. Whilst we may not acknowledge the entire second list, we would agree that some of them matter to us.

So what happens when a circumstance forces us to choose one

value over another? Find a solution that meets all the values, is the answer employees are usually given. I used to believe this was easy, but experience and observation has changed my mind. We all actually have a hierarchy of values, even if we do not like to admit it. And this hierarchy becomes transparent at times when we cannot fulfil them all.

The clearest occasions are those where we have a limited resource, and have to choose how to use it. Time and money are a finite resource. We spend them on what we believe is most important to us.

Have you made sacrifices to fund your children's education? Perhaps fewer holidays or a smaller house? In this instance you are demonstrating that you value education ahead of pleasure, your children ahead of yourself. Some of the bitterest arguments in a relationship can be about money because through spending money we reveal our values. If you and your partner have different values, you are likely to disagree about how to spend money. Talking about the values, rather than today's manifestation of them, can help build understanding between two people in a relationship.

Similarly time. Do you watch television, or turn it off to spend time talking to your family, or ringing up friends? A values-based decision.

The same applies in organisations. Nobody has enough time, and meetings tend to get squeezed. Which items get taken off the agenda? A values-based decision. What we value most will get airtime, what we value least gets bumped.

When costs are tight, what gets cut first? Values at play again.

Choices of this nature reveal that we all – as individuals and organisations – have a hierarchy of values. We will fulfil as many of these as we can at any one time, and when we have to make a choice, we do so based on our own hierarchy.

It is the precise nature of your own personal hierarchy that determines your unique stand in the world. It shapes who you are and how you operate. Similarly, it is the way the hierarchy plays out that makes each organisation unique. Although the proclaimed value statements of many organisations look similar, the balance and weight they place on each value, as well as on a larger number of un-stated values, creates the organisation's stand in the world.

This concept is not well understood. In not appreciating the impact of this hierarchy, many efforts to drive values through an organisation fail.

Imagine your organisation has three values:

- Break the mould
- Act with integrity
- Support one another

Each individual in the organisation filters these three through their own personal set of values, which is much longer and more complex than those three. As a result of this filter, two things occur:

1. They interpret the three organisational values in a particular way.

One person might interpret 'act with integrity' to mean that if an individual is not performing, it lacks integrity to leave them in the role. This person's view is that supporting people means supporting the broader team by not allowing a non-performer to stay in a role where he is letting others down. Another might say that the act of highest integrity is to provide that individual with lots of coaching and support, because integrity in their eyes is edged with another value of supporting individuals to succeed.

2. They judge others' interpretation of the values according to their own hierarchy.

Someone else is perceived to 'not support the values' because their response to a particular situation does not line up with their own. A different ranking of the three values will cause one person in this organisation to respond slightly differently to another.

When we come to discussing how to develop your organisation so that it aligns with its values, working with these hierarchies becomes very important.

You will find this concept of the hierarchy of values extremely useful as you lead your cultural change. Understanding and working with it provides the vehicle for teams to understand each other, and become less judgmental about one another's actions.

Your culture is the result of behavioural norms that establish what is acceptable. These norms reveal what is *actually* valued. A hierarchy of values in your organisation is picked up through the messages people receive. They receive these messages from behaviours, symbols and systems. They show what is really important; they are your 'walk'. Through their observations, people draw conclusions about what is valued. If these conclusions do not align with the stated values, leaders are accused, with some justification, of not walking the talk. You will now appreciate why taking the broadest interpretation of the word 'value' is important in managing a cultural journey.

YOUR CORE INSTINCT

Embedded deep in your values is the essence of your organisation. The choices you make over time combine to make up your individuality, or your core instinct. Sometimes I am even inclined to call this the organisation's soul. There will be one or two characteristics so fundamental that they form the basis of your organisation's personality.

We often uncover this during the course of our work with a client. When we present our findings, we can always tell if what we have found is a real core instinct, part of the organisation's DNA. In the room there is a collective sign of recognition as people hear played back to them something they knew instinctively, but may never have heard articulated. One core instinct we found was 'frugal' and 'dependable'. When we presented this to the IT team, they groaned. They knew it was so true. They had been hiring high-flying, innovative IT folk, and when they arrived they became incredibly frustrated. The insight made them realise they needed to find IT professionals who could do the job required, but whose style was a little more toned down. These people would be much more credible with their internal customers, and settle in better.

A core instinct will not change, regardless of how much cultural change work you do. You can change the CEO, the whole top team, the strategy, the remuneration policy and the brand positioning. Still the instinct stays embedded. If you can find what it is, you have a tremendous asset in your cultural change work. Because you can use this instinct to allow you to go with the flow, rather than push against it.

Recently I had lunch with the 80-year-old founder of an organisation who is now an icon. He told me of the early days of the organisation, when he and a few colleagues had been recent immigrants to a new country. When the organisation won its first contracts – it was in the construction industry – they brought entire villages of men, and later their wives and families, out to work for them. Even the priests came. Because these people were strangers in a new country, they formed very close bonds together. The company felt like a family because in many cases it was a family. It still feels that way today. The company has a core instinct of looking after each other that runs very deep. Sometimes this is useful, sometimes, when it prevents taking tough decisions, it is not. But their culture work is to use this instinct to their advantage, because it will never go away.

BEHAVIOURS, SYMBOLS AND SYSTEMS: YOUR VALUES IN ACTION

Your values underpin what happens in your organisation, but your people are probably not aware that this is occurring. It takes a certain skill and a disciplined way of looking at the world to see the values that underpin everyday actions. They play out through three channels: behaviours, symbols and systems. I'll give you some examples here, and we will go in to them in more depth when we start to develop your culture plan.

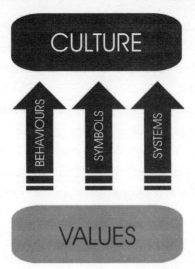

Behaviours

Everyone's behaviours reflect their values. If I value harmonious relationships then I will be polite, considerate and perhaps sometimes avoid telling others things that might cause friction in our relationship. The strength of my value of harmony will be tested when someone who is close to me really provokes me. If I value harmony very much indeed, I will resist the urge to get angry. If I only value harmony a little, I will blow my top when under extreme provocation.

If I really value customers, I will not sell them something that I do not ultimately believe they will benefit from. This value is always tested at times when there is pressure on sales targets; so many organisations have that 29th of the month feeling, when sales people are tempted to sell anything that will enable them to achieve the month's target.

During your culture change process you will need to work hard at changing behaviours, your own and those of others, and this will require some shifts in your value-set.

Leadership values and behaviours are your first priority, because until leaders are seen to be walking the talk, you will get limited traction on culture.

The behaviour of a senior leader has a two-fold impact. It

impacts the immediate surroundings. It also tells everyone that this is the behaviour of someone who has reached senior position in the organisation. Others then adopt a similar behaviour, and thus the culture is reinforced.

You must recognise the links between the behaviours of those in positions of influence, including yourself, and the culture these behaviours encourage. There are millions of behaviours displayed in any one day in an organisation. Here are some of the ones we have found have the most significant culture impact.

Behaviour in a leader	Culture it produces
Humility, being willing to admit mistakes	Openness, learning
Seeking out and listening to the views of the front line	Customer focus
Asking for and following up on commitments	Accountability
Saying no, and taking no for an answer	Discipline, control of risk
Accepting justifications for non-performance	Avoidance
Favouring one person over others for reasons not based on performance	Politics
Shooting the messenger	Cover-ups

You will also hear about behaviours that have been interpreted in a negative way, despite the individuals themselves feeling the intention was good. This is frustrating, but it is important to hear what is being said, and to accept that, in relation to culture, perception is everything.

The senior team of one of our clients was perceived to have been undisciplined and lacking in strategic focus ('blowing in the wind' was how it was described). This was because of an external appointment they had made. They had amended a structure to accommodate the seniority of the person involved. This was perceived by staff to have reversed a structure decision made a year previously regarding the strategic focus of the business. This behaviour had been interpreted as an example of a 'who you know' culture. This perception of the culture actually had some merit. However, in the discussions that formed part of their culture process, it emerged that their rationale for the appointment had been to strengthen their succession bench strength – a recent senior departure had left this very weak. But they had not communicated this, and cultural norms had led others to jump to conclusions.

We must understand different behaviours because theoretically they can be changed quite quickly. They do not require a two-year investment and a change process in the same way as would, perhaps, the development of an accurate, transparent mechanism for displaying performance data. However, changing human behaviour comes with a different set of challenges, to be covered during the course of this book.

Many are tempted to believe that culture is something that occurs separately from the mainstream of business activity. A crucial shift in thinking is that culture is formed and reformed by everything that is done in the business. Every behaviour and each decision sends a message, and that message is in turn interpreted by people in the organisation as a reflection of what is valued, which in turns moulds the behaviour and decisions of others. It really is about walking the talk.

Symbols
Symbols are events or decisions to which people attribute a meaning, which may well be beyond the scope of the original. A symbol is created when one event is seen to be an example of a larger pattern, and thus symbolic of that pattern. For example, the

size and location of offices has a symbolism which extends far beyond the total square metres they occupy. Who gets which office is interpreted as a sign of favouritism, or status, of the power hierarchy.

Symbols are important to understand, because the interpretation of events will usually follow a pre-existing perception of what is valued. As in the example of the external appointment creating a restructure, a decision will be seen through the filter of how the culture is viewed. They are used as a validation of perceptions of values – sometimes with validity, sometimes without.

Typical cultural symbols are situations where a choice has to be made – usually by leadership – and all potential values cannot be met. Thus the use of time and the allocation of resources become powerful symbolic acts. Physical space, offices, etc., become symbolic because choices are being made within an overall limited amount of space. Not everyone can have the corner office! The decision not to have an office at all displays another set of values.

Other powerful symbols are the rituals which have been built up over years. Many strong cultures understand the binding power of rituals and use them as an effective way of bringing a community together. Think of the rituals associated with most of the world's great religions. Rituals form an important part of building a new culture, and their existence in your culture today will tell you a great deal about the influences of the behaviour and sense of identity of the group. Many organisations in the last ten years, with the increasing rise of women in the management hierarchy, have had to examine rituals so habitual that men simply did not notice them. Working habits which are not child friendly, for example. To change a male-oriented culture required changes to these rituals.

Finally, symbols become accentuated through the telling of stories. Storytelling turns symbols into legends: the defining moments of your organisation's past, the great heroic events and the people caught up in them. The telling of the story becomes even more important than the event itself. The very best culture masters understand the power of storytelling and the symbolic acts.

They work because they are a manifestation of the value-sets that sit underneath the stories. How an individual or an organisation behaves at times of pressure demonstrates more fully than anything else where the values really lie. In our society fairytales are used to educate our children. In our religions, stories – parables, legends – describe the values in action. David McClelland, in his pursuit of the values that sat behind an achievement culture, studied the fairytales and children's stories of cultures and empires throughout the ages, and correlated these to times of economic growth (McClelland, 1961). His findings, outlined in his book *The Achieving Society*, are wonderful examples of how values and cultures create economic outcomes.

So, to understand the symbols of your organisation, you should look in the following areas:

- Where is time spent?
- Where is money spent?
- What gets priority in times of pressure?
- Who (individuals and groups) are favoured, and why?
- What are the themes of your rituals and legends?

Symbols become a key platform of your culture development process. They are the most difficult to plan for. Symbolic gestures spill outside from within a manager's values. They could be gestures of generosity, or of unconventionality, or of standing true to a belief under extreme pressure. Above all, they are the measure of how deeply held certain values are. For all of us, it is easy to uphold a value during times of peace. In times of strife the strength of our value-set is tested. Such times are the defining moments of an individual's and an organisation's life.

Every great company has such stories. They talk about them all the time and they become, in the telling, the most powerful booster of culture you can have.

Systems

The third source of messages is that of the systems that underpin your organisation. I am using the word systems in a broad sense, covering those mechanisms of management which control, plan, measure and reward your organisation and its people.

Systems are different from behaviours and symbols because they are the result of historical decisions that were made. Someone in your organisation's past made a series of decisions which designed your systems. Changing those decisions and designing new systems takes time. Systems tend to lag behind the changes to mind-sets and values.

Your leadership team may genuinely adopt a new set of values around the customer and how they are to be treated. You then realise that your entire technology systems are designed to collect information along product, rather than customer, lines. How can you truly understand and support a customer focus when you cannot even tell which products your customer uses, or view the customer's history with you? An employee in one area, or at one moment of time, cannot be equipped with the information about the customer which the customer, naturally, has in her own head. Implementing a Customer Relationship Management system to better understand the requirements of your customers, might take you two years, even if you put it at the top of your priority list. Meanwhile, the government of your country has introduced a new tax system which is going to involve another set of system changes, and this simply has to take priority or you will not be in business in a year's time. So the customer system gets pushed back a little further.

You inherit the systems of the past value-set of your organisation. They will influence both the behaviour and the mind-set of your people. The systems may well force your people to behave in certain ways, even if they, and you, know that these ways are not what you want in the future. This becomes a bigger problem the larger your organisation is, and the further away from the owners of the systems you are. If, for example, you are trying to change the culture in one country, in a global organisation, this will be a frustration. But you must understand how the system influences behaviour.

The system also influences the values, particularly if your people see you as still supporting it, and thus apparently endorsing the values the system encourages. Sometimes the systemic components can be used as a justification for cultures not changing. They are actually given more power than they deserve. An aligned value-set in relation to behaviours and symbols will do more to change culture than changing the remuneration policy. However, systems do form a part of the whole.

Many of your organisation's systems form part of the cultural tapestry and will come under review as you drive culture as an enabler of performance:

- The HR systems
- The planning system
- The measurement and reporting systems
- The communication systems
- Customer processes
- Feedback loops
- Structure

Companies usually have the systems you would expect, based on their past priorities and values. When they truly shift the way they think and therefore their values hierarchy, they can and do change their systems fairly quickly. If they have started believing new things to be important, however, but have not shifted at a fundamental level, then the investment in systems will not be made. For example, organisations with high avoidance cultures inevitably have poor management information. Why? Because it has not been important enough to them to really know how each individual is performing. If they knew, they would have to do something about it. Having the justification of poor information systems allows them to continue avoiding tough decisions about performance. A company we knew had a division that looked, from the outside, as if its economic drivers did not stack up. But it was the CEO's favourite. He had grown up in that division, and had something of a blind spot about it. At a subconscious level he did not want the data to prove that the division had to go. Conveniently, investing in the technology to give him that data never got to the top of the priority list, despite the pressure from other divisions seeking the funds to grow. It was not until the CEO retired and a new one was appointed that the required data was collected. As expected, it resulted in a radical restructure and a shift of strategy. But several years had been lost in the competitive environment. A typical example of the cost of a poor culture.

On other occasions the systems get ahead of the values. This typically occurs when an individual who has carriage of a particular system comes into the organisation and implements a leading edge upgrade based on his experience from a previous organisation. Such a move reveals a fascinating feature of a strong culture. The culture, and the individuals within it, will distort the new system to such an extent that it finally fits the cultural norms.

Let's take the example of a new performance management system we saw implemented in a bureaucratic and unaccountable culture. The process is designed, and the managers trained in how to use it. The new system of objective-setting generates more paperwork than the entire customer research department. Every employee gets around 35 objectives as managers attempt to follow the rules and measure everything that employee does. Rather than focus the employee's efforts this sends them into a complete spin. A mass of work is generated trying to work out how to measure all of these objectives. Finally a process is generated, but, after huge fanfare, it starts to die as the year progresses.

At the end of the year many managers continue to give all of their team threes and fours in their evaluation, on the basis that the measurements were not valid. And then to cap it off, the CEO decides to issue bonuses using his own system of evaluation, which bears no resemblance to what has been implemented during the year. And the top team do not receive a performance evaluation at all.

By year two things are getting back to normal, and by year three the HR director has left in disgust and the whole thing settles down. Until the new HR person arrives with another set of cutting edge ideas.

The Relationship between Behaviours, Symbols and Systems

None of these three can get very far ahead of the others before they are dragged back to the norm. Certain circumstances, in particular the arrival of new people with a passion for change, can cause one of the three to get ahead for a while. However, unless there is a comprehensive attack on the culture as a whole, the norm will gradually bring everything back to an equilibrium. This is an important fact to understand as you absorb what you are learning from your diagnostic stage, and plan your next steps.

In the end, it is the shift in the hierarchy of values amongst a critical mass of people in positions of influence and power that will achieve permanent change. The rest of this book is about how you achieve this shift, and then underpin it by changing enough of the sources of messages, simultaneously, to establish the realisation in the organisation that things have really changed. Once this occurs, the culture change process speeds up incredibly. For a while it feels as if you are pushing a huge rock up a steep slope. Suddenly, almost overnight, you reach the top and the rock starts to move very fast indeed. This usually occurs sometime in year two or three. So hang in there.

2

The Journey at a Glance

In broad terms, your culture journey will look like this.

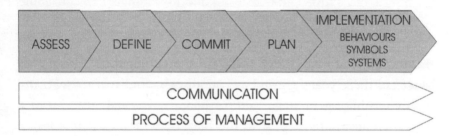

You first understand the culture you have, and its impact on your performance. Then you describe the culture you need, and the values which underpin it, and set goals for its achievement. You then build and implement a plan, based on behaviours, symbols and systems. Throughout, you must have a communication strategy, and ensure the process is managed with discipline and rigour. Each of these are described in detail in this book. This chapter gives you an overview of the process as a whole.

Plan for three years to make a serious, measurable, palpable shift in your culture. You will get movement in less time than this, but to start this process with less than a three year time-frame is to risk your investment. A cultural transformation in a large organisation will take longer than that.

This means three years from the time you make the decision to tackle culture in a conscious, funded and focussed fashion. You have already been on this path for some considerable time. Most organisations that make the conscious choice to invest in the culture option have made a series of decisions over previous years, which in themselves have moved the culture. In fact, to be in a position to make a conscious decision about culture you have to have moved some way down the path of self-awareness.

A client of ours came into his organisation as a CEO and immediately saw that there were a number of changes he wanted to make. His first three years as CEO was about making tough decisions. He cleared out a lot of dead wood. He sold off several businesses. He re-structured the company to give a greater line of sight with regard to accountability. He set some strong performance standards, and put in place a level of measurement transparency not previously apparent.

Three years later he turned his attention to culture. Do you think the culture we found in our diagnostic was the same one this CEO inherited three years previously? Absolutely not. Instinctively, and without thinking of it as culture change, he had introduced a culture of accountability, at least in the senior levels.

But now he wanted to achieve a lot more. He wanted to create a customer focus. He wanted to take his instinctive approach to accountability right through the organisation. He wanted to leave a cultural legacy that would live beyond him. We planned his three-year journey with him from the time he made that decision.

A typical journey
There isn't a cookie cutter formula for changing a culture. However, there are some elements which are essential for everyone. Think of these as phases, each will take a year or two, some organisations get through the first phase quickly and then take much longer on the rest. Or vice versa. It depends on the size of your company, the level of commitment, and the strength of your case for change. Chapter 15 describes a company which transformed their culture in a period of around six years. Whilst they are pretty exceptional now, they would be the first to say they have so much more to do. It is a never-ending journey. However, there are

some definite milestones which will let you know you are making good progress.

Phase One

Phase One is about creating momentum, and putting wedges in place which make it hard to go back.

You should gain insight as to who you are as an organisation and what makes you tick. Research into your current culture is required to do this. This involves data collection through a survey and some in-depth conversations with some of your people. It will give you both the benchmark for measuring improvement, and enough detail to enable you to understand the key drivers of your culture thus selecting the levers you will pull to change it.

Armed with the results of your research, you can then refine your picture of the kind of culture you want to create. There are several attractive options to consider, and you will move from nice words to a much more substantial description.

Building the plan is the big task for this phase. This includes the business case, the activities for the next two years, the process for managing the plan, measuring progress, accountabilities and cost. Your Culture Development Plan is the mechanism through which you will ensure you turn your vision into reality. It takes the 'fluff' out of culture and delivers the business benefits.

There is a large engagement process to be completed in this first phase. This process requires leadership. The more people understand what you intend to create, the harder it becomes to change your mind when other priorities crowd in. Your organisation needs to be engaged in both the results of the diagnostic and the intended end state. The Board and your senior team need to be engaged in the plan. All of this engagement has two purposes: to get people involved in what needs to be done, and to ensure there is enough support that the momentum will not be broken by unexpected changes in key leadership positions, or a short-term cash crisis.

By the end of Phase One you must have the following in place:

A clear picture of what you have and what you want

A funded plan for change over the next two years

A 'stake in the ground' communication to all staff

The top team feeling as if something has shifted in their approach to each other

Commitment by the Board, CEO and key executives to this three-year journey

Phase Two

Phase Two is about changing the way people think, feel and behave and putting in place the key enablers to lead the culture into the future. For some organisations, this year stretches to two or three, because of their size.

During this period your focus is introducing initiatives designed to help your people to rethink their beliefs and values so that they can change their behaviour in-line with the culture you have targeted. This is a major education programme, targeted initially for leaders, and cascaded through your organisation as you build confidence in your leadership capability.

Then bring in some new people, selected because they represent your cultural aspirations, and exit some who obviously don't fit.

You must work intensely with the senior teams. This really is the phase of walking the talk. You have to get visible change at this level, and until you are confident you have achieved this, hold back on further steps.

The work you have done to date gives your leaders confidence that they will be supported in taking more radical cultural steps themselves. As a result some will take decisions with positive cultural impact beyond anything you could have planned.

Phase Two requires the introduction of new rituals. Rituals influence behaviour without necessarily requiring everyone to be on board initially. Examples of organisational rituals include: new meeting disciplines, communication forums, shared techniques for learning and problem solving.

Functional teams who have responsibility for major organisational processes with a cultural impact – HR, finance, planning, risk and legal – should spend Phase Two using the feedback from the cultural diagnostic to redesign those processes so they reflect the desired culture.

By the end of Phase Two you should have the following in place:

Observed behaviour change in 80 per cent of your senior leaders and 40 per cent of your managers

The big ticket items associated with performance management designed and in place

An epidemic of local initiatives which go far beyond your original plan

New rituals in place which support new behaviours

Phase Three

This is the beginning of a much longer process to continually refine and lift the bar in relation to culture. Phase Three involves holding the line about the new expectations and using peer pressure to accelerate your transformation. By this stage you have given all of your people the opportunity to align to your cultural goal. You have articulated the behaviour required, you know how to measure it, you have provided support and education. Those who are capable of changing will be doing so. You now have to focus on those who are not going to make it from a cultural perspective. Some of these

may be performing in other areas. Their presence in the organisation holds back your culture, and if your business case stacks up,
their cost exceeds their contribution.

This process is a gradual one, and accompanies the implementation of new HR, finance, reporting, planning and risk management processes which support the culture you want.

Education, communication and rituals continue to evolve, and
will be introduced in Phase Three to new groups of employees, or
with refined emphasis.

There is a moment during this phase where the whole process
suddenly seems to get easier. It is as if you have been cycling up a
long hill, and you suddenly come round a corner and realise you
have reached the top and the road starts to wind downwards. You
pedal less, and yet momentum builds. The burden of building the
culture becomes spread across a much wider group. This tipping
point often happens quite quickly. Enough people have come on
board, and suddenly a whole lot more become engaged, and the
resistance decreases. As you feel this moment arrive, you can
capitalise on it. Accelerate the work. Make bold decisions. Use the
momentum to carry you forward.

By the end of Phase Three you must have the
following in place:

No one remaining in the organisation for more than six
months who does not fit the culture's new standards

Everyone articulating clearly what is so special about
this culture, and how what they and others do builds and
reinforces the culture

Evidence of a competitive advantage in both the
customer and employment market based on
your culture

THE INVESTMENT

The cost must be measured in both time and money.

Changing a culture requires mental energy and thinking time, it needs planning, but above all it needs time put aside when groups of people in the organisation can work through what the emerging values mean for them. Culture change is very much a team process. It requires people to change, and they do this best when they are in good company – the company of others who are going through the same process and aspiring to the same values. In the same way as going on a holiday enables us to look at our lives afresh, taking time out together allows us to examine and realign our values.

For an initiative that is going to have such an impact on your organisation, you should expect every employee to take two to three days out each year dedicated just to this, and for managers probably six to eight days per year.

Teams must also assume they will need time together focussed on how they behave, the messages they send with their behaviour. Say another two days a year.

Your regular meetings may also need a short agenda item specifically referencing your intended culture. Communication forums of all types will increase.

You will need some dedicated resource to manage your culture plan, and to ensure the process has the rigour required for such an important piece of work.

All in all, then, to be successful, culture would need to be amongst the top three or four key priorities for your organisation over the period of intense change. If it does not have this priority, then it will lose the war for time in your organisation, and this will probably cause its failure.

Finally the financial investment. It's hard to put a figure on this, but consider how much you spend each year on changing customer perceptions and behaviour through your marketing budget. Investing the same sum on achieving the same results with your employees would be a good yardstick. Many organisations spent more money changing lines of programming code in their computer systems last year than they would ever invest in changing the way their employees think and react. It is little wonder that few organisations have successfully achieved their cultural aspirations.

When pushed for a figure I offer US$1000 per employee per year. This will cover:

- Dedicated resources to plan and implement your Culture Development Plan
- External support to help with this process, the diagnostic and the mind-set changes required
- Changes to key cultural enablers (such as the performance management system)
- Communication processes

I will show you how this investment should be spent during the course of this book. It is important to give you a sense of the scale of the undertaking, and then to relate it to other activities. Do this little exercise to help firm up in your mind where your culture change project will stack up in relation to other major spends in your business:

Culture: No. of employees × $1000 × three years

IT projects over three years

Marketing spend, customer brand positioning

Process re-engineering projects

Cost of replacement of employees (search firms, training)

Of course you can go into the first phases of a culture change process without spending anything like this amount of money or time. It is perfectly valid to undertake a cultural diagnostic, do a business case of the potential benefits of change and decide not to proceed further. The issue is that most organisations do not necessarily follow such a logical path. A more common route is to start with all guns blazing, values statements communicated everywhere, and then either think the job is done, or get distracted by other priorities.

If you decide to take the process step-by-step, the important thing is to communicate it to those employees who are involved. In this way, you don't heighten expectations unrealistically, and have to deal with the subsequent disappointment and cynicism.

IS IT WORTH IT?

Some leaders come to their particular role – as CEO, as divisional or country manager, or as an HR manager – with an already formed conviction that they want to focus on culture. There seem to be many causes for such a conviction. If you see yourself in this category, see if you recognise one of these experiences in your past:

- You have already been through a cultural change process, and saw first hand sufficient benefits to convince you that this is an investment that will deliver ample returns to your new organisation
- You have experienced considerable frustration in executing your chosen strategy, and all the evidence you see leads you to conclude that the problem lies in the culture – your people are simply not behaving in a way that will enable this strategy to be successfully implemented
- You have experienced some of the costs of a poor culture – difficulty in attracting or keeping good people, a lack of speed relative to your competitors, and ability to respond well to change
- You have a deeply held belief in people, and in their almost infinite potential given the right set of circumstances and cultural environment

Other leaders are considering culture as one of a number of possible investments over the next few years. If you believe you fit into this category, perhaps:

- You have read of others undertaking a process of this kind, and believe it is important to evaluate its potential return to your own business
- You have adopted a new strategy, or undergone a significant change, and know that logically this is going to require some focus on culture. Examples would be a merger, a globalisation/ nationalisation process, a major re-engineering process, a change in distribution strategy
- You have others in your leadership team keen to take this path, and wish to gain more information to make an informed management decision as to whether to support their position

Most organisations I talk to describe its culture as one of the potential limiting factors to the implementation of its strategy. Very few describe the culture as a competitive advantage, or an enabler.

Some organisations do not tackle the challenge because their leaders describe culture as 'all that soft stuff'. This is simply a convenient way of deflecting the fact that they either do not understand what culture is, or are so scared of what it would require of them personally, that they are making sure their organisation does not get them anywhere near such a personally threatening situation.

If you work in an organisation with a leader who falls into this camp, read on, because often people are afraid of what they do not understand, and this book will give you the techniques to describe what needs to be done and the benefits in terms of real returns.

Putting these aside, we are left with a very large number of organisations who see their culture as an impediment, and a very few who see it as a competitive advantage. We put time and effort into the things we value highly. If we do not value something highly, we dedicate fewer of our resources to it, and it is less cared for, less functional. Compare what your organisation spends on culture to, say, technology, or even advertising. One would have to conclude that most organisations do not consider culture to be important. If culture is unsatisfactory, it is the result of many years of neglect.

There are not many people in the business world who have a real understanding of corporate culture, its impact on the business and how to change it. Most HR professionals have to be generalists, and do not have culture as a specialty. Some business leaders understand leadership and engagement, but do not, for the most part, understand the relationship between everything they do, every decision they make, and the company's culture. Experience in leading successful culture change is limited. Perhaps this is why really outstanding cultures are few and far between, despite the business benefits they can deliver.

To reverse this will require focussed investment over a period of time. How can you determine whether putting your attention on culture will deliver the return you expect? It is worth putting a lot of effort into resolving this question, and in order to answer it, you will probably have to take the steps outlined in the next two chapters.

You will be looking for evidence to know whether investment in culture is worth it for your organisation.

Are your competitors faster, more innovative, and leaner than you are?

Do good people leave, or choose not to join your company because it is a frustrating place to work?

Is there an opportunity to really differentiate your company in your industry on the quality of customer experience?

Do you waste time and money on starting too much, failing to complete successfully, or have to rework?

Are you confident your employees could not (and would not) act in a way that would destroy your organisation?

And the most important question of all:

Have those individuals in key leadership positions shown an openness to the possibility of learning and changing themselves?

Could they walk the talk?

(If you are one of these individuals, this means you!)

You don't need a large number of leaders like this when you start, but you need a few, and the belief that others can change.

The first chapters of this book will enable you to put a real business case together, understand the size of the opportunity, and the level of investment (financial, personal, effort, time) that will be required to get the return.

If you then make the decision that this is not the right move for you, you have made a smart business decision. You can consider yourself an organisation that has exercised prudent management practice in the examination of culture as a potential investment opportunity for a medium-term return.

You will no longer be in the camp of the ignorant, the mis-informed, the over-enthusiastic, the fad-follower, or the cynical. My first task is to put you in a position where you can make a rational decision about if, when and how you will change your culture.

If that decision is no, consider this book an excellent investment. You have just saved:

- Millions in investment in the superficial elements of culture
- Lots of embarrassment as you gradually back down from initial lofty statements
- Lots of time talking platitudes about culture to a bunch of people who cannot really say they are not interested because it is such a lofty topic
- Recruitment fees as people leave your company because the reality does not live up to the promise

Saying no is a good thing. It is actually one of the characteristics of many great cultures, so you took an important step in any event. Saying yes is good too, but only if you really mean it!

WHAT WILL IT FEEL LIKE?

Leaders who tackle culture seem to be motivated in two different ways. Rational and intuitive. Your business case will deal with the rational. For those who are more intuitive, here is what it feels like to take on this challenge.

Firstly it will be your most memorable leadership experience. Our memory is forged by experiences which contain emotion. This is certainly an emotional journey.

You need faith that this road will actually deliver returns. Despite many indications, it is hard to find absolute proof that better cultures consistently deliver better returns for shareholders. We all know, even if we don't admit it, it is possible to deliver returns to shareholders using a whole range of short-term devices. These are not necessarily delivered in the spirit of highest values. Not that they are out of integrity (well, with some exceptions), but they do not send messages to employees about behaviours which line up with values of teamwork, accountability, customer focus *et al*. In other cases favourable market conditions – a profitable industry, an advantageous government policy, deliver returns.

Culture is a strategy to produce both long and short-term returns, but it is certainly not the only strategy to produce short-term returns. Thus while we can demonstrate the business case for culture, we cannot confirm that those returns could not have been delivered through other means.

So, faith is required. And a sense of legacy – a desire to leave the company and its people a gift of being a great place to work, a great staff to lead and a great company to deal with. This legacy may or may not be recognised in your tenure.

Faith and a desire to leave a positive legacy are emotion-based motivations, which leave one feeling good inside. The legendary Australian cricketer Donald Bradman believed players should always remember that they are custodians of the game, and it is their job to leave the game in a better state than when they began. If you are motivated by these kinds of thoughts, you are well positioned to take up a role in leading culture.

Great Place to Work

Changing cultures is also a selfish act. It just makes life so much easier and more fun. A good culture removes many of the emotionally draining and stressful elements of work. I once read about a president of a country undergoing a *coup* describing the experience as pulling levers of power that were disconnected from the engine. Nothing responded. I have talked to many CEOs who have that feeling sitting at the top of their organisations. How to get traction? To make it happen and turn strategy into execution. Culture is a great tool for this. When your culture starts to hum you start to feel that you have your hand on a lever that connects.

Work has become the main outlet for our creativity, the place where we get to express ourselves and achieve great things. It's important that as leaders we provide the best possible outlet for this creativity. This motivated me to focus on culture change – the vision that work could become a place where people were uplifted.

The culture process provides many moments where you see this happening. That feels pretty special. It also ensures you become the best you can be, and that personal journey is evolutionary in its own right.

One of my favourite organisations is a manufacturing company where I feel the cultural buzz the moment I walk into the place. Every one of our team feels the same thing. My assistant, Christine, struck up a friendship with her counterpart in the Divisional Manager's office, and got an invitation to spend a day over there. Every little thing shouted out that this was a great place to work. Everyone treated her as an equal – there is no sense of hierarchy; in the factory everyone said hello as she walked past, small huddles of people pull chairs together to plan changes to the way they checked each other's safety procedures. Whilst I could give you lots of details, it was the atmosphere that stays with me. Christine told me that it had all changed over a period of about three years. For the first time, people at the front line were asked for their opinions, treated as equals and given the authority to fix the things that frustrated them. Over a period of time their confidence grew, and they started to believe in themselves.

I compare this to my daughter's first few weeks at her first big job as a management trainee at a large multinational. She went in full of enthusiasm, dedication and confidence. Receipt of her first report, meticulously written and full of ideas, was not even acknowledged by her boss. Her second was rubbished by her colleagues containing recommendations which would involve them having to change things, and that was too much trouble. By her third, her confidence and energy was waning. The culture was getting to her. As her mother, this was particularly troubling to witness. As a professional, I knew how much this culture was costing her employer.

Leading a culture change provides an extraordinary opportunity to grow yourself. You receive feedback about yourself, which you are asked to respond to. You look deep inside your own value system to see whether what you say you value is actually reflected in your decisions and behaviours. You attract people who challenge and stretch you. You learn to stand up for what you believe in, even when your colleagues, your Board and your owners do not yet share the same vision as you. And you pull on great inner strength to hold what Jim Collins and Jerry Porras in their book *Built to Last* called 'the genius of the *and*': transforming the culture *and* delivering short-term performance.

So the journey can feel lonely. It makes you the target of blame and resistance. You are challenging people at a very core level: A good culture change process will challenge people's sense of security and put them firmly outside their comfort zones. So you need to be sure you are up for this for at least a three year period.

Worse than not starting is to start and then lose interest. Aside from the wasted investment, the process awakens hope in your people. If you generate this feeling, and then do not follow through, you will leave many crushed dreams. Cynicism masks a fear of hope, and those who are let down tend to move into cynicism, not only now, but also the next time a leader comes along with promises of change. You may encounter some of this yourself if there has been a history of such start/stop activity in your organisation.

You will almost certainly have to make some tough calls on people who have been around for a long time. Not everyone will come with you, some will leave of their own accord, but some will need to be nudged, or even pushed. Are you up for that?

Whatever the business drivers of your organisation's decision to consider culture as a competitive advantage, if you are taking a leadership position in favour of this decision, you must be sure of your commitment. This is true whether you are the CEO, the Organisational Development Manager or a line manager intending to advocate change of this nature.

It is a decision only you can make, and it is not related to whether you feel you have the support of others. Externalising responsibility for your decision will lead to problems later on. This concerns your intuition and the extent to which you believe you have the passion for this task. Can you walk the talk?

3

Holding Up the Mirror

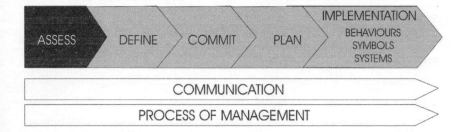

ASSESS DEFINE COMMIT PLAN IMPLEMENTATION BEHAVIOURS SYMBOLS SYSTEMS

COMMUNICATION

PROCESS OF MANAGEMENT

UNDERTAKING CULTURAL RESEARCH

A Culture Diagnostic is a special piece of research that reveals the current culture. This chapter will show you how to carry it out, and why it is important. It is really worthwhile investing in the research, even though you may be champing at the bit to get moving forward. You can use the list below as a basis for the objectives of your diagnostic, when you are briefing the team responsible for doing it.

You need an independent person or firm to undertake this research. All of your internal people are themselves part of the culture, and so are you. Even a new member of staff is not best placed to give feedback if they are to be effective in their future role. Politics is probably still alive and well in your organisation, and you want this person to succeed and help you further down the track – giving culture feedback can create some enemies. The messages from the research may be difficult for senior management to hear, and outsiders are the best people to deliver these.

There are three main reasons for doing your Culture Diagnostic:

1. To understand what messages your people believe they are receiving about how to behave.
2. To learn the sources of these messages – be they behavioural, symbolic or systemic – in as much detail as possible. This is essential if you are to build a targeted Cultural Development Plan later on
3. To provide a benchmark against which you can measure progress in a year or so

1. Understanding the messages

Understanding the messages people receive is important if you are to change them.

There is logic to how people behave in your organisation. They behave in the way they believe will enable them to fit in and succeed. You are the tribe to which they belong, and it is important for them to make sure they are accepted by their tribe.

Most of this is going on quite subconsciously, which is why the Culture Diagnostic is very important. In order to hear the messages your people are receiving, which will almost certainly not be the messages you think are being sent, you have to keep a very open mind.

It is much easier to assume that it is your people's 'fault' they are behaving the way they are, and this is the challenge associated with hearing this feedback. I often hear leaders talk about the lack of skill, the poor attitude and inappropriate behaviours in their organisation. And implicit is that 'they' have to change.

A fundamental principle of this book is that people behave the way they do primarily because of the influence of their environment. Change the environment and most people will change their behaviour (or leave the organisation). This position puts the responsibility in the hands of those who are sending the messages, and who have the power to change messages. You have to take responsibility for the current behaviour.

2. Pinpointing the sources of those messages

There are thousands of sources of messages in any organisation. Every behaviour, every decision and action sends some kind of message to others. However, there are always a number of sources that scream louder than the rest. Some of these can be anticipated in advance: Top team behaviour, remuneration policies, for example. Others are very organisation-specific.

Your Culture Development Plan, when you write it, will be targeting those message-sources which are the strongest, and which can therefore have the greatest impact if changed.

Pinpointing the sources also helps key influencers to understand their role in culture. It holds up a mirror and allows managers to see their actions and behaviours as others interpret them. So often, this interpretation is different from our intent.

3. Providing a benchmark

You must be able to measure the progress you are making. You will be making a considerable investment, and its return has to be measurable. Culture is such an emotional experience, that it is essential to be able to provide objective proof of the subjective feeling that things are getting better.

When you are in the process of change, it is quite difficult to remember what things were like before. Change can look like failure when you are in the middle of it. The culture journey tends to leave one with a sense that there is more to do. It is easy to forget how much has actually been achieved. Repeated measurement of change is a morale booster if progress is being made. And if the objective measure does not register change, it can be a useful jolt if a small group of individuals feel real progress has been made.

HOW TO DESIGN YOUR CULTURE DIAGNOSTIC

Qualitative and quantitative

Qualitative research solicits opinions from people through conversations with them, or in written form. Its findings are descriptive.

Quantitative research asks people to answer questions selecting from several possible responses (for example no, not sure, yes). Its findings are numeric. Your diagnostic must contain both qualitative and quantitative elements.

The quantitative element is required for benchmarking, and for establishing the differences between the cultural perceptions in different parts of your organisation.

The qualitative provides nuances which require interpretation, and detailed examples, which you will need to build your Culture Development Plan. Some organisations believe their quantitative tool will achieve this objective – we have never found one that gives enough detail to allow targeted interventions.

Quantitative Measurement

In evaluating quantitative tools, you understand the difference between culture and climate. Many organisations use a tool that is more a measure of climate than of culture, and therefore their solutions lack the rigour achieved when a real understanding of the culture is accomplished.

Climate describes how people are feeling, how satisfied they are, and to what extent they feel engaged with the organisation. There has been extensive research done on the relationship between employee satisfaction, customer satisfaction and profit. Thus measuring employee satisfaction and opinion is important, and a good measure of leadership competence. A survey that measures satisfaction will contain questions such as:

- Would you recommend this organisation as a good place to work?
- Are senior management doing a good job of setting a future direction?
- Do you have the resources you need to do your job?

Climate surveys are influenced by the mood of the organisation, affected by events such as rumours of a downsizing, or a cut in budget. Responses to specific questions in a climate survey can be shifted through specific interventions targeting that question. For example, a question about the extent to which people understand the vision of the organisation will improve through extensive vision communication exercises.

Culture questions centre on people's perceptions of what is valued around here and hence the messages they are receiving.

For example:

- To what extent are people expected to do what they say they will?
- Does the environment encourage people to support each other's success?
- Is it easy to keep your head down and stay out of trouble?

And thus go to the heart of the messages.

Culture surveys measure the net effect of a series of behaviours, symbols and systems observed by people in the organisation. Specific interventions will influence this net effect. A series of interventions will tip the balance towards the perception of a new message. Let's take an example:

- To what extent are people expected to play politics to gain influence?

This question would be a crucial one to shift if you are to create a culture of transparency and meritocracy. What would you need to do to improve your score on this question? Let us imagine the following things happened within a six-month timeframe:

- There is an individual known for their tendency to 'suck up' to the managing director in large forums by saying all the things known by everyone to be what the MD loves. The MD visibly changes his response to this person, and tests whether their words are actually followed through with actions and results

- A quiet achiever, never prone to playing the political game, is promoted into a key role
- In a number of teams, performance data of each individual against plan is published and discussed, and justifications and sweet talk, previously accepted, are firmly rejected by the leaders of those teams
- The practice of 'having a meeting before the meeting' to get caucus support, is reduced, and disagreement occurs publicly, and is resolved in a vigorous, but constructive manner

Four changes to messages. A mix of behaviours, symbols and systems. These would change the 'play politics to gain influence' question, and would serve to take an important step to changing the culture.

In contrast, a climate survey might include a question such as:

- Do you believe promotions in this organisation are fair?

This question goes to a particular piece of the 'political' message, but will not capture the range of informal mechanisms that support the political agenda. If the organisation has put a lot of effort into changing its promotion process, the climate question will be able to measure whether this effort has been successful, but this is not enough for your purpose.

We are often asked whether there is a link between the results of climate and culture surveys. There is, but it is not always direct. Climate survey results can improve if specific issues targeted in its questions are addressed. But the culture survey may not yet show change, because many of the informal (behaviours, symbols) areas are counter-balancing the good work achieved by the specifics. Often an improvement in climate is a predictor of future improvements in culture, but only if the broader cultural issues are being addressed.

On the other hand a climate survey may show dissatisfaction because people are resisting change, and yet this change is part of the process of shifting some fundamental values that will change the culture. As the culture starts to change, some of your people will be unhappy. But these may well be the ones you want to be unhappy: the ones holding on to the old set of values and resisting the change.

The culture you aspire to will not always contain satisfied people. Studies have shown that a constructive culture is a much more satisfying place to work, but this does not mean that people are happy all of the time. A specific event can cause blips in a climate survey.

As a general rule, if your culture survey is improving, your climate survey will probably also be improving. However, the reverse is not always true.

Selecting your survey

Most organisations use a proprietary survey for measuring culture. Proprietary surveys have three advantages:

1. They are backed by the research and validation required to be sure that the questions asked really do elicit responses that can be used to describe your culture
2. They provide an external benchmark against which you can compare your results
3. They enable you to describe the nuances of your desired culture as you measure the existing position

When examining the benchmarks used, consider what you are trying to achieve and how your organisation thinks. Some organisations believe it is important to compare themselves to their competitors, others are more concerned with setting their own path and measuring themselves against it.

When choosing the tool for use as both a measure of existing culture and of desired culture, make sure it has the flexibility to allow you to design a future that is uniquely you. Some tools point all users to the same desired future, which does not give you the opportunity to define that special 'wow' factor!

Setting up the Quantitative Survey

There is a tendency when undertaking a survey to set up the demographics so that they can be cut every which way: gender differences, age differences, length of service, levels, divisions, etc. Sometimes with culture surveys too many splits are not as valuable as they might first appear.

To determine the splits you need, consider what information the data will provide for you, and how it will be combined with the qualitative results. In most organisations the essential pieces of culture are experienced by everyone within the community, regardless of division, level or gender. What differs is the strength of what is experienced and the balance between one message and another.

The sources of messages cast long shadows and individual parts of the organisation will not be shielded from this shadow. For example, the budgeting process will touch everyone in some way. The technology systems also. The accessibility and visibility of senior leaders may touch everyone, or may be experienced differently in different parts, depending on the size of your organisation, the way it is structured (degree of autonomy of business units) and the style of leaders.

So your demographics can identify difference, but in planning your approach, try to keep the main focus on the whole, rather than the parts. To really shift a culture, you have to affect the whole eventually. (See Chapter 12 for more information on this topic.) The most useful demographics are the division splits and the splits by level.

The divisional splits will identify best practice in your organisation. They will enable you to follow up to see how one division has created cultural magic within a whole that has not. This observation of best practice is a valuable input to your culture plan.

The splits by employment level provide key information on how culture plays out in your organisation. Sometimes the front line has a better experience of culture than senior management. Other times it is the reverse. Some organisations have a dip in the middle. The splits by level will be very important to your design of the plan. They are also crucial when you re-measure, because they show you how the changes to culture are flowing through your organisation.

It is best not to split the organisation into too many levels, or your analysis of the results will get lost in detail. Culture change is an experience for a whole community, and it is in these larger groupings that you can really measure change. Get too lost in detail and your results will be influenced by idiosyncrasies that, whilst interesting, can actually distract you from the main game.

Our recommendation for most organisations is four levels:

- Senior management (the top team and their direct reports)
- Middle management
- Front line supervisors/management
- Front line

A large organisation might insert a fifth level in the middle somewhere.

Determining who to send your survey to
If you keep your demographics fairly broad, technically you do not need to survey everyone. You can get a valid response surveying 25 per cent of the front line, and perhaps 50 per cent of the management levels. It is always advisable to survey all of senior management, because you need their engagement very early if you are going to get traction on your plan.

The senior management results will give you vital information about where your cultural challenges are going to lie. If the senior management result is bad, you have a particular set of challenges we will cover later. It is important to avoid senior managers disassociating from this result, saying that they did not get to participate and therefore they cannot trust the data. (Yes, I know this may sound unbelievable to some of you, but I assure you I have heard this response a number of times!) You will have enough to deal with without this one, and it is easily fixed by having all senior management participate.

There are good arguments to support surveying 100 per cent of every level for the same reasons, especially if the overall cost of the diagnostic is not heavily weighted towards a cost per survey respondent. (Which it shouldn't be, since this is not where the bulk of the value lies.)

You might consider doing the cultural diagnostic in a layered fashion. By this I mean tackling the senior and middle management population first, and either leaving the front line till later, or doing a very small sample for both interviews and surveys.

I suggest this because once individuals are involved they do expect a quick response. There will be some significant work to be done to make changes in senior management behaviour and any glaring sources of misaligned messages. One very valid approach to culture change is to tackle these first and get some wins on the board before expectations within the organisation become too high.

On the other hand, front line people are the ultimate recipients of culture and they are the interface between your culture and your customer. They will have the clearest experience of how your culture impacts the customer.

An influence on your decision will be the extent to which, in your judgment, you will be able to get traction on your culture agenda quickly. Another will be the level of cynicism in the front line to this kind of initiative, which could have been caused by previous aborted efforts.

If you are expecting strong resistance to even getting behind a proper culture change process, especially if this expectation is based on past failed attempts, you might be better taking the softly softly approach. If, however, you already have some momentum, you are confident you will be able to come back to your whole workforce with the results of the diagnostic and a credible commitment to action, you can then involve everyone. You get a clear picture of the whole culture dynamic, and involve people who later become your greatest supporters.

Qualitative Research

Qualitative research elicits the opinions of people through talking to them, individually or in groups. The purpose of your qualitative component is two-fold:

1. To understand the subtleties of your culture – the unique pieces that make your organisation what it is. No matter how good your quantitative work is, it will be based on some form of generic survey, and may not identify unique characteristics, e.g., a top line culture and a cost culture; different ways of being people orientated; winning together versus winning alone. These distinctions become crucial when you come to design your culture plans

2. To understand what underpins and sustains your culture – the behaviours, symbols and systems from which your people pick up messages about what is *really* valued in the workplace. You need specifics in order to achieve change later. Your team will be very frustrated if your diagnostic comes back and says that your culture encourages the avoidance of accountability, but cannot give specific examples about why this is, and therefore what needs to occur to stimulate change

We have found that one-on-one interviews are the best way to conduct the qualitative component. We have experimented many times with focus groups, in an attempt to involve more people at a lower cost, but have found that on this particular topic, focus groups become 'group think'. The data received from them is far less than the sum of the data received from interviewing the same people individually and is often influenced by the most vocal negative voice, especially when the overall culture is quite dysfunctional.

Selecting the people to participate in the qualitative research
For this piece of work, you need to select people with a very specific set of characteristics. Unlike other polls, you are not looking for a representative sample of views. Your quantitative data will provide you with this. Here are the criteria for selection:

1. An ability to observe the culture at work. You need to speak to people who can be both in the culture and simultaneously see it working. This requires good observation, the ability to see patterns and to link cause and effect

2. A reasonably healthy attitude to life. People who are completely negative will not be able to make observations. This certainly does not mean you need people who are rosy-eyed about the culture. But someone with an axe to grind is probably not the best selection

3. A position or a history in the organisation, which gives a breadth of view. People in interface roles are good; the PAs to key leaders have a great perspective

4. People new to the organisation are invaluable for two reasons. Firstly they have worked in other places, and therefore have the ability to compare and contrast. And secondly new people sit outside of the cultural dynamic – this usually lasts for about three months

5. Some old-timers. They give a great perspective on how the culture developed. They can track through the historical events, the people and legends that have influenced the current position

6. People who know how the key systemic cultural drivers (finance, HR, risk/compliance and technology) are meant to work. Then ask similar questions of the people on the receiving end of these processes

7. A mix of levels and divisions. If you want to highlight the differences between divisions you will need to take a sample from each

Finally, consider interviewing customers and suppliers. Customers' experience is the ultimate result of your culture. They will also be able to compare their experience of you with that of other organisations with whom they do business, including those in different industries.

Suppliers offer the same service to a range of organisations and can therefore provide you with some very useful comparative information. Suppliers often get the rough end of the culture deal – they are frequently undervalued as a key part of the mix.

How many people do you need to talk to?
These days we interview fewer people than we used to when we first started doing this work. We have always been amazed how much commonality comes through in the interviews. By the time you have done 20 you usually have 90 per cent of the picture. But include more than this to cover the times when there are very different cultures running in different parts of the business. When one considers that culture is actually about the behavioural norms of the tribe, it should not be surprising that there is a significant amount of commonality. However, it is always extraordinary for us to watch the diagnostic process unfold.

Conduct between 30 and 60 interviews. Go back to some interviewees and ask them more specifics about certain themes that are emerging, or perhaps ask these questions of a new group.

Structuring the questions
We call this process Message Mapping. As its name suggests, the questions probe the areas that reveal what people believe is actually valued in their organisation. You are looking in the areas of behaviours, symbols and systems. Examples would include:

- Performance management systems in practice
- Priorities for spending money and what gets cut when things are tough
- What gets most airtime in meetings
- How leaders spend their time
- Recent promotions and exits and what they symbolise
- Senior management behaviour – examples of the best and worst
- Who has the power in the organisation and why
- Myths and legends – the stories of excellence, of trouble, and what they symbolise

Don't focus too much on the written documents. It's how the interviewees view these that matter.

Making the performance links
Ask interviewees for examples of how the cultural traits they are describing link to performance. They will have no difficulty in giving the interviewer examples. Areas to look for are:

Accountability	and the cost of avoidance
Rigour and learning	and the cost of arrogance or superficiality
Speed and nimbleness	and the cost of bureaucracy and delay
Attractiveness to customers and employees	and the cost of losing them
Simplicity	and the cost of complexity and duplication
Discipline	and the cost of poor governance

Drawing conclusions
When we analyse interview findings we follow this process:

1. Listening to what was actually said
2. Looking for the underlying values behind what was said
3. Comparing the findings from the interviews with the survey results
4. Finding common themes
5. Tracing these themes to see how they are linked, looking for root-cause
6. Finding the elements that will probably never change and need to be used constructively
7. Finding the more superficial habits which can probably be changed
8. Identifying the differences between areas and levels, and confirming whether these are of degree or of values differences

9. Building a picture of the behaviours, symbols and systems which sustain these values
10. Finding examples of performance impact and hypothesising on the broader cost of culture

REPEATING YOUR CULTURE DIAGNOSTIC

Quantitative data on culture is best collected once a year. A year is long enough to see change, but not so long that people don't feel the urgency to deliver an improved result. On the repeat occasions, your qualitative analysis can specifically test whether the initiatives you have undertaken have contributed to changed messages about what behaviour is expected.

How you will use the methodology of your Culture Diagnostic to measure change over time is covered in Chapter 11, which discusses the management disciplines required to sit behind your culture journey.

SUMMARY

The Culture Diagnostic gives you an insight into your organisation that you did not have before. It becomes the first part of the education process for your leaders. To interpret the information well, you need to understand the elements that make up a culture. In coming to terms with this, leaders have to take personal responsibility for the culture. Through their behaviours and decisions, they are supporting a map of messages about what is valued. Whilst many of your leaders may not have been around as the culture was being created, today they are sending messages which demonstrate that they tolerate the way it is.

The diagnostic report may be the first time leaders have been given research-based information which can provide them with the catalyst to change, and suggest how this might be achieved. It is worth doing well, because you will refer to it often over the coming year or two.

4

Defining the Culture You Want

You can define the culture you want before or after you do a Culture Diagnostic. You can also, of course, describe it beforehand, and then refine it later.

Some of you will already have a view as to the culture you want, even if this is not fully syndicated amongst your colleagues. Your task now is to refine, engage and build on the vision already formed in your mind.

Those who start this journey already convinced of its value and the approach they intend to take, more frequently define the desired culture before undertaking their Culture Diagnostic. If you are building a culture, rather than changing one, this would also be the case. Those who are considering culture as part of a broader change strategy may find it more useful to understand the current position before setting their target culture.

In every case, your desired culture must be the one that will support the implementation of your business strategy. If you need product innovation, your culture must embrace challenging the *status quo*. If low costs are a priority, you will need to kill bureaucracy and fiefdoms, or siloes, which add duplication of costs.

I have found both approaches to be successful. The already convinced group needs less evidence to build their case for change. Its diagnostic focuses more on what will bring about change, rather than the impact of culture on performance, or predicting the impact of culture on some future event (such as a merger). A good diagnostic will show you the path of least resistance for your culture development. You will get faster results with much less risk if you design your future so that it builds on the strengths of your past.

The early stages of your culture – perhaps the first six months – will take you to the point where both groups can make the best decisions for their organisation. The risk that the convinced group has is that it will go down a path of culture without the evidence to support it becoming the top priority in the company. The risks for the unconvinced group are that it will not invest enough to really understand the business case for culture in its organisation.

A VALUES-DRIVEN ORGANISATION

There are actually two parts to the change process. The first is to become a truly values-driven organisation. A values-driven organisation holds to its chosen values during times of pressure. This is integrity. If you go back to our original lists of values on pages 9–10, a values-driven organisation upholds the first list, the Enriching Values, even when the temptations of the second list, the Selfish Values, appear.

To understand this, think of friends and colleagues you know. Remember that old fashioned phrase: 'he was a man of principle.' One does not hear this expression very often now – it certainly predates the time when using the male gender for such phrases was considered appropriate. A 'man of principle' describes someone who holds true to an inner set of beliefs or values at all times. He does not sink to behaving in a way that only serves his own interests.

An organisation of principle is a values-driven organisation. Even when times are tough, performance is poor and time is short, there are certain principles from which it will not waver. It is actually such times that determine whether an organisation really is values-driven. It is easy to uphold good principles when there is no pressure to do otherwise. This is why tough times bring out the true character in us.

My father was a prisoner of war in World War Two. He speaks very eloquently about watching the behaviours of his colleagues. Within days it became clear which fellow prisoners were 'men of principle'. Some, he noted, gave up all principles in the desire for a cigarette. Others when they became hungry. Others, simply through the frustration, fear and boredom of camp life began to steal, to betray, to put their own interests ahead of others. Most values involve some element of upholding the well-being of others as well as yourself. Their role in society has been to ensure that as a community we live in a way that looks after the whole, not just the individual.

A values-driven organisation achieves this. There may be some members who do not always behave in this way, but the community norm is that values will be upheld. Tolerance for repeat offenders is low, because their behaviour threatens the strength of the whole. The values become the glue that holds the community together.

Values are different from vision. A shared vision or purpose will also hold a community together, but in a different way. The vision is shared aspiration of what we are going to do, achieve or contribute together. The values provide the trust that, as colleagues, we are doing this as a group, rather than as a set of individuals. Values give us a sense of identity; vision gives us a sense of purpose. Together they are a formidable pair.

Your culture today is the result of what has been valued in the organisation over the past few years. If you have not bonded through a shared set of uplifting values, individuals will have reverted to the self-centred needs on the second list: control, power, status, looking good.

The biggest step you will take is to become a values-driven organisation. This means lifting yourselves as a group out of individual or organisational selfishness, the pragmatic approach which says there are no rules; we will achieve our goal at any cost at all. This is the most difficult work of the process, and also the most important.

The rest of the work centres on your chosen thrust – be that customer focus, performance, teamwork, innovation or people, or some combination of the above. We have found many managers surprised by this balance and some resistant to it. People get very attached to the work associated with developing their list of values, and see this as the main component of the definition stage. In fact, the main component is looking within and determining whether you are up for being a values-driven organisation. This also requires determining the same of yourself.

There is little point spending three days debating whether teamwork or customer focus is the most important value for your organisation, if, as a group, you are not up for being values-driven at all.

MAKING THE CHOICE FOR YOUR CULTURAL FOCUS

Most cultural aspirations fit into five main categories. They are described with many different words, but when it comes to planning your path, it is useful to understand the fundamental thrust of your intention. From this you can add the unique characteristics, which will distinguish you from everyone else. The five dimensions are:

Dimension	Other descriptions
Achievement	Performance, accountability, focus, speed, delivery, meritocracy, discipline, transparency, risk mastery
Customer-centric	External focus, service, responsive, community, environment, social citizen, sustainability
One-team	Collaboration, globalisation, internal customer, teamwork

| Innovative | Entrepreneurial, agility, creativity, challenging status quo, learning, continuous improvement |
| People-first | Empowerment, development, safety, care |

There are linkages between each, and to some extent each depends on at least one or two of the others for its success. In our experience if you make considerable progress in one of these dimensions you will inevitably pull yourself up on most of the others as well.

Personal values – in particular integrity and honesty – spread across each of the above categories. Every culture change process must include these, either implicitly or explicitly, because it will be hard to achieve any of the others without them.

Some organisations target all five dimensions, or a mix.

By taking this approach you tackle all the dimensions that are integral to an outstanding culture. The approach recognises that there are links and dependencies between each. You need elements of the achievement culture to deliver consistently for your customers. A focus on people will encourage innovation and teamwork.

Others find that it is more effective to give their cultural efforts a single focus. Making change in any one of the five dimensions requires a lot of effort and investment. Focusing on one for a year or so until you see some traction can be a better use of resources and a clearer message to your people.

Your business imperative may suggest that one of the five should be your priority. Some leaders are more naturally attuned to one of them, and will therefore be most credible working on this dimension. Your Culture Diagnostic may have highlighted one as being particularly troublesome.

On balance I would tend to recommend a tighter focus initially. I believe that a contributing factor for the difficulties organisations have in changing their culture is a 'kid-in-the-candy-shop' desire to have everything on offer. Later chapters will demonstrate how much there is to do to change one dimension of behaviour. Changing all five at once may just be overload.

To begin, look through each of the main cultural dimensions as they are laid out, and ask yourself some hard questions about your affinity with, and willingness to really drive, each one. Once you have done this, spend structured time undertaking the same exercise with the leaders of your organisation.

The first culture I will describe is the Achievement Culture

1. The Achievement Culture
Different organisations use slightly different terms to describe elements of this culture. For simplicity I have grouped them together.

Other words
Accountability, performance, focus, speed, delivery, discipline, meritocracy, good governance, transparency, rigour, risk mastery.

A definition
A culture in which individuals, teams and the organisation are expected to deliver what they agree to deliver.

A description
I like the word Achievement to describe this culture, rather than the more commonly used 'performance culture'. To achieve means to do something successfully. To perform has two meanings in the dictionary: to put on a show, and to undertake a task. Neither actually includes the concept of successful completion.

Accountability is required for people to achieve within an organisation. Accountability is a relationship between two people – one is being held to account by another to achieve an outcome. Thus accountability puts achievement into the organisational context. In an organisation each individual enters an implied contract. The contract, which in too many organisations is never clearly defined, is to achieve certain outcomes in exchange for a salary.

Accountability can apply to outcomes and to standards. The 'what' and the 'how'. Discipline in approach is visible in Achievement Cultures. People understand the parameters within which they can operate. They are held to account for clear performance outcomes, and at the same time for complying with policies. Achievement is defined as both of these combined.

Managers know how to hold people to account, and are expected to do so. Achievement cultures have learnt how to maintain accountability within the complexity of a matrix structure, and people may be held to account for different things by different people. They take responsibility for managing the paradoxes inherent in such situations. Not having full control over all the inputs is not a valid excuse for non-delivery, and people learn to influence as well as direct to get what they need to deliver.

Meritocracy lies as a value within an Achievement Culture. Meritocracy means that reward (monetary, promotion or other) is handed out using a system that is based entirely on merit. Thus meritocracy does not allow for favouritism, prejudice against individuals based on gender, age or any other criteria. It also does not allow for the rewarding of individuals who are not performing.

Discipline is strong in an Achievement Culture. Things run to time, projects stay on track and people come to meetings with the information they need to make a decision.

Achievement Cultures are neither gung-ho nor fearful when it comes to taking risk. They work hard at anticipating and mitigating for risk. They will take planned risks if they consider the reward great enough. But they do it in a controlled way.

Keeping your word is another value within the Achievement Culture. When an individual signs up for their objectives, which become their contract to perform to a certain level, the organisation is depending on them to deliver. When they say 'I can do this', in an Achievement Culture, it is considered to be a promise. And people do keep their word. The same applies to delivering requirements to colleagues whether these are a report on a certain day or the action items from a meeting.

Openness and transparency are values within the Achievement Culture. Achievement requires a rigorous attention to the facts. Accurate, realistic and simple data is valued because it enables better decision-making, good assessment of risk and measurement of success. Achievement Cultures provide this information for everyone.

Speed and focus occur in an Achievement Culture because when meritocracy and keeping your word become the values sustaining a community, then people become much more conscious about what they say yes to. They know that once a yes is committed, the expectation will be of delivery. Thus carefulness about what is undertaken results in the focussing of effort. The distractions of new ideas, demands or requests become fewer. Speed occurs because decisions are not reopened. It may take longer to reach a decision because everyone becomes so conscious of the do-ability of a proposal. They wrestle with options, time-frames and risks. This is valuable debate. When a decision is made, everyone owns it and no one reneges. So the length of time from decision to completion is much shorter. One of the characteristics of organisations with Achievement Cultures is that they always finish what they start.

Here are some of the practices that occur in an Achievement Culture, which in turn send messages about what is valued and thus further reinforces the culture.

Behaviours

- Vision, strategy and a priorities framework is agreed and communicated
- Trade-offs are surfaced and explicitly resolved in teams
- Rigorous debate prior to signing off of targets
- The bar is lifted every year with support of the organisation
- The line is held on non-delivery – no excuses
- Individuals do what they say they will, delivery on promises
- No surprises – mistakes and non-delivery is communicated

Symbols

- Vision, strategy and priorities stay consistent long enough to determine their success
- Individual performance is transparent to others – metrics and milestones
- Meetings start and end on time, and in agreed actions which are followed up
- Individuals who do not meet targets are exited, no more than one year of non-performance

Systems

- Individual contribution to strategy and team targets explicitly defined
- Top-down stretch targets are communicated at the commencement of the budgeting process
- Simple, assessable management information for each major metric against which individuals perform
- Information used is fact-based, realistic and straightforward
- Reward structure allows for large variation between top and bottom performers
- Complete alignment between reward and performance

The business rationale

The Achievement Culture will deliver you many benefits. It:

- Increases the overall performance capability of your organisation
- Decreases the risk that you will not achieve performance targets
- Increases speed of decision-making and execution
- Makes you more focussed, doing fewer things very well, and completing them
- Makes you the employer of choice for high achievers

Supporting characteristics

It is always useful to build on strengths you already have, and some organisations have characteristics which naturally pre-dispose them to certain cultural aspirations. Traits in their culture, with some positive reinforcement or slight adjustment, can form the basis of their cultural aspirations. In thinking through your desired culture, consider information you collected in your Cultural Diagnostic which showed existing strengths.

Traits in your existing culture that will facilitate the Achievement goal

- A desire to win
- The pursuit of excellence
- Genuine effort and hard work

Other motivators for targeting an Achievement Culture include frustration with the lack of focus or speed, and performance crisis.

Organisations that are attracted to the Achievement Culture will often operate in an environment where growth is not easy to come by, and performance depends on squeezing every ounce of value from the existing business. Such organisations are under intense pressure to continually perform to higher standards, they know costs are too high and are not confident of exceptional revenue growth.

Beliefs that you need to champion an Achievement Culture

- That there are no excuses – by taking personal responsibility you can find a way around obstacles to deliver
- That the employment contract is a contract for outputs, not just effort
- That transparency of individual performance and its consequences is fair

---

Values you will need high on your values hierarchy

- Meritocracy
- My word is my bond
- Truthfulness

The deal-breakers

There are certain factors which make a particular culture an almost impossible stretch for some organisations. I call these the deal-breakers. If you believe these factors apply in your case, it might be better to target a culture which you are more likely to achieve. In the case of the Achievement Culture, the deal-breaker is a CEO who is not prepared to hold people to account and act on the consequences. If this person is you, and you can admit to this, you must consider whether you are prepared to overcome whatever it is inside you that has held you back. If you are not the CEO, consider the chances of influencing this person. A CEO who does not act on those who consistently do not perform will undermine everything else you try to do to create an Achievement Culture.

Over the years I have got to know Tony very well. He is the CEO of a company with around 25,000 people in the financial services industry. The business has grown well and delivered acceptable returns, but recently they have faced a downturn in market conditions which is making it harder to deliver the great returns of recent years. Tony is a great leader in every respect, but has had one Achilles heel – difficulty holding people to account. This became clear to me when I facilitated a session with the team and discussed with them their individual contribution to an overall target that had been promised to the market. Tony felt promises had been made. The team considered the numbers to be more like intentions – there were a number of circumstances which would challenge the achievement of the targets, and no one really felt accountable for addressing these. There was an unspoken assumption that the CEO would pull something out of a hat to ensure the overall number was achieved.

The lack of clarity was typical of the type of discussion this team commonly had. Tony's style allowed this to happen, although unconsciously. He squirmed when he had to speak directly to one individual and clearly assign accountability to that person for delivering a particular outcome, or fixing a particular problem. If he got over this hurdle, he squirmed again when an individual came back with a 'reasonable' reason why the target would have to be adjusted. There was one conversation I heard when the competitors lowering their price was put forward as a reason for non-delivery. Tony accepted this argument too easily. Were he to have held his ground, the team would in all likelihood have found another way to deliver the required targets. Once Tony had given them the easy way out, they did not bother.

Tony will probably never find these conversations easy. However, the personal turning point that enabled his company to develop a much stronger Achievement Culture, was his recognition that he had a problem in this area. Once he saw it, regular coaching enabled him to develop techniques, phrases and disciplines to have these key conversations with his people. Without his willingness to change, pursuing an Achievement Culture would have been of little benefit, because the team at the top were not being held to account.

The second culture for you to consider is the Customer-Centric Culture.

2. The Customer-Centric Culture
Other phrases are used to describe this, but all with a focus on the outside world.

Other words
External focus, service, responsive, community-oriented, care for the environment, social citizen.

A *definition*

A culture where an intimate understanding of the needs of those outside the organisation form the basis for all decisions.

A *description*

The Customer-Centric organisation is designed from the outside in. Everyone understands the customer, or other external stakeholders such as the communities within which the organisation operates. They care about their impact on the outside world. There is profound empathy, which, in his book *Emotional Intelligence*, Daniel Goleman describes as the ability to feel what another person is feeling. Employees know how their external stakeholders think and what they want, and can understand how their individual jobs impact them and how their decisions will be received.

The driver for decision-making is whether it will make it easier, faster, cheaper or more pleasurable for the customer. With this single-mindedness, a great deal of waffle and 'activity-itis' just falls away. When improvements are made to internal processes, and costs are reduced, these savings are invested into improving things for the customer or passed on directly through lower prices.

Listening is a primary activity. The front line, who have direct contact with the customer, are listened to continually, and encouraged to feedback their experience of customers' responses. Customer research is rigorous and presented at the highest levels of the organisation. Management meets regularly with customers, engaging them in conversation and listening to their complaints. Customer feedback is taken very seriously; themes and implications are drawn together and given back to those with the authority to respond. The antennae into the external world are so active, that these organisations are in a position to hear shifts in customer views even before the customer has picked them up.

Empowerment has been well thought through, with the

customer-facing staff in mind. Customer-facing staff are given as much authority as possible, so that they can respond to unique customer circumstances. Speed, flexibility, reliability and relationship – whatever is the driver of customer satisfaction – the front line is given every support to deliver this. Where the offering is not flexible, the impact of this has been carefully communicated in many ways so the customer's expectations usually align to what they receive.

Customer-Centric organisations have a strong external focus which extends beyond their customers. They understand the importance of the media as a communication tool to both customers and employees; they recognise brand value and are obsessed about maintaining the integrity of their brand. They appreciate that the communities within which they live have rights, and that they are often customers or influencers of public opinion. They care about sustainability. They value and work on their relationships with governments and regulatory bodies. In short, these organisations are attuned to the feelings of others, and this competency makes them responsive and easy to do business with.

They are acutely aware of the implicit or explicit promise that exists between a supplier and its customer. They hurt when this promise is unfulfilled. I use the word 'hurt' deliberately. Their relationship with customers is an emotional one, and when they let them down, they feel bad. The passion is palpable throughout the organisation. It provides the impetus to go the extra mile, and leads to inventiveness, continuous improvement, responsiveness and reliability which customers value highly.

The characteristic we notice first in Customer-Centric organisations, the one that sets them apart from the rest, is the attitude and approach of employees whose positions do not directly interface with the customer. Their knowledge and mind-set makes them indistinguishable from their customer-facing colleagues. For example, the finance team of a government services organisation we work with knows exactly how much time their requirements for financial data take the front line to input. They know the impact this has on the individual customers, and one of their priorities is to reduce this distraction for the customer, and find ways of being less demanding, of simplifying and co-ordinating their requests. Their motive is not cost-saving, but improving the customer experience.

In another retailing company, the head of legal gave me a lengthy explanation of shoppers, their trolleys and their children, and what this meant in terms of their requirements for car parks. As he negotiated contracts with shopping centre owners, his perspective on what was negotiable was based on an intimate knowledge of customer needs. Not a superficial knowledge from a couple of market research reports, but an in-depth understanding of what mattered to them, and the implications for his work.

In Customer-Centric organisations, everyone has the same depth of knowledge of the customer – people apply this knowledge based on their position, experience and authority.

If the customer refers to a broader community group – for example a focus on the environment – the same focus and interest is applied to understanding these needs, and then finding ways to meet community expectations *and* still satisfy customers *and* meet financial targets. Operating in a sustainable manner, without harming the outside world, matters. The genius of the 'and' described so well by Jim Collins and Jerry Porras in *Built to Last* is a key attribute of these organisations. The mind-set is not 'either, or' but 'both, and' and once this becomes an accepted norm, ways are found to fulfil the needs of apparently conflicting customers.

Here are some of the practices that occur in a Customer-Centric culture, which in turn send messages about what is valued and thus further reinforce this culture.

Behaviours

- Management spends enough time with customers to speak with authority about their needs
- Individuals go the extra mile to satisfy customers
- Listening and relating are common behaviours
- Supporting and delivering to colleagues is a high priority, and the hand-over points work well
- Customers are talked about as decisions are reached in every meeting

Symbols

- Top of the investment priorities are initiatives that will improve customer experience and prepare for their future needs
- Untrained staff are not put in front of the customer
- Stories and legends of exceeding customer experience are widespread

Systems

- Structure allows for the maximum amount of flexibility and responsiveness to the different customer groups and needs
- Customer research and satisfaction measures have equal weighting with financial performance
- Customer satisfaction is driven through process improvement, as well as face-to-face contact, and is embedded in the design of organisational procedure
- Training is extensive
- People are rotated through customer-facing positions
- Procedures demonstrate trust in staff and in customers

The business rationale

Each of the five cultures described is supported by reasons why it will deliver benefits. The Customer-Centric Culture:

- Facilitates customer loyalty, allowing you to win at customer retention
- Positions you to quickly pick up and respond to customer needs
- Builds pride at every level, especially the front line
- Forces empowerment and simplicity, which in turn reduces cost

Traits in your existing culture that will facilitate the Customer-Centric goal

- A front line whose loyalties lie as much (or even more) with the customer than with the organisation
- A relationship bias, a liking for people
- Humility, a lack of arrogance

Organisations who are attracted to a Customer-Centric Culture operate in an environment where there is little product differentiation. Differentiation exists within the service experience and the human touch – financial services, professional services, public service, and retailing.

Beliefs that you need to champion a Customer-Centric Culture

- That those closest to the customer know more about their needs than you do
- That it is possible to satisfy customers and have low costs
- That customer perception is the truth (the customer is always right)
- That one day, a competitor will emerge that cracks the customer satisfaction challenge in your industry

---

Values you will need high on your values hierarchy

- Listening
- Honour
- Relationship
- Learning
- Reliability

The deal-breakers
The killer for the Customer-Centric Culture is arrogance, the 'we know what's good for you' attitude which results in forcing the customer to behave, buy and comply with what is best for the organisation, and reject feedback. If you believe the arrogance in your key players cannot be influenced or changed, don't take this option.

3. The One-Team Culture

Other words
Collaboration, globalisation, internal customer, teamwork, boundary-less.

A definition
A culture where the good of the whole is placed above that of the individual or sub-group.

A description
A One-Team Culture is one where people are expected to always think of the team first when making decisions. A 'We:Me' approach. A One-Team Culture is becoming more essential as technology and process re-engineering make isolated units much rarer. There are few pockets in an organisation where staff can complete their work without depending on others. And yet, in a large organisation, One-

Team is counter-intuitive. We bond most naturally with those who are geographically close to us, and this means our immediate team, rather than the broader group.

Building a One-Team Culture requires considerable effort to increase the extent to which the component parts identify with the whole. I like to give the example of the European Union: being French or Spanish can feel more important than being European. The more people relate to being European, the easier it will be to make the EU work. To do this requires reasons to feel European. Aside from the Ryder Cup in golf, for example, the Europeans do not come together to play as one sporting team.

One-Team Cultures develop their common identity strategies effectively. They may not operate under one brand name, but their people identify with the whole. A lot of work goes into building pride in the achievements of the whole. People talk about 'our way' and 'this is how we do things' when referring to the whole organisation. Processes, rituals, terminology and disciplines are shared across the business, and this makes it easier for people to communicate with each other. There are many opportunities to see the world through the eyes of colleagues from other units. People are trained to lift their thinking and see the organisation from the balcony, as well as from the dance floor. They have dual citizenship, and switch between the two at will.

Sometimes it is appropriate for people to argue from the perspective of their unit. As a team they have to represent the views of their people, and the needs of their stakeholders. But they can simultaneously see the bigger picture, and recognise when a decision for the good of the whole is the right one.

These organisations normally carry matrix structures, but more importantly, they have matrix mind-sets. Their interest in their horizontal relationships is as strong as in their vertical ones. They care about one another's success, and support it accordingly. They pass on information and opportunities and share resources.

Individuals are good team leaders, but also good team members. The team is the basic organisation unit, and teams are formed and reformed frequently. Team effectiveness is high. Debate is rigorous, and people challenge each other, but once a decision is made, team solidarity is assured. Team processes are solid, and common, roles within teams defined; the organisation makes it easy for people to behave as good team players.

Because silos, or fiefdoms, are not a part of the culture, the power bases which accompany them are absent. One benefit is that the balance between functional and line roles and the value of both, is recognised. People trust other units; that their intentions are good, and they are competent to do their job. As a result they are happy to allow others to do work on their behalf, and can accept accountability for results where some of the inputs are not within their sphere of control.

Here are some of the practices that occur in a One-Team Culture, which in turn send messages about what is valued and reinforce the culture.

Behaviours

- Problems are resolved with the big picture in mind, units do not design short-term solutions which leave difficulties for the broader business
- Conflicting priorities caused by the matrix are resolved openly and constructively
- When a decision is made, individuals speak and act in support of it

Symbols

- Work is done by one group, on behalf of the whole, unless there are strong reasons for variation
- People are moved across the business, managers give up their good people to other units, and receive others in return
- Common rituals and language are used across the business

Systems

- The remuneration system encourages people to facilitate the success of others
- Structures and reporting lines recognise dual citizenship, people are held to account by different people for different deliverables
- People are not penalised financially for giving up something for the greater good
- Peer review is an important part of performance evaluation

The business rationale
- Customers experience a seamless service and cross-business processes work effectively
- Cross-referrals occur between different sales and service teams
- Best practice is picked up quickly across the group, so standards rise quickly
- Effort is not duplicated unless there is a strong business rationale – a leaner cost base
- Resources are easily focussed where most needed – underperforming areas, opportunities for quick wins in the market
- Mergers between companies, divisions or teams can occur quickly, and planned synergies are realised

Traits in your existing culture that will facilitate the One-Team goal
- A love of sharing
- A desire to be involved
- A bias towards big picture thinking
- A social environment, a human touch

Other motivators include
- Serious budget cuts, meaning people just have to depend on each other
- A common enemy

I have not found an industry-bias in relation to organisations that naturally tend to a One-Team Culture. However a shared characteristic is often that the management population is biased against high egos and machismo. Women seem to be more naturally collaborative and more inclined towards this type of culture, which is often the natural state of organisations with a high female management population.

Beliefs that you need to champion a One-Team Culture
- That what goes around, comes around – helping others succeed will facilitate your own success
- That most people are well-intentioned – their actions have a worthy motive, even if you haven't quite figured it out yet
- That people can be accountable for things they don't control

Values you will need high on your values hierarchy
- Generosity, sharing
- Co-operation
- Trustworthiness
- Openness
- Diversity

The deal-breakers

The deal-breakers are the barons, the ones who hold on to their little fiefdom, turn their backs on everyone else, and encourage separateness. You will find lots of these in your organisation right now if silo-thinking has been a problem for you. To move down this path, you need to be confident you will have the courage to stand up to, and, if necessary change these individuals.

4. The Innovative Culture

Other words
Entrepreneurial, learning, continuous improvement, creativity, enterprising, pursuit of excellence, growth, a better way.

A definition
A culture which strives to do what has never been done before, to improve, be unique and to operate at the highest standards.

A description
The words which describe this culture – entrepreneurial, learning, innovation, improvement, pursuit of excellence – may seem to describe different activities, but I have found the underlying cultural and personal value-sets very similar. The defining factor is a love of learning, a desire to create something new, to become better for its own sake. The feeling in these organisations is one of fascination for the products or service with which the organisation is associated. Teams talk about them all the time, they brainstorm in the coffee shop as much as in formal sessions. They are almost obsessed with finding a new and better way.

Innovative organisations tend to be ahead of their customers, rather than responding to them. They are the inventors; the innovators who create customer needs and who often advance the progress in the process. Frequently there is a commercial gain from this position, but the culture is not only driven by this. It is also driven by the pure joy of the pursuit of excellence.

In such an environment, mistakes are expected, welcomed and used. People are used to failure; they measure it, discuss it and work with it. The acceptance of failure is a requirement to work here, although failure is not seen as such, rather it is seen as a part of the journey toward success. These organisations have worked hard to redefine success. They recognise that human beings need a sense of achievement, and use milestones along their processes as measures of success to be celebrated.

However, because Innovative Cultures expect to take steps into the unknown frequently, they have also developed very good risk-management procedures. They could be called masters at managing risk, because they know they have to continue to take them. An innovative retailer we worked with was excellent at piloting new products or store lay outs. They would design how they would be introduced, put them into three or four stores, measure everything associated with them, and then pause. If signs were good, continue, if not, can the idea, or change it. There was no shame in this. It was expected. This one process became a beacon for their Innovative Culture.

Strong visions are an important part of this culture. They are able to hold to a vision for a long period of time without knowing how to get there, and often without evidence that the vision will ever be fulfilled. The belief that anything is possible is underpinned by rigorous realism in evaluating the success of experiments or pilots.

The Innovative Culture does not have room for strong egos that hang on to a point of view and cannot back down. The courage to act, and then to quickly correct, is the key to success. There is a love of ideas and curiosity, a 'what if' mind-set. Good ideas come from anywhere, and therefore hierarchical status is not valued. Leaders in Innovative organisations see their role as one of sourcing good ideas, and providing broad frameworks within which people can work with authority and autonomy in pursuing excellence in fields in which they have more knowledge than their bosses.

The pursuit of excellence for its own sake builds tremendous pride. In one of the first assignments of my career, I had the privilege of working with a large hotel whose standards of excellence were renowned. Several months into the assignment I met the head steward. One of the roles of the stewards in a hotel is the washing up. They work in the bowels of the organisation. This man had a passion for excellence which he had learnt through growing up in this culture. He considered that the quality of the silver – how it was polished, the continuous ways his team found to improve their standards of removing streaks, working more efficiently – was the most important thing in the hotel. He talked, with a quiet pride, of being the backbone of standards in the hotel. If his team could sit in their hot, dark den and turn out silver of immaculate quality for the guests, then all was well with the world. Quality spread out from his centre in the bowels of the hotel to every part of the operation. That was his view of his job.

These organisations usually use teams very well. Teams are formed and reformed around an idea or a project. They are given lots of autonomy and expected to measure their progress and self-manage. Ownership is therefore high, along with self-belief. People 'have a go' – the 'can do' is strong. The entrepreneurial spirit presides.

People are expected to help each other and to ask for help. One client held global 'support weeks', where people from all over the world flew in to provide a think-tank to help a unit who put up their hand to ask for assistance. It was expected that the individual unit shall ask for help, and that those who could provide it paid for their own expenses to come over and lend a hand.

Learning is transferred across the organisation. Internal best practice is measured, and knowledge is shared and asked for. If someone is doing something good, everyone wants to know about it and communication and knowledge management systems are used to facilitate this.

In another organisation a process called a 'bounce' session was an established ritual. Anyone with a new project or plan was expected to call a bounce session made up of a diverse group of people, in order to 'bounce' their ideas off them before going any further.

Innovative people are not proud or arrogant with regard to learning. If they hear about someone else doing something better than them, they find out how they're doing it. But they are equally confident with inventing something themselves if it is not out there to learn from. A client told me recently that they had just won an award, and there was an immediate flurry of employment offers from one of their competitors. They recognised excellence and wanted to buy it by hiring the people who had been responsible for achieving it, so they could learn how it had been done.

Here are some of the practices that occur in an Innovative Culture, which in turn send messages about what is valued and thus further reinforce this culture.

Behaviours

- Experimenting encouraged
- Ideas are challenged, people speak their mind
- Mistakes are considered opportunities for learning
- Best practice is transferred across the business
- People ask for help

Symbols

- Rituals associated with learning are common (post-implementation reviews, quality circles, help meetings)
- Resources are assigned to think-tanks for development of embryonic innovative ideas
- Experience is valued and not allowed to walk out the door in times of downsizing – mentoring is common, and 'elders' are valued

Systems
- Rigorous measurement (inputs, pilots, tests and small chunks of process) for the purpose of improvement
- Knowledge management systems are extensive and well-used
- Innovation, idea-generation hard-wired into performance management
- Structure designed to encourage delegated authority and empowerment

The business rationale
- Delivers product innovation and industry leadership
- Attracts and keeps unconventional people with original ideas
- Removes the costs associated with 'not invented here'
- Allows early correction on mistakes, reducing escalating costs of unsuccessful strategies, projects or new products

Traits in your existing culture that will facilitate the Innovative goal
- Informality
- Intellectual rigour
- Willingness to change

Organisations that embrace this culture are often from industries where product innovation is a real potential source of differentiation, for example technology or pharmaceutical. Smaller organisations seeking to carve a niche for themselves against much larger players can often do so through this approach. Creative and artistic people are at home in this environment, and their organisations tend naturally towards this type of culture.

Beliefs that you need to champion an Innovative Culture

- That there is always a better way (if it isn't broken break it anyway)
- That you are not always right
- That not knowing is a sign of strength, not a weakness
- That mistakes are an opportunity to learn

Values you will need high on your values hierarchy

- Curiosity
- The pursuit of excellence
- Openness
- Courage

The deal-breakers

The Innovative Culture requires the willingness to have a go without all the information, to take controlled risks. If key players in your organisation have a strong risk aversion, and find it difficult to take the first step without all the facts, this culture will not fly. A penny-pinching mentality also makes innovation very difficult as a meanness of spirit will kill off an idea before it has developed its own momentum.

5. The People-First Culture

Other words

Empowerment, delegation, development, safety, care, respect, balance, diversity, relationships, fun.

A definition

A culture in which people are valued, encouraged and supported.

A description

A culture which values people places the humanness of employees at the centre of its operation. It never considers its people as an 'asset' or a commodity which belongs to the organisation, but rather as human beings who have chosen to participate in its activities. To value people requires understanding them, and this means applying all of those human skills which make any good relationship work: listening, supporting, appreciating, enjoying, respecting.

In a People-First Culture employees feel good, they want to contribute and they go the extra mile that comes from a relationship of mutual respect and trust. Because they are treated well, they treat the organisation and its customers well – there is a sense of a fair exchange occurring, and such cultures have much lower instances of selfish behaviour such as theft, legal suits or the manipulation of rules to capitalise on personal financial gain.

When an individual feels valued they give their best. People-First Cultures lift the performance of individuals, and make great performers out of people previously tagged as mediocre.

Many factors contribute to an individual feeling valued. Their contribution is meaningful, and recognised. Their opinion is asked for and listened to. They are trusted. Their individuality is encouraged and supported. Time is dedicated to developing and supporting employees, whether through ensuring their safety, providing flexibility of working arrangements or encouraging their training and study. People are given the authority, resources and training to make decisions – they are empowered.

Underlying all of this activity is the basic belief that human beings respond and contribute best in an environment in which they feel valued. This applies to all employees, regardless of gender, race, religion or seniority. Such organisations do not consider punishment or 'sink or swim' to be the best approach to motivating people. This does not mean they are soft, but rather caring in their approach.

Diversity is a value within People-First organisations. Diversity does not allow one individual, or group of individuals to impose their beliefs, way of life and style on to others. It does not recognise one group as being superior to another. This approach provides the organisation with the benefits of a wide range of opinions, approaches and views on problems and challenges. It creates a natural curiosity for the ways of others which gives these organisations an advantage in their empathy with customers, their ability to partner with others, undertake mergers or expand into other countries.

The safety, health and well-being of employees are a natural outflow of this value-set. To kill an employee through unsafe work practices is the ultimate sin of an organisation with people at the centre of its value-set. Reading this, you may consider that it is the ultimate sin, period. But practices in many organisations would suggest that care for the lives of employees is not at the top of the values hierarchy. For many the drive for safety has been the trigger for a change in mind-set with wide ranging benefits in relation to caring for each other. The financial benefits of a safe workplace are a natural outflow, but not the driver, of a people-centred culture.

People-First Cultures are usually fun. There is a lot of laughter, employees enjoy each other's company, they have forged successful relationships with one another, and they recognise that one of the benefits of coming to work is to be in the company of great and talented people. Even when times are tough, the sense of humour prevails.

Because people are seen as human beings rather than positions, there is a strong egalitarianism in cultures which value people. More senior people may be paid more, but they are not seen as better people, and are not afforded status or privileges which do not add to their ability to do their job.

People feel safe to speak up. They are not intimidated by their bosses, and they know they will be listened to. Problems, illegal activities, non-performance will be raised. 'Whistle-blowing', the term used for individuals who report activities which they believe are outside of company policy, will occur.

Some organisations with a strong people-centricity have a

flavour of paternalism, a family feel where employees are looked after, loyalty is strong and senior management play a caring benefactor role. Such cultures were more prevalent twenty years ago. Others have a more modern interpretation of valuing people, and the relationship with the company is more one of equals.

Caring for people is the most powerful win-win cultural option. An organisation that truly puts its people first bypasses the unease many employees feel about whether the cultural process is just another word for delivering to business owners at the expense of employees.

A 5-star hotel we worked with over a period of years tracked a direct relationship between how their staff were treated by their supervisors, and how they treated customers. If they were shouted at in the kitchen, they would go straight through to the dining room and be hostile or cold with customers. The hotel called this 'back of house, front of house'. Staff stepped through those big double swing doors, and took with them the atmosphere of whatever had been going on behind the scenes.

Here are some examples of practices that occur in a People-First Culture, which in turn send messages about what is valued, and thus reinforce this culture.

Behaviours

- Leaders coach, support and listen to their people
- Junior people are treated with the same level of respect and interest as their senior colleagues
- Any form of disrespectful behaviour (bullying, lack of performance feedback, aloofness, taking credit for the work of others) is stamped out very quickly
- Constructive challenge is encouraged – everyone's opinions are valued

Symbols

- Non-traditional and diverse people choices are made for key roles
- People are given responsibility and the chance to prove themselves (with safety nets in place)
- Employee benefits are equally spread across the whole hierarchy
- Symbols of status are rare (large offices, differentiated travel policies)

Systems

- Performance management is treated seriously and based on the importance of giving feedback, learning and development
- Training is broad and well-resourced
- Work-life balance policies are well-developed
- Diversity is built into all HR policies and visible
- Employee well-being metrics are robust and meeting standards is expected (safety, employee satisfaction, etc.)
- Trusted mechanisms exist to report non-compliance behaviour (sexual discrimination, stealing, etc.)

The business rationale
The People-First Culture will deliver:

- A strong employee brand, reputation as employer of choice
- Enhanced performance from individual employees
- Reduced turnover and recruitment fees
- Access to the total spectrum of talent – true meritocracy
- Compliance to policy, which allows empowerment within defined limits

- Outstanding commitment at the front line, which customers love
- Abundant, high quality communication, including access to problems (no surprises)
- Reduced unethical behaviour (stealing, etc.)
- Reduction or elimination of cases of unfair dismissal, discrimination or sexual harassment

Traits in your existing culture that will facilitate the People-First goal
- Paternalism
- Loyalty
- Progress on safety
- A relationship bias, a naturally social environment

Organisations that are naturally attracted to the People-First Culture will often have a workforce with a large number of front line people. The untapped potential here gives real service or performance advantage. Examples include retailers, service providers, industrial and manufacturing environments.

Beliefs that you need to champion a People-First Culture

- That people are inherently trustworthy
- That other people can always add to my original ideas
- That diversity of age, gender, race, sexual orientation add to a team's effectiveness

Values you will need high on your values hierarchy

- Trust
- Egalitarianism
- Diversity

The deal-breakers

Some people have a distrust of others, or an inflated view of their own importance, which makes it almost impossible for them to value their colleagues. If you or a key player in your culture (for example your CEO) display these characteristics, you will really struggle to gain credibility on this path.

This completes the description of five cultures which can add tremendous value to the achievement of your organisation's goals and aspirations, be they strategic, financial, social or sporting. From these examples, you can develop a detailed sketch of your desired culture, which may draw pieces from more than one of the five I have described. You may decide to go for the whole lot (although I would encourage you to focus on one or two, at least in the early stages).

LINKING YOUR CULTURE TO YOUR UNIQUE BUSINESS DRIVERS

Many culture initiatives fail because they lack a strategic context. The piece of work to link broad values statements to specific business drivers is not undertaken. The two remain separate in people's minds. Under pressure, the business drivers take over.

Let's say you have selected One-Team to become one of the values of your desired culture. The work you now need to do is to define the 'why', the 'what' and the 'how' of One-Team.

We have a client in the mining industry. They have a number of mines scattered over a wide distance with several hundred kilometres between them all. Their raw material is shipped through one port to customers. Each mine worked fairly well as an intact entity. Because of their remoteness, communities grew around each mine, and a good mine manager led an effective team. Performance was measured by how many tonnes were produced.

The next big performance step for this company lay in the amount of material they could ship from the port. Ships arrived each day to be loaded. The trick to extra performance lay in ensuring that there was always the correct grade of raw material in the correct quantities waiting for each ship as it docked. This required a new level of co-ordination and a new definition of teamwork. Teamwork had previously meant working well within each mine. It now had to mean co-ordinating well between mines, so that transport of materials to the port occurred in an orchestrated manner, according to the needs of the ships arriving. The customers determined the ships' needs. This co-ordination meant that sometimes mining had to actually stop at one mine whilst another over-produced. It spelt the end of the mine manager as ruler of his own kingdom.

In one move, this organisation's challenge was to redefine teamwork. In doing so they also had to become more customer-focussed and redefine performance so that it came to mean tonnes shipped rather than tonnes mined. Suddenly their culture efforts had a real business bite. Their tonnes shipped increased by 20 per cent over three years. All through that soft fuzzy thing called teamwork.

Lion Nathan, the organisation profiled at the end of this book, has 'sociable' as a core value. This value is linked to their product, beer. It is also linked to their great threat, the misuse of their product through over-consumption. They want consumers to see their product as a part of the broad social fabric of their life, and consume it in moderation within this framework. Their customers, mostly hotel and pub owners, are a sociable bunch. Their vision is to make the world a more sociable place. They found that through talking to each other, they passed on internally best practice and improved performance. The whole picture linked together revealed how developing a sociable culture would benefit employees, customers and shareholders.

This is how to get culture to the top of your business agenda. As the leaders of the culture change, you must build your own version of this story. It must have all the specific business references that only you possess.

DEFINING THE SPECIFICS

In addition to the values attributed to the five dimensions of culture described, there are others you will find at the core of every great organisation. They are also present in fine leaders, and these values inspire others to follow that leader. They include:

- Integrity
- Openness
- Loyalty
- Honesty
- Humility
- Generosity
- Commitment

Some combination of all of these will be right for your organisation.

You will probably want to describe your culture with some specific statements which you call values, principles, 'our credo' or some other expression which your team likes. As you develop these statements I encourage you to use unusual words to describe what you mean. One organisation I know uses the word 'elbow room' to mean 'empowerment'. They find it much more effective because it is descriptive, quirky and not an overused term, which empowerment has become.

When presented with broad values statements, everyone will agree that these would be excellent aspirations to follow. You will find that people will 'sign-up' but you will not get the traction you need. You now have to develop the picture of your desired culture. There is an important piece of work to do before you plan any major change initiatives.

You must decide what specifically you want to change. Assume that if you say 'teamwork' to your people, they will believe they are already doing it. On each cultural dimension – Achievement, Customer-Centric, One-Team, Innovative, People-First – people will tend to believe they are personally strong.

A study asked managers to rank themselves as communicators. 100 per cent of those asked ranked themselves in the top 50 per cent. Half of those asked ranked themselves in the top 10 per cent. When it comes to these descriptive terms, we all see ourselves in the OK–excellent range.

In doing so, answer these questions:

- Why, specifically, are we doing this? What is the business driver, how does this fit in to our strategy? Why do we think we will beat the competition by taking this approach? How much money do we think we will save? How will it contribute to winning more customers? You will have gathered a lot of this data when building your business case for culture

- What, specifically, will each value mean in our context? For example, if customers, why customers? All customers? The profitable ones? The internal customers? What if my internal customer makes a demand that takes a lot of time, and takes me away from another demand that I believe has more external customer benefit? How does customer-focus tie into selling? Should I tell a customer if they could benefit from a cheaper product of ours? What if the competitor's product would suit them much better? If we stop product pushing and start responding to customer needs will there be a short-term loss of revenue? Will we wear that?

- How will this work for me? What are you expecting me to do differently? In what way will this change my decision-making? My prioritisation? What do you want me to do when I get pressure from my boss to act in a way that does not line up with this value? What will you do with those who do not act according to the values? How will you know?

Describing behaviours

Your job is to describe what you want, so specifically that when one of your people hears you talk about it, they realise that they are not operating in this way yet. This description will involve describing the culture in terms of the behaviours it expects, and does not expect. You can use the three types of behaviour described in Chapter 6 to do this. Your list will never be comprehensive, and will evolve as the organisation starts to discuss the desired culture. It will also serve to provide the specifics people seek, and to define your expectations of them.

It can be useful to add some negatives. As a general principle, I am not in favour of negatives in the context of culture because they can seem like the antithesis of a values-driven organisation. However, they can be easier to observe than the more positive expression of the same statement. 'Never leak information' for example, is much easier to understand, and to evaluate, than the more commonly used 'maintain cabinet solidarity'.

SUMMARY

Building the picture of the culture you want is an exciting phase, and one in which you should involve as many people as possible. The description may seem very ambitious, compared to where your organisation is now. Some cynics in your team may call it a 'motherhood statement'. Persevere. The statement of your cultural intent becomes the anchor for your future work. It tells your people that this is what you want, and that these behaviours will be promoted. It gives hope and encourages people to join and stay with your organisation. The more detailed the picture is, the more alive it becomes. Over time, all of your leaders will be expressing it in their own way. The essence, though, remains the same.

5

Signing Up to the Journey

HOW TO START – THE WORK OF THE TOP TEAM

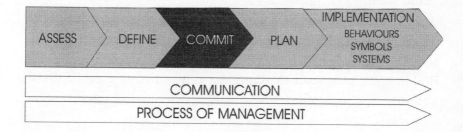

IGNIFICANT culture change can only occur when the behaviour and mind-set of the top team changes. Culture change is not something that you can drive from the bottom up. Organisations are by nature hierarchical. Those at the top have more power than the rest, and their opinions, decisions and behaviour impact on more people than those in any other part of the organisation. Culture is about messages. People read messages and adapt their behaviour to fit what they see as the required norm. Who sets the norm? More than any other, it is their boss. After all, in a hierarchy the boss ultimately has the power to determine his or her people's future career, remuneration and continuation in the organisation. For all the talk, there are few people who will continually and consciously displease their boss. This does not mean people will never challenge their boss – they will challenge their boss if they believe that ultimately the boss will think well of them for doing so or thinks well of them in other ways, such as performance, that they can get away with it.

The top team is important because they are the ultimate bosses. Their decisions ripple through the organisation and send signals about what is important. They determine where resources will be assigned. For example, in a limited budget situation, they will decide whether to invest in a CRM Customer Relationship Management system or a new general ledger this year. The extent to which your systems are customer-friendly now is the result of decisions that were made over the past few years. The top team made these decisions, either directly or through the targets they set for particular systems.

And finally the top team's decisions have a powerful symbolic impact. The team casts a long shadow. Their actions are amplified and more is read into them than is necessarily intended.

> Walking the Talk
> The top team impacts the culture through behaviours,
> symbols *and* systems

For our purposes, the top team refers to the group who have the most impact, through behaviours, symbols and systems, on the culture you are trying to change.

If you are a small organisation – say fewer than 50 people, that means the CEO and one or two others. In organisations between 50 and 500 people it probably means the CEO and the senior team. In a partnership structure, such as a professional services firm, you have to consider the whole partnership group as the top team, which means you have a big job on your hands to get the initiative going, because there is no single CEO with authority to act.

Above 500 employees it is possible to change the culture in one part of the organisation without tackling the whole thing. This is particularly true if the part concerned is fairly self-sufficient. So, for example, if you are heading up a division which has geographic separation, or P&L accountability, you can make a reasonable go at changing many elements of your culture.

As we move into organisations of 5000 employees or more, the divisional leader can make a considerable impact.

The limiting factors are the global or organisation-wide, systems. One of our clients is a country head of a large global organisation. This organisation, like most of its kind, has a number of policies and practices that are standard around the world. The planning and budgeting process is one. This process does not lend itself to creating high ownership of numbers by the individuals who are expected to deliver them. Our client has worked very hard to create a local process that allows the teams to redistribute numbers between them, but this has run into difficulties because the matrix nature of the organisation means that although he is the country head, his people report to a global head of product lines. These individuals are not brought into the cultural aspirations of the local country manager.

Many of you will face versions of this in your workplace. Don't despair. Culture change is never the clinical operation we all plan for. It is important to understand which of the message sources you can influence, and which you have to accept and work with. Chapter 12 covers how to change culture from the middle.

You must take an analytical view and determine which organisational unit or level is the right place to drive the piece of culture change you are planning. This decision will depend on:

- Your level of independence and how many of the levers for change you can control or strongly influence
- The amount of effort it will take to influence upwards – is it worth doing this upfront or waiting until you have some runs under your belt?
- The nature of the culture change you are intending – will it primarily be dependent on behaviours (which you can influence more strongly) or systems (which may be out of your control)?

So, work out who your top team is going to be for the purpose of this work. Got them in mind? They are your first piece of work. And that includes you since I am assuming you are in there somewhere. If not, I'll show you how to influence them.

The first piece of work with the top team

It is best to get going with the top team before you get into too much detail with planning how you are going to drive a broader culture change process. Whether you are the leader of that team, a team member, such as the HR role or an influencer, such as an organisational development specialist, how far you can take the team in these early stages will determine the kind of plan you create.

There are four objectives you want to have achieved with this team very early:

1. Acceptance of the current cultural state
2. Confidence that the desired culture will deliver business outcomes
3. Understanding the process
4. Recognition of their part in the culture, and what will have to change

Your fifth, and long-term objective, is that their values and behaviours align to the desired culture.

My experience is that the last, and most important, does not happen overnight. You have to get going without complete confidence that this last one has occurred. We will hold this last one until Chapter 8 which describes how you change values and behaviours, and focus on the first four.

Choosing your influencing strategy
Let's assume that you, the reader, have already accomplished the objectives outlined above. Our task is to work out how best to bring your colleagues to the same place. Here I have to make a distinction

between those of you who are line managers leading the team, and those who are in a functional role with culture as an imperative.

As a team leader

If you are leading the team you are in a strong position. Remember we talked earlier about the reasons for embarking on a culture journey. You are already convinced, perhaps because of past experience, an intuitive sense or a strong strategic rationale that this is the path to take. With this, as the leader, you will find you can achieve the first three objectives, with perhaps a little outside expertise to help define the steps in your process.

Your challenge lies in the fourth objective, having the top team recognise how they contribute to the culture as it is now. The key to this lies in the quality of your cultural diagnostic, and thus the acceptance that it achieves your current state. The best approach here is to be very logical, using the Behaviours, Symbols, Systems framework, and using hypothetical examples. You will need to find people the team trusts to give them feedback. This might be your HR person, an external firm of advisors or a group of more junior people whose opinion is listened to.

The key is to be aware that most people are pretty unaware of the impact of their behaviour on others. That we cast long shadows is not something we think about much. There is usually a good explanation as to why a particular course of action was taken; it was not done to deliberately send an undesired message. Thus an attacking stance is less effective than an exploratory one.

In the early stages, aim for a general recognition that there is a link between our behaviour and decisions, and the broader culture.

Find your early adopters. These are the individuals who already believe this approach is the way to go. You may only need one or two in the early stages. It is easy during this process, to focus on those who are not 'getting it'. Focus on those who do get it. Strengthen their belief; build their confidence to go out on a limb. They are the people you will need to help you build critical mass.

As a team influencer

If you are in a position of influence, but not team leadership, your challenge is greater but still achievable. We have worked with many HR professionals and line managers who are seeking to bring about cultural change and finding that the greatest apparent barrier were the team leaders themselves. How much can be achieved without these individuals fully on board? The answer is that some progress can still be made, but you have to take the leader's style into account as you plan.

I have seen a team with a very withdrawn leader, lacking in the skill and will to drive accountability, and unwilling to make decisions, make considerable progress towards an Achievement Culture by working together around the boss. It required great collaboration between them, but increased the effectiveness of their respective divisions, as they became a virtually self-managed team. It only happened, though, because they pulled together, and did not play politics to gain the leader's favour.

Your best approach is to find a way to win the heart and mind of your leader. Using the processes outlined here, you should achieve objectives 1-3: gain acceptance of the current culture, the benefits to performance of the intended culture and an understanding of the journey.

Both team leaders and team influencers must look out for the tipping point. There is a magical moment during this process when the norm for behaviour in your team tips from supporting the old culture to supporting the new one. For a while it may feel it will never happen, and then suddenly it happens really quickly. You may find one new person in the team can swing the balance or perhaps a shift in thinking in one influential player.

When this tipping point occurs, you may find there are still two or three team members who are not on board. But social opinion has moved against them. From being the ringleaders of the past, they have become somewhat ostracised. You will find that in the next few months either they will leave, you will find it in you to ask them to go or the team will move them into a position of little influence, perhaps needing them because of a particular skill or knowledge they have.

All of your efforts with the team must be towards this moment. The best way to achieve this is to focus on those who are the easiest to get there. The tipping point is a factor of critical mass – you don't need everyone with you to reach it.

BUILDING A BUSINESS CASE FOR CHANGE

Some organisations have a crisis on which to base their culture work. If your organisation has been through an extraordinarily difficult time, and the events which contributed to this can be fairly easily linked to culture, then building the business case is easier. Some people believe that the impetus for culture change can only occur as a result of having hit rock bottom. The shock of this provides the catalyst that forces bold decisions previously avoided or perhaps brings in a group of new leaders with a clear mandate for change. This situation can definitely produce a new culture, as long as the new leader understands the levers for culture and does more than just fire a lot of people. Change stems from an emotional response. A crisis certainly provides one of these. But the case for change can be built without a crisis, and culture can be led by inspiration as well as in the aftermath of a disaster.

Those who are not excited by culture are more likely to be won over by logic than by emotion. Thus the business case becomes very important. Here's how to build the case for culture change.

The business case for culture becomes more substantial when the benefits move beyond making this a 'nicer place to work'. There seems to have built up in parts of the business community a belief that culture is that 'soft, fuzzy thing' we do in addition to running the real business. Wrong. Culture is what you do every time you make a decision. Culture is what makes your projects run over budget, your strategies ignored, your customers frustrated and your business blind to a major threat until it knocks you over. Culture is your business, not something you have on the side.

Your business case for culture should focus on these six areas. They are the ones in which culture has the greatest impact:

Speed	• Responsiveness to market changes • Decision-making • Implementation
Accountability	• Consistency of delivery • No excuses • Compliance
Rigour	• No group-think • Risk-management • Challenge
Simplicity	• Reducing complexity • Reducing waffle
Collaboration	• Avoiding duplication • No silos • Group benefits overrides individual
Attractiveness	• Staff loyalty • Strong employment brand • Having customers feel your people care

To build your business case for the benefits of changing your culture, calculate the cost of some of these items, and then assume they improve by 20 per cent. You will find you arrive at a fairly large number, well in excess of the amount you will need to invest in your culture change process. I am picking 20 per cent as a fairly conservative number. If you really transform your culture you will generate some much larger numbers than this.

To do this you have to understand the characteristics of your current culture, which cause some of the problems. Your cultural diagnostic should pick these up in detail, but here is an overview, in the five areas of potential cultural transformation covered in Chapter 4.

If you are a shareholder of a publicly listed company you may be horrified by the next section. But I assure you that what I describe occurs every day in many organisations. The cost to the shareholder of culture is higher than most realise.

Characteristics of a non-Achievement Culture

(See pages 64–66 for a description of an Achievement Culture)

Avoidance is the strongest feature of non-achievement. In Avoidance Cultures the norm is that nobody is held accountable for specific outcomes. Such cultures evolve when it becomes obvious over time that mistakes will be punished, but success not rewarded. Thus the priority becomes to stay out of trouble. The game becomes a very sophisticated form of pass-the-parcel, where the aim is to make sure that nobody ends up holding the parcel when the music stops.

This plays out in day-to-day life in many ways:

1. A huge amount of activity. Activity covers up for a lack of accountability for outcome. Being busy is a good way of keeping out of trouble. Doing a bit of everything means that you can never be accused of missing something, and so Avoidance Cultures tend to jump on to every new strategy, opportunity or market segment

2. Measurements are complex and objectives are fuzzy which makes it hard to tell if they are achieved. Confusion is the best form of lack of accountability. Avoidance Cultures have usually not mastered their metrics, and will tend to measure too much to accompany the multiple activities

3. Decisions are slow and complexity is everywhere. Presentations are long, responses to questions obtuse; there is a love of the intellectual. There is much talking. When decisions do arrive they are often without conviction, and are unmade

soon afterwards. A decision sets me up to fail, and this must be avoided

4. Lack of individual accountability. Teams are used instead of individuals. Everyone gets involved in everything. It is rare that an individual takes accountability for something on his or her own. Meetings take over, diaries are packed full. Consultants are used in ways where they virtually run the business, projects grow in scope

5. Justifications are given and accepted. Avoidance organisations develop a sophisticated set of reasons why performance is difficult. These justifications describe true events (the market is down, the competitors changed tack, IT did not deliver), and deflect from management's job of anticipating and mitigating these risks

6. Non-performers are not clearly identified, and action is not taken to remove them. If people are removed, they are moved to another area where their non-performance continues

Impact on performance

In building your business case for an Achievement Culture, look to the following areas:

- A lack of focussed strategy, doing a little of too many things, failure to invest primarily in one area and gain a competitive advantage there
- Failing to stop something, remaining in an unprofitable sector/product for too long, not cancelling projects that are not turning out well
- Non-compliance, which in extreme cases can lead to illegal practices or decisions by individuals to play outside the rules and lose the organisation large amounts of money
- A decision that took too long to make, and the accompanying rework associated with further researching or redrafting of the proposition. The loss of competitive advantage or cost reduction, caused by this

- Individuals being allowed to under-perform over a long period of time, and the impact of this on the area they head up
- Overuse and misuse of consultants

Each culture I have described will require a different business case. The next is the Customer-Centric Culture.

Characteristics of a non-Customer-Centric Culture

(See pages 71–73 for a description of a Customer-Centric Culture) There are two types of non-customer centricity. The primary feature of the first is an inward-looking bureaucracy. In this case it is as if the customer does not actually exist. The culture is built around the needs and politics of the employees. Rules are built to serve internal needs of control, and habits become entrenched. Success is defined through internal order; through not making mistakes, not taking risks and fulfilling the requirements of internal masters. Such cultures breed obedience and conventionality, combined with a passive acceptance. In monopolies, be they government-owned or commercial, such organisations can succeed over a long period of time, and the voice of the customer becomes unimportant.

The other is the more aggressive product-pusher. Such organisations are characterised by arrogance and confidence, as they drive customers to purchase their goods and services. This approach can also be successful especially if the competitors use a common approach, sales skills are strong and products reasonable. These organisations understand their customers, but they understand them in terms of what is required to sell more to them. Selling is a stronger cultural push than service. Their approach to the market is push, rather than pull.

This plays out in day-to-day life in many ways:

1. Change is slow. The organisation does not respond to customer dissatisfaction, and in many cases does not collect it in any meaningful way. Customers experience the same

frustrations over long periods of time. When change does occur, it may actually make life worse for the customer

2. A lot of time and money is taken up with activities that gain a life of their own, but are not necessarily adding any value

3. The organisation spends a great deal of money persuading its customers to do what it wants – buy its products, use its services. The answer to falling revenues is increased sales effort, rather than improving service and causing customers to return of their own volition

4. The customer is treated as a series of products, rather than as a person. This is confusing for the customer, and costly for the business, which does not get the benefits of integrated solutions

5. Customers become incredibly frustrated and feel trapped, for example by a monopoly or government service, for which they have no alternative. Community perceptions, and lack of funding, make it difficult to hire good people, and service suffers further

6. Members of the organisation behave in a way which is insensitive to the expectations of the broader community. For example, a number of sporting codes have recently been damaged by the attitudes of their players to women, the media and drug-taking

7. The service mentality is not strong, so internal service to colleagues is also weak

Impact on performance

The business case for a Customer-Centric Culture will focus on:

- The cost of not understanding at decision-making level what makes the customer tick. Decisions made that repel or frustrate customers, and consequent loss of sales
- Times when you have not responded quickly to competitor threat – either not seen the threat or been unable to change tactics to respond to it

- A shift in customer habits that you completely missed, when a sector of your market moves away from your areas of traditional dominance
- The relationship (and relative costs) between customer acquisition and customer retention
- The damage to your brand, and reputation of insensitive behaviour by your people
- Blow out in costs in non-customer-facing areas, roles which create activity to justify their existence
- Difficulties with hand-offs between back office and front office, and the consequent cost of rework

An organisation without a One-Team culture is very disjointed:

Characteristics of a non-One-Team Culture
(See pages 76–78 for a description of a One-Team Culture)

Looking good is the primary feature of a culture which does not operate as One-Team. The culture is built around the glory of the individual, and in the process attracts and builds some very large egos. These cultures develop as it becomes obvious that by looking good as an individual you can win big time, and that this is not always accompanied by performance. The priority becomes to build up an individual's image and status, and to provide whatever they need to succeed.

The extent to which this success is actually linked to financial or other real outcomes will be a factor of the level of achievement in the culture. The less achievement there is, the more the individualism will play out as shining rather than actually producing outcomes. It is here that the definition of 'perform' meaning to put on a show, can really come into its own.

With a reasonable level of achievement, it is possible to deliver financial outcomes with a non-team based culture. However, this does not occur if the environment requires collaboration across the business. Most organisational strategies do.

This plays out in day-to-day life in the following ways:

1. Empire building within individual fiefdoms, resulting in duplication of effort and an unwillingness to share information, or resources with others. Individuals are often good team leaders, but hopeless team members, preferring to focus on leading their own area. Different areas may be pulling in different directions, with different priorities

2. A lack of affiliation with the bigger picture. Difficulties with globalisation, nationalisation or any structure that requires people to play on multiple teams. Lack of collaboration with people from other areas or units. A reluctance to be accountable for numbers over which they do not have complete control, and thus difficulties with any form of matrix structure

3. One-upmanship, or internal competition, with a lot of time being spent proving how good we are to each other. There will be many meetings taken up primarily with presentations, and if there is discussion, it tends to take the form of comments or questions to put down others. Meetings do not leave with anyone in a better position than when they came in, and are therefore a waste of time. Goal setting becomes a bidding contest

4. Lack of support between peers. In the non-team culture the best management activity occurs between a manager and the individual subordinate. There is little resolution of issues between colleagues, with such resolution usually having to be cascaded upwards. A struggling area is left to struggle alone, individuals cannot rely on their colleagues support to help them succeed or to get a new idea up and running

5. Internal customer/supplier relationships are weak. Performance targets are not negotiated with colleagues, and in many cases individuals will prefer to create their own means of getting things done, rather than rely on colleagues. Internal customers do not see themselves as responsible for helping their internal suppliers succeed. Suppliers tend to struggle with the balance between the service role and the policeman or expert role

6. Reinvention and redefinition of the wheel. Learning from

others and adopting their methodologies occurs rarely, with multiple versions of the same activity occurring across the organisation. Common vision and strategy is hard to sustain, people leave meetings where an agreement was made, and continue with their own approach

7. Disrespect for the value of others – both as individuals and for some roles. A feeling of top dogs and underdogs. Difficulties with diversity, such as during mergers and acquisitions, towards women, certain lower profile roles being undervalued

All of this impacts on the performance of these organisations, and it is here that you will find your case for change.

Impact on performance

In building your business case for a One-Team Culture, look to the following areas:

- The cost of duplication of effort – IT solutions, training programmes, etc. being invented in many places simultaneously
- Gung-ho goal-setting – over-optimistic sales figures and other demonstrations of individuals outshining each other
- Adoption, at a divisional level, of strategies not in-line with the overall vision. The cost of market confusion or cannibalism, such as winning customers from each other
- Difficulty in implementing projects that are led in one area but need collaboration and input from others – such as new product design and customer-billing systems
- Customer complaints regarding hand-offs from one area to another, such us between phone and face-to-face distribution channels
- Loss of good people from the out-of-favour tribe, for example in a merger or out of service/operations in a sales focussed culture
- The wasted investment of one group not knowing what the other is planning, such as advertising campaigns with no front line warning (or training), and thus sales opportunities lost

Where organisations do not have the entrepreneurial spirit at the heart of their culture, they exhibit some distinctive characteristics:

Characteristics of a non-Innovative Culture

(See pages 81–84 for a description of an Innovative Culture)

Organisations that do not have a culture of learning and growth get left in the past. They take a position on how the world is – their customers, their competitors, their products and services, and they work hard to make the world fit into how they want it to be. They are often, and to their mind unexpectedly, overtaken by others who have a greater willingness to learn.

Employees will find external reasons to explain when things go wrong. They blame, justify, deny and defend. They are not open to feedback, whether it is direct or indirect. Feedback from their market is unco-ordinated and does not reach the people who are making decisions about the future. Staff pick up quickly that attempts to give feedback to management will be met with a defensive response.

When I was a child we used to do lots of jigsaw puzzles. There would always be a puzzle laid out on a table with a green baize cloth, and we would all sit around and talk and place a few pieces. The family was fanatical about jigsaws – we were such purists no one was allowed to look at the picture on the lid! Every Christmas my grandmother, a formidable woman who we called Gar, would arrive and settle herself in front of the jigsaw. Gar had one fatal flaw. Once she had decided a piece would fit in a particular position, she could never be convinced otherwise, no matter how strong the evidence was to the contrary. She would just jam those pieces in, complaining about the poor quality of modern jigsaw manufacturing. We quickly learned not to question her wisdom, although we did used to sneak downstairs early in the morning to correct her mistakes so that we all had some chance of finishing the jigsaw. I often think of those evenings with Gar when we are invited to an organisation with a non-learning culture.

A non-Innovative organisation exists in a bubble of its own making. This is particularly challenging if the organisation is fairly successful. The seeds of their future failure lie in the arrogance brought about by the current success. Many consider the entrepreneur to be leading trends, rather than following them, and this is indeed the case. But what is not visible to the outsider is the amount of learning and correcting that goes on in order to become such a trendsetter. These organisations try lots of approaches before finding the one that brings them success. They don't become rigidly stuck on one path.

A blinkered approach leads to a tolerance of mediocrity and blindness to declining standards. Near enough becomes good enough. The organisation lacks the desire to pursue excellence, and will therefore deliver services to its customers which may be adequate, but not delightful. Success will depend on the state of the market: if competitors are also mediocre, if the organisation has its position in some way secured through government or regulatory influence or if the cost of entry for new players is prohibitive, these organisations can be successful. But the moment the opportunity arises, customers will move to a competitor who is more innovative, modern and exciting.

This plays out in day-to-day life in a number of ways:
1. The organisation lags behind the opinions and needs of its external communities. When indicators start to reflect this, it responds by pushing harder on its existing position or products
2. There is an unwillingness to back down and admit to being wrong. This results in becoming trapped in unsustainable contracts, partnerships, merger talks, strategies or continuing with projects which are clearly never going to succeed
3. Mistakes are made a number of times by the same group of people, who did not take responsibility in the first instance. Different parts of the organisation repeat the sins of their colleagues and predecessors

4. Feedback that would facilitate learning sits in the wrong part of the organisation – the data does not flow back to those who could take action
5. People are not allowed the opportunity of learning from their mistakes – accountability and authority sit in different places

Impact on performance
The cost of this culture will lie in:

- Delays in coming to market with innovations or failure to do so at all
- Repeated rework, caused by the same mistake being made over and over, whether in product design, project implementation or errors for the customer
- Re-inventing the wheel. Different divisions undertaking the same type of work because there is no knowledge transfer across the business
- Bureaucracy, high costs associated with a failure to improve cost standards
- Poor quality goods being manufactured or services delivered, resulting in a high rejection rate which does not reduce over time. Lack of consistency in quality and wide variations

Finally, it is easy to spot the organisation that does not value its people:

Characteristics of a non-People-First Culture
(See pages 87–89 for a description of a People-First Culture)
When an organisation does not value its people, it is quite simply a horrible place to work. Those people with initiative and high self-confidence just leave. This is not a place you would choose to work if you had other options. But the state of the employment market may mean this is not an easy choice for many people.

These cultures seem to wear people down slowly. Employees enter the organisation with enthusiasm, and gradually their life spirit seems to be ground out of them. After a few years they may no longer see the leaving option as a possibility, which might be as much a reflection of their own state of mind as of the employment market itself. An abusive culture produces a feeling of helplessness. People enter into a victim mind-set.

Resentment sets in. Employees moan about their lot. Their conversations with each other about management and the company are bitter. They check their mind out at the door, and go through the motions through the day. This is often particularly true at the front line, where the perks of work – status, power, money, are least, and so there is little compensation for living in an unsupportive environment.

People are seen to be the problem. If a problem arises with a customer, supervisors will blame the customer-facing staff member. Systemic or process solutions are not thought through, because management is in the habit of blaming others. Their lack of respect for their people, and failure to see their willingness to contribute, is at the root of the culture.

The culture's beliefs about its people becomes a self-fulfilling prophecy. It breeds disloyalty and low-self esteem. As a result, people become selfish, and they focus on getting what they can for themselves. These cultures become the opposite of values-driven, and people look after their own needs.

This plays out in day-to-day life in the following ways:
1. People will do the minimum requirement and no more. They will not go the extra mile, for their colleagues, their boss or their customers
2. A lack of investment in people development and training results in poor quality service. Employees do not have the knowledge required to do their job well
3. Standards are sloppy, people do not carry through on commitments, return phone calls, pass on information to each other
4. As people gain some position of authority, they build walls around themselves, and find ways to meet their own needs by

increasing their financial reward, building their empire and treating their subordinates as they have been treated

5. Opportunities are taken, when they present themselves, to abuse the system, through stealing, cheating or lying
6. Discrimination, sexual harassment, and bullying are common, as those who reach positions of authority use their power
7. When there are employment opportunities, people leave. Because people are not coached and trained, vacancies often have to be filled from outside, because internal candidates are not available

Impact on performance

In building your case for a People-First Culture, look in the following areas:

- Recruitment costs, and the cost of training up new people
- The loss of corporate memory, and relationships, that is a result of losing good people
- The cost of stealing and other ways in which employees abuse the system
- Changes to process or product not picked up and used, because people did not buy in to the communication they received
- Lack of feedback about problems or potential problems, an environment where whistle-blowing cannot occur. (It has been established that people further down the NASA organisation knew about the potential problems with the 'O' Rings on the Challenger spacecraft, but did not raise these up the line prior to the disastrous launch)
- Law suits from badly treated employees

I have outlined a range of ways in which you can build the case for culture, in your quest to bring your whole top team with you on this journey. It really is essential that you feel you can achieve this if you are intending to drive a major culture change process, rather than work quietly from the sidelines. There is one more line of argument.

SUSTAINABLE PERFORMANCE

In describing how to build a business case for culture, I have focussed on those elements which can directly flow to the bottom line in a fairly short time-frame. The return on investment should be within a short enough time-frame to persuade the most challenging director or CFO that there is a case to invest in culture change. There is enough evidence on this basis alone to undertake this work.

There is another argument for building a great culture and that is that it supports performance on the triple bottom line. The triple bottom line concept – that organisations have a responsibility that goes beyond that of their shareholders – is taking root quickly in the business community. To believe that an organisation has a responsibility to the communities in which it operates, to the environment and to its customers and employees, suggests a values-based approach. There is a fundamental change happening in the values hierarchy of both the business community and its stakeholders which is evolving at this time.

If companies are expected to consider more than their own bottom line, then, according to the definitions of values covered in Chapter 1, they must move from a focus on the second, selfish, list of values, to the first, more other-centric ones. If the values in the community move to the point at which companies are expected to behave in this way by everyone (including investors), then their performance will only be sustainable if they do so. This would make the business case for culture even stronger than it is now.

Sustainable performance requires a values-based approach. It requires holding fast to certain values even under great pressure to produce short-term performance, and ideally to achieve both. Sustainability is the art of plotting this path. If your organisation has taken steps to consider sustainability as a business priority, then your business case can focus on the importance to this strategy of building a values-based culture.

With all this information, building your business case becomes easier. It is important to show how culture causes people in the organisation to behave in ways that have a performance impact. And how what we value affects how we choose to spend our money and how we make decisions. With this concept well-framed up front, the impact of culture on performance becomes much broader than most people who see your business case may have previously imagined. The greatest enemy of cultural work is the idea that it is just about making our people happy. People being happy is merely a by-product. And many will not be happy as the culture starts to change: those who have been comfortably sitting in one of the cultures described above may feel like lifting their game is all a bit too hard!

SUMMARY

This brings us to the end of the first phase of your journey, and the first section of this book. At this point you should now have:

1. An understanding of your present culture
2. A description of what you want
3. A case for change
4. A broad outline of the journey
5. A top team who are signed on, at least intellectually
6. At least a couple of completely committed advocates.

This process will probably take you around six months. You are now in a position to move on. The second section of this book shows you how to move from where you are now to your defined cultural outcome.

SECTION 2:

THE CULTURE DEVELOPMENT PLAN

UILDING or changing of a culture must be tackled with the same amount of vigour and discipline that you would use to change any other component of your business, be it your marketing strategy, your IT platform or your cost structure. You will need a plan, to which you dedicate resources and manage its implementation. However passionate you are personally about all this stuff, and even if you are the CEO, the charisma of your conviction is not enough. Many CEOs have failed to change cultures, and analysis of those failures suggests a failure to understand and manage the complexity of the task, as well as, in some cases, an unwillingness to understand that in this instance, you are a part of the problem as well as a part of its solution.

I will call this plan a Culture Development Plan. It will lay out how you will move your organisation from its current position, which you've identified in your Culture Diagnostic (Chapter 3), to your intended position, as described in your Desired Culture (Chapter 4). How to build the business case for the investment your plan will require was described in Chapter 5, and you will by now have commitment to proceed. The purpose of your Culture Development Plan is to deliver the return on that investment, through achieving the Desired Culture.

Your Culture Development Plan will show how to change the messages people receive about behaviour in your organisation, so that the culture changes. It will focus on those levers at your disposal: behaviours, symbols and systems. It will also outline how you intend to manage the process, who will be accountable for it and how you will measure progress.

The plan should cover three years in broad outline, with the first year in detail, and be updated every year. The nature of change to the thinking and behaviour of human beings is such that you have to expect changes to your approach as you progress. It is hard to anticipate the pace of change, which groups of people will move ahead fastest and which will resist the hardest. As your leaders become more values-driven in their thinking, they themselves will pick up the ball and initiate a range of changes far beyond those you considered in the early days of writing your plan. This, of course, is just what you want!

This section of the book will start with a framework on how people think, feel and behave, which will give you the understanding to construct a plan to influence them. The following chapters will cover how to change behaviour in yourself and others, how to use symbols and systems to build your culture, and the processes for communication and management.

6

A Framework For Change

| ASSESS | DEFINE | COMMIT | PLAN | IMPLEMENTATION BEHAVIOURS SYMBOLS SYSTEMS |

COMMUNICATION

PROCESS OF MANAGEMENT

BEHAVIOUR lies at the heart of any plan to build culture. It is also the key to your organisation's performance.

Your culture is continually reinforced through the behaviours in the organisation, in particular those in positions of influence – the role models. Everyone watches their behaviour to figure out what is normal and expected. You can see that in order to change your culture you are going to have to change the behaviour of a number of people, especially those in positions of influence. Leadership behaviour is your top priority.

All people behave the way they do because of how they think and feel. Our thoughts, beliefs, values and feelings – some deep and subconscious, some superficial and transient – cause us to behave the way we do in any given moment. This jumble of thoughts that goes on inside of us I will call our *mind-set*. I will explain them each in more detail shortly. If you want a person to change their behaviour, you have to influence their mind-set.

So to change your culture you have to change the behaviour of leaders and to do this you must change their mind-sets. But, as you know, your leaders' mind-sets are influenced by the culture as it currently stands, which is continually telling them to behave the way they are at the moment.

> Your plan has to figure out how to cause enough people to behave counter-culturally for long enough to establish a new norm and bring the rest along with them

This is the fundamental strategy to changing culture.

If you achieve this, there is a domino effect:

Change in the mind-sets of leaders

Leads to

Change in the behaviour of leaders

Leads to

Different decisions being made by leaders, in-line with their new beliefs and values

Leads to

People attributing meaning to decisions (symbols) associated with a change in values

Leads to

New messages being received throughout the organisation about what is now valued

(supported by changing enablers which have simultaneously been redesigned)

Leads to

Other people in the organisation changing their behaviour to fit into the new norms

Leads to

Further reinforcement that the culture and its values have now changed

Leads to

New performance outcomes, the effect of the chosen values

So, there you have it. That is how it works, and your job is to design and implement a plan that will facilitate this chain of events.

WHAT IS BEHAVIOUR AND WHAT IS ITS ROLE IN PERFORMANCE?

When it is said that people are an organisation's greatest asset, it refers, of course, to the fact that nothing occurs in the business context except by and through people. Each person in your organisation spends a certain amount of their waking life at work. What they actually do in that time determines their contribution to the organisation's performance. All effort associated with leadership, motivation, organisational development, culture and other such activities have as their goal to influence how employees use their time at work.

Everything that occurs in your organisation is activated through the behaviours of your people. How you and your colleagues behave will determine the type of strategy you adopt, your discipline in executing that strategy, how you allocate resources and how you lead your people.

Clients will often ask us to prove the relationship between culture and performance. We find the challenge is not so much to prove the relationship between them, but to find anything in an organisation where the outcome is not influenced by behaviour, which in turn is shaped by the culture.

The picture looks like this:

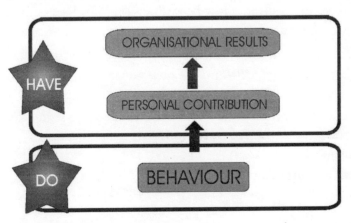

What we **DO** (behaviour) produces what we **HAVE** (outcome).

Each behaviour produces a particular outcome. A different behaviour will produce a different outcome. If you want different performance outcomes for your business, you will need to adopt different behaviours. They say a good definition of insanity is to continue to do the same things yet expect a different outcome!

The purpose of having the best culture possible is to create an environment that draws out the behaviours from your people that are most appropriate to the aims of your organisation.

What is behaviour?

Behaviour is how I act in the world. It is what I do, and what is visible to others. The words 'behaviour' and 'action' are used quite imprecisely to cover the whole range of what people get up to at work. To design your interventions, you need to be very clear what these terms mean, and what you are actually seeking to change.

We have analysed many lists of behaviours used by organisations to define what they want from their people. We have found that everything that people do at work can be grouped into one of three categories.

1. Interactions with others
2. Use of time
3. Decisions made

I will describe each to show how changing mind-sets changes the behaviours, and therefore the performance outcomes.

1. Interactions with others

This category includes the *quality* of our interactions with others:

- Friendly
- Brusque
- Clear communication
- Honesty

- Hostile
- Inspiring

And the *content* of our interactions with others. Content is what we actually say or write, and what we do with our body (touch, laugh, strike, look away, etc.).

Here are examples from the millions of behavioural interactions:

- Tell someone you are unhappy with their performance, keeping eye contact as you do so
- Object to a proposal being put forward, in writing
- Smile, and inquire in a friendly manner if a customer is happy with your service
- Talk with excitement about recent successes in a team meeting
- Question your finance person on the rigour of sales figures

Although some of our behaviour is fairly instinctive, certain mind-sets increase our ability to monitor and adjust how we interact with others. For example, if you can build trust with someone, your behaviours towards each other will change. Most people are capable of building trust under the right circumstances and with the right support. Your Culture Development Plan will build initiatives to provide those circumstances.

Similarly, we tend to avoid behaviours in which we lack confidence. Often this lack of confidence comes from a lack of skill. If you teach people the skill of giving feedback, for example, you increase their confidence, and they are more likely to do it. Your plan will include training programmes in such skills.

2. Use of time

We all have a certain number of hours a day we spend at work. What do we choose to do with that time? Every minute of every day we are making choices about how we use our time. Say I have half an hour before the next meeting. I could:

- Phone a customer (which customer? The one who likes me or the one who is unhappy with our service?)
- Phone my boyfriend
- Do my expenses for the month
- Talk to a colleague about a problem I think is coming up
- Do another revision of the presentation I am making to the boss tomorrow

And a million other choices. Which choice I make determines the outcomes I will achieve that day, and ultimately my performance.

How an individual spends his or her time is determined by what they think is important, which in turn is influenced by their hierarchy of values. For example, if you believe that achieving your own sales targets is more important than helping your colleague by supporting her new project, and you have very limited time, you will probably avoid going to the meeting she has called, and instead make another sales call. Your Culture Development Plan will include initiatives which reshape the hierarchy of values of your people, and thus change the choices they make about how they spend their time.

How time is spent determines an individual's performance. No one has enough time, so we are continually making choices about where we focus our attention. For many people these choices are quite subconscious. Some delegate the task of allocating their time to others. Their PA or their colleagues get to fill their diaries without a rigorous set of criteria. The battle for one's own time in a large organisation is one which, if conquered, will drive enhanced performance in-line with values.

Here are a few examples of the thousands of important behaviours related to the use of time, which will contribute to building your desired culture:

- Coaching team members
- Building and communicating vision
- Visiting customers

- Planning for and mitigating risks
- Finding best practice, and learning how they do it
- Giving performance feedback

3. Making decisions

We draw upon our past experience, and our beliefs and values, to make judgments all the time about the best course of action. Examples include:

- What recommendation shall I make in this report?
- Shall I hire this person or that one?
- What goal shall I set for this team?
- Shall I spend money on this?
- Which supplier will I use?
- How will I price this?

Decisions are made based on experience and values. Experience tells us what has worked before, and accumulates to allow us to predict the best course of action for the future. Values tell us what should be our priorities and our decision-making criteria. Changing beliefs and values will influence the latter part of the inputs to a decision.

The strength of the integrity and diversity values with one of our clients helped them to make tough decisions regarding sacking an individual whose behaviour towards women at the Christmas party was overtly sexual. This individual was one of the top team and had in every other way been a great performer. He was sacked as a result of that night. A CEO with a different set of values and beliefs would have found another way of dealing with the situation. (As you read this, notice how your personal set of values is considering which course of action you would have taken in that set of circumstances.). Sacking that person was a behaviour.

Here are some examples of behaviours in this category you might want to have in your organisation:

- Rejecting sub-standard work
- Favouring internal promotions where candidates are available
- Considering the needs of the broader organisation when making a decision about IT software
- Supporting and sticking with a team decision once it has been made
- Removing non-performers from the team
- Closing a division which has been losing money for years

Within these three categories lies everything that each one of us contributes to our organisation on a day-to-day basis. I will group them together and call them 'behaviour' for our purposes here. If you review the lists of behaviours you already have in your leadership evaluation tools or your descriptions of desired culture, you will find they fit.

You can see the relationship between these behaviours and the performance outcomes that an individual delivers, and how these then impact the overall performance of the organisation. Our diagram now looks like this:

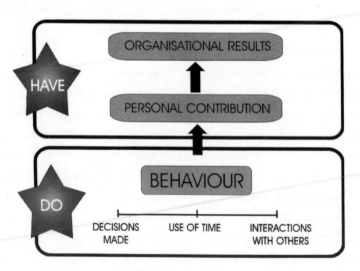

How behaviours group together to impact performance

Jo runs a government department which provides a number of

services. Some deliver excellent service standards, others do not, and yet the poor performing divisions are also running the highest overheads. For many years the department did not have good data on service standards, but a technology upgrade a couple of years ago made this information available. Jo is a good manager of her people, well-liked, supportive and fair. But she hates making tough decisions. She's a classic 'Ms Nice Guy'.

Since the data became available, she has been avoiding making any decisions on non-performing parts of her portfolio. This major behaviour – avoiding decisions – has a whole lot of sub-components. She believes presentations which sugar-coat the truth (category 3 – making decisions), she pulls resources from another efficient area to prop up this division (again, making decisions), she closes off the discussion when the one member of her team who is prepared to challenge her, raises his concerns about the matter (category 1 – interactions with others), she spends a great deal of her time reassuring her minister that all is well (category 2 – use of time). This has been going on for a year. She displays a whole range of behaviours, all underpinning her major character flaw of avoidance. Unsurprisingly, a culture of avoidance has spread through the department.

Let's take another example and work it through to see what mindset changes would need to occur to produce a different behaviour (and a different outcome). Tim has a team who need to talk to each other frequently to be successful together. In particular, his marketing manager is responsible for product promotions which require front line sales people to be prepared to talk through options with customers when they ring in. Last time a promotion was run, the first the sales people heard about it was when the customers started calling. One of them even had to ask a customer to fax in the ad they had seen with the pricing deal! They estimated that this lack of information had caused sales from the promotion to be 10 per cent lower than anticipated.

Several people had tried to raise the issue of a lack of communication with Tim, but he cut them off with jocular remarks about everyone being big people and capable of sorting things out for themselves (category 1 – interactions with others). There was an item on a management meeting agenda about product promotions, but the previous agenda item concerned a presentation Tim had to give to the Board on financials, and he had allowed this item to go way over time so he would be confident of the figures he was presenting (category 2 – use of time). This was not the first time marketing had not let the rest of the organisation know what they were up to, but Tim had been avoiding having this performance conversation with the marketing manager (category 1). At performance review time he scored the individual 4/5 (category 3 – making decisions) and continued with this person in the role for several years, despite average performance in a number of areas. Overall impact on organisational performance – considerable.

What would be the mind-sets – the beliefs and values – required in Tim to enhance performance, and send new cultural messages? He would have to believe strongly that:

1. Communication between his team members matters, and it is his role to ensure that it happens by asking key questions and showing his expectations in this area

2. Agendas are an important way of respecting the relative importance of everyone's job. They can become a part of the 'keeping our word' commitment of the team. As the boss, Tim does not have the right to override an agenda in order to ensure that he looks good in a presentation to his boss

3. Honesty in performance reviews is at the heart of a performance culture. Scoring someone a 4/5 who is not performing is dishonest and letting the team down

If Tim held these three beliefs strongly, there would have been a very different outcome for the organisation. In addition to the direct benefit of having the marketing and sales functions operating as a cohesive whole, Tim's behaviour would have been noted by others. In displaying behaviours based on the three beliefs described, he would send messages to others about what was valued and expected, thus setting a cultural norm associated with:

- Performance
- Teamwork
- Holding to commitments (agendas)

One simple example, where once we start to unpick the pieces, the relationships between behaviour, culture, beliefs and values and performance outcomes become apparent.

MIND-SETS: THE DRIVERS OF PERFORMANCE

This brings us to the most challenging and most important piece of your Culture Development Plan which is changing the mind-sets of your people. Because what people do, is caused by who they are. This third level of our model is called BE. How someone is at the BE-level determines what they DO which determines the outcomes they HAVE.

BE-DO-HAVE.

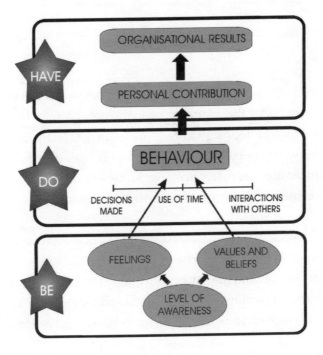

The BE-level, which I have collectively referred to as the mind-set, contains three elements:

1. Feelings
2. Beliefs and values
3. Level of awareness

In order to shape the behaviour in your organisation, you need to understand each element at the BE-level, because behaviour change is caused by changes in mind-set.

Feelings

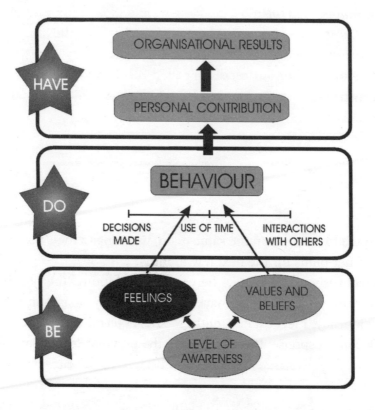

How I am feeling determines my level of engagement, which means how involved I feel. This determines the amount of energy that I am willing to invest in any given situation. It determines my motivation. Motivation, from the Latin word meaning 'to move', comes from the same root as emotion. If I am emotionally engaged in a situation I will respond to it more strongly than if I am only intellectually engaged in it.

Engagement becomes the energy charge behind my behaviour. If this charge is positive I will display behaviours that are constructive. If the charge is negative or if there is very little charge because I am not emotionally engaged at all, my behaviours will probably be less useful, or potentially destructive.

There are many feelings that are influenced by behaviour.

Examples of the types of feelings that impact behaviour and performance outcomes

• Excited	• Cynical
• Energetic	• Driven
• Frustrated	• Appreciated
• Anxious	• Tired
• Nervous	• Focussed
• Confident	• Angry
• Trusting	• Distracted
• Mistrustful	• Stressed

Imagine two people in the same team, listening to their boss laying out her plans for the next few months:

First response: I'm new here, I am ambitious, this job is the opportunity to make my mark, and I'm ready to sign-up for this new journey. I feel excited, enthusiastic, determined.

Second response: three years ago the previous leader said all of these things. We just had a terrible performance year because his team made some stupid decisions. As a result a lot of people were let go. I am very cynical about going down this path again. I feel let down, mistrustful, unconfident.

Clearly these two people will behave very differently in response to their leader's requests.

Beliefs and values

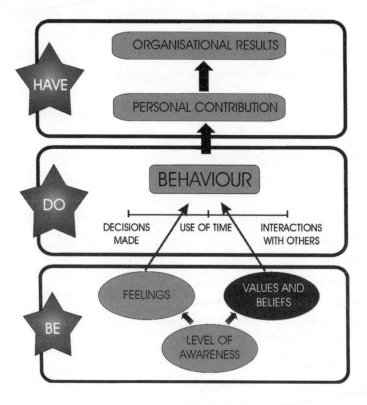

My beliefs and values then direct this energy charge in certain directions. Some of these beliefs are quite superficial and conscious, and others are much deeper and I may not even be aware of the extent to which they drive my behaviour. Often, because we are contrary and illogical animals, our values and beliefs do not line up with each other, and we carry a superficial belief about something, but our behaviour does not line up with this belief, because we hold a deeper, contradictory belief. The more deeply held, and often subconscious, a belief or value lies, the more likely it is to be the stronger one if a conflict exists – the driver of the actual behaviour.

An old friend of mine believes that developing good people matters, but he continues to hold on to work, and not delegate. He and I have long conversations about this, because I have some of the same challenges myself. Over the years, as we have both become more self-aware, he realised that whilst he superficially believed people matter, he held a much deeper belief of his own superiority. He basically thought he was better than everyone else, so naturally assumed that he would do the task better than others. It is this latter belief that drove his behaviour. In my case, I had a pretty strong belief that I needed to prove my own competence all the time. Holding on to work enabled me to do this. So we both had to change our deeper beliefs so that our value of developing people could shine through.

Examples of the types of beliefs which impact behaviour and performance outcomes
- You can't trust other people – if you want a job done well, do it yourself
- The finance people don't care about customers
- If you make enough sales calls you will make your numbers
- The market will come good soon
- My boss doesn't want to hear bad news
- To fit in around here I am expected to raise concerns openly

These beliefs have been formed from experiences we have had, from which we have drawn conclusions. These conclusions may or may not be the same conclusions that another person would have drawn from the same experience. And just because a large number of people believe something, this does not make it any more or less true, or necessarily any more valuable than an alternative belief. Notice that I have not used the words 'right' or 'wrong' here. Some conclusions, and therefore beliefs will prove to be more useful than others to us in the future. 'Useful' in this context means delivering the outcomes we want.

Some beliefs are more rational, and therefore can be changed through logical argument. Others are more emotional, and can only be changed through alternative emotional experiences. These are experienced more as knee-jerk responses than as beliefs, although they come from a deeply held view of the world. These are more difficult to shift.

Unfortunately, when I have a certain belief I may behave in ways that cause the outcome that my belief predicted. A vicious circle is therefore generated. For example, if I believe people are untrustworthy, I am likely to withhold information from them which will make it harder for them to perform. Because they have not performed, they will have proved to me that they are untrustworthy.

In addition to these beliefs, we have our personal values. These are our deeply held beliefs about what is important in the world. Some people hold values very strongly, and we call them values-driven or people of high principles. For others, values are less significant in determining their behaviour, and they are more influenced by their feelings, and beliefs about what they need (for example, money).

Examples of personal values which impact behaviour and performance outcomes

The value of looking after one's mates or affiliation. This resonates through almost every part of our society, be it national pride, allegiance to a football team, the desire to be a part of some club or a group of individuals with a common set of beliefs and purpose. This value is strongly activated when we work for an organisation.

The value of being true to one's word. This plays an important part in being accountable, delivering what you say you will, following through on promises. It is a fundamental piece of organisational life, and of the relationship between an organisation and its customers and owners.

The value of learning. This lies at the heart of a willingness to pick up ideas and successes from other parts of the organisation, of acting on feedback, of continuous improvement.

The value of integrity. This will cause me to act honestly even when I have the opportunity to do otherwise, to abide by the policies of the business, to keep confidences, to stick with a decision we made together, and act in the interests of the organisation which has employed me.

Think of feelings, beliefs and values as the engine and the steering wheel of a car. Feelings (the engine), determine the power behind your driving. Beliefs and values (the wheel), steer that power in a particular direction.

Level of self-awareness

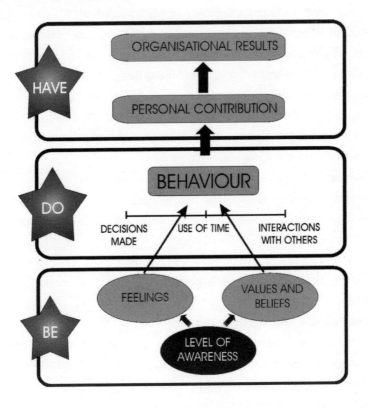

At the base of the BE part of each of us is our level of self-awareness. This means literally how aware we are of ourselves and what makes us tick. A person who lacks self-awareness goes through their life feeling a victim to circumstances. They are unable to see the connection between themselves and the outcomes they experience in the world. A person who is cognisant can make these connections. They know that, for things to change, first I must change. They can observe the workings of their own minds sufficiently to change their attitudes if they are not useful. Consequently, these individuals are more likely to have beliefs and values which are useful and uplifting to both themselves and those around them. They are also more likely to produce outcomes that are satisfactory because they are not operating in a world of luck, chance or magic, wherein some miraculous outside event will occur to make everything work out.

If our level of self-awareness is high we become aware of the game that is being played out by our values, beliefs and behaviours that produce the outcomes in our life. We are observers of our lives as well as participants. We dance on the dance floor, and also watch the dance from the balcony. If we can do this, then the web of our values, beliefs and feelings entangles us less. We are in a stronger position to adjust them when they are not producing outcomes with which we are satisfied.

High self-awareness over time leads to an inner confidence that Abraham Maslow described as self-actualisation in his book *Motivation and Personality*. He describes people who are highly self-actualised as:

- Having a realistic view of situations, not personalised and neither overly optimistic nor pessimistic, and able to distinguish between the fake and the genuine
- Relatively independent of culture and environment, and less susceptible to social pressure
- Open to individual and ethnic variety
- Accepting of self and others
- Having a freshness and ability to see things with wonder, which leads to originality and creativity
- Spontaneous with a sense of fun and humour which is not hostile to others

An altogether valuable set of attributes for any organisation.

An enhanced level of awareness comes from mindfulness, when you watch the other parts of your mind play out their routines. The split second taken to step back is often enough to enable you to choose different behaviours. You actually get to watch yourself playing a part in your own movie of your life, and to be the director of that process. Like the movie *Groundhog Day*, in which Bill Murray tries out different behaviours in the same situation to get different results, a higher level of cognisance lets you experiment with behaviour to produce better outcomes.

Level of awareness determines the degree of defensiveness in your response. It allows you to create rather than to react to your life circumstances. This ability is extremely important to the process of changing yourself. Without it, you are indeed a victim of your own established mind-sets, and it will feel as if you are at the mercy of what life throws at you. We sometimes call this 'being a victim'. This is a permanent state of BE-ing for some people.

A huge side-benefit of raising your level of awareness is an increased sense of well-being. As you develop the ability to step back and watch your own behaviour and reactions, you feel more centred, less overwhelmed and happier. There is a real win-win bonus to culture work!

BE-DO-HAVE: THE FRAMEWORK FOR CHANGE
I will use BE-DO-HAVE throughout the coming chapters to provide a framework for building your Culture Development plan. You HAVE a certain culture, which is producing the performance you HAVE. A major influence on this culture is the behaviours of leaders in your organisation, what leaders DO. You will have to reshape how your leaders BE if you are to change what they DO, and thus the outcomes you HAVE. This reshaping is called changing mind-sets. It will form the major part of your Culture Development Plan.

To change culture you have to change mind-sets at the BE-level of a critical mass. This critical mass is probably about 30 per cent of your workforce in the first three years, and 60–70 per cent of your management population. There are two ways to change mindsets – 'change the people or change the people'. Either convince your people to change their attitudes or bring in replacement people. You will need to do some of each. As you build towards the critical mass number, the expectations or cultural norms change. It becomes clear what is now expected. At this point those who have the capacity to behave differently, but have been holding back from doing so because they wanted to fit in, start to display behaviours you want, they change at the DO-level. This is a great pleasure to behold. The shift in this population is what moves your culture change process into top gear.

At the same time, those who have deeply held beliefs or values that lock them into one, inappropriate pattern of behaviour become very apparent. This is the group you will have to remove from the organisation, through nudging or something stronger, over the next period of time. Some of them will actually leave of their own volition, because they can see they no longer fit in. Others will cling on.

PRIORITY TARGET GROUPS IN YOUR CULTURE DEVELOPMENT PLAN

When your objective is to change culture, your priority target groups for mind-set change in the early stages is your leadership population. The hierarchical nature of organisations means that the messages sent by leaders are the most influential in terms of creating the culture. The early stages of your work must therefore be to change the messages they send about what is expected. Work with front line staff will always be hampered by the culture within which they work. For reasons we have already discussed, staff are likely to adapt their behaviour to fit with their perceptions of what is expected. Your investment will be diluted by the counter-influence of the supervisors and managers on the day-to-day job.

The influence of leadership is particularly strong around what one could call organisational values, such as customer-focus, teamwork, innovation and performance. In these instances individuals have fewer personal values outside the work environment, so the influence of the values around them is stronger. In the case of more personal values, such as integrity, loyalty or caring for others, an individual is more likely to behave according to their own values, rather than those of the culture.

So, as a general rule, start your in-depth efforts with the leadership population. Also, include people who have strong influencing positions with their peers, because they are respected for their experience, technical expertise or performance.

Involving the front line

When an organisation starts to involve the front line in a meaningful way, it can truly be said that the desired culture is gathering momentum. Great cultures feel as great at the front line as they do at management levels. Involving the front line is a significant step, which is best taken at the point when you have the leadership population on board with your cultural aspirations, and are seeing behaviour change. Do not hold back, however, believing you have to wait until the leadership population have got everything handled. Intent and evidence of change are the triggers to take the next step.

Involving the front line requires a major investment in time and money, which is why it is best left until leaders are convinced that the culture journey delivers business benefits. Once the front line is involved, culture becomes a passion and a core feature of what your organisation represents. Culture is talked about in the corridors. Pride builds in what has been achieved and where you are going. Business benefits are communicated and understood.

Management sometimes considers that a different approach should be used for the front line because they are more junior, paid less, belong to unions or don't have career aspirations. I have not found this to be a valuable line of argument. There is a slight arrogance I see creeping into such thoughts. 'Because we are leaders we have greater capacity to cope with advanced programmes.' In relation to your core components of the Culture Development Plan behaviours, values, symbols, communication, your front line will respond as favourably as your leadership population. Often the front line has a freshness and enthusiasm missing amongst the more jaded management group who have been through more programmes of various kinds during their career.

Staff at the front line have the same experiences – trust, fear, frustration, enthusiasm, values dilemmas, responsibility, blame, etc. They display the same range of behaviours and responses. They benefit in the same way from building their life skills, becoming more values-driven, engaging more fully with their work. Universally, we have found that, initially, leadership does not display a superior set of behaviours or values than that of the front line. In defining a new set of standards and expectations, previous measuring sticks become less valid, and in this regard everyone goes back to zero.

FRAMEWORK FOR YOUR CULTURE DEVELOPMENT PLAN

Now that you have the framework to understand how change will occur, you can think through all of the elements of your Culture Development Plan.

You must lay your plan out in six segments:

1. Desired culture, existing culture, gap, business case
2. Initiatives to change the mind-sets of your people, starting with the leadership population
3. Changes to symbols and systems, to reinforce the message of your new values
4. Communication strategy
5. How you will measure change
6. Governance structure for the cultural journey

The first point was covered earlier in the book. The coming chapters provide the detail to enable you to build and implement the rest of the plan.

7

How to Change
Your Own Behaviour

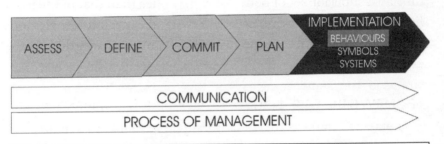

| ASSESS | DEFINE | COMMIT | PLAN | IMPLEMENTATION BEHAVIOURS SYMBOLS SYSTEMS |

COMMUNICATION

PROCESS OF MANAGEMENT

> 'Don't say things. What you are stands over you the while,
> and thunders so that I cannot hear what you say to the
> contrary'
>
> Ralph Waldo Emerson

THERE simply is no culture change without walking the talk. Whatever role you hold in this process, you have to be an example of the behaviour you want. This doesn't mean you have to be perfect in every way, but it does mean that, when your behaviour is inappropriate, you can be aware enough to notice this and acknowledge it to others.

This is challenging for many leaders, because they will argue, quite rightly, that they have already been very successful in their careers, and therefore their behaviour must be working. Many leaders are successful despite their style. But no leader successfully changes their organisation's culture without aligning their own behaviour to that required by the desired culture. Many leaders I know, for example, are aggressive, competitive go-getters, who are better at leading a team than being a member of one. They have struggled with collaboration throughout their career, but their organisations rewarded them because they produced results within their own area, even if at times this was at the expense of the whole. Such leaders could not lead a One-Team Culture without changing their behaviour. I worked extensively with Greg who was a country head for a multinational pharmaceutical company. He wanted a One-Team culture. As the country head, one could believe that he did not have to be a good team player. But he was a part of a global team. And whenever he spoke about his colleagues in Head Office, it was in derogatory terms, believing that he was doing a better job than them. His people were not stupid. They could see he wasn't walking the talk. When we did a leadership assessment on him, the data said the same thing. I got this message through to him eventually, but it took a while!

To play a leadership role in culture, you have to understand on a personal level what is involved in making the type of change required. You personally need to be moving faster than anyone down this path. At the very least you need to be working on yourself as hard as you are working on everyone else.

Walking the talk requires you to change your behaviour at all times, not just when you are putting on your 'best behaviour' show. The only way to do this is to change your mind-sets. If you do not change at the BE level, you may be able to adopt some new behaviours for special occasions, but the mind-sets you still hold will exert themselves when you are not concentrating, and others will see you revert to type. When you change your feelings, values, beliefs and level of self-awareness, the behaviour change at the DO level is automatic, because the force that sat behind it has changed. This is the only way to be sure you walk the talk.

Here are some of the best techniques for changing your own mindsets. They will also form a part of your plan as you determine how you facilitate other people pursuing some of these paths. Remember, you have an advantage here, you wanted this to happen. You are what is known as 'change ready'. Despite this, you will find some of this work quite challenging. This is because it will take you outside your comfort zone.

There are five paths you can take to change mind-sets. You will probably want to pursue all five at some point.

Area of focus	Type of technique
1. Changing rational, intellectually held beliefs	Exposure to alternative, rational data and arguments
2. Changing less-rational beliefs and responses with an emotional underpinning	Increasing emotional intelligence through self-analysis, feedback, coaching or therapy
3. Becoming more values-driven and changing your values hierarchy	Increasing self-confidence and listening to intuition through coaching and thoughtfulness
4. Changing your feelings	Increasing positive motivation through trust, relationship and meaning
5. Changing your level of awareness	Opportunities for, and practice of, self-reflection

For many people these paths, loosely called the paths of personal development, are a life journey in their own right. For some, the path of raising self-awareness has a spiritual tone which makes it a quest. For others, getting comfortable with emotions, a process often entered into as a result of emotional pain of some sort, leads to a voyage of self-discovery that brings much joy and satisfaction.

I must confess to a personal bias here. My early years were spent in the pursuit of spiritual and emotional development, and I was very practised in these techniques before entering the world of corporate change. Bringing the two disciplines together has been a life's work for me, and the corporate world is becoming more attuned to the potential that such an approach has to transform, rather than merely change culture and behaviour.

Transformation is a process from which there is no return. Once I know and have seen that I can produce a different outcome by behaving in a different manner, I can never go back to not knowing that. Thus I am transformed. I have become a different person because of this new knowledge. This is more than change. Change has the potential to change back or to change to a third position. Transformation is permanent, and involves an added dimension that embraces the previous one. The internet, for example, has transformed how we feel and think about information, as well as changing our behaviour. Were the internet to disappear tomorrow, we would recreate another way of achieving what we now know about the accessibility of information.

It is this level of transformation that we all aspire to in our culture change initiatives. To ensure its permanence we need an inner shift that changes forever the way we view the world.

So, this personal journey comes with a health warning! Once you shift what you know to be possible both within yourself and within teams and organisations, you cannot go back. You may find your quest takes on a life of its own beyond the requirements of your immediate business priorities. Some organisations have taken the step of offering programmes for their employees' partners, to satisfy the enthusiasm generated back at home for what was occurring at work.

UNDERSTANDING WHAT NEEDS TO CHANGE

You will almost certainly need some help to understand the impact you have on the culture, and how your mind-sets cause behaviour that does or does not support what is required. You have to find a way of seeing yourself through other people's eyes. Remember we are looking for the messages people receive from your behaviour, and this will usually be different from the messages you were intending to send.

There are many sources from which you can receive this feedback:

1. From a 360-degree feedback instrument

Pros: Anonymous and therefore likely to be truthful

Can be designed for the culture you want

Provides a measure of change

Depersonalisation of data less threatening

Cons: Often somewhat vague, raising the desire for more specific examples

Data can depersonalise and reduce impact and sharpness

Mixed quality of instruments

2. From your Culture Diagnostic

Pros: Strong links to the impact on culture

Picks up a broad group view – the long shadow you cast

Cons: Unless you are the CEO, more likely to relate to the senior management group than you personally

3. By asking colleagues you trust

Pros: Will give you a supportive, balanced view

Further questioning will elicit specifics, which makes it easier to take action

Cons: Colleagues may hold back some feedback, desiring not to hurt or displease you

Individuals may hold a view that is not universal

If you become defensive, collateral damage to the relationship

4. Direct feedback from your people

Pros: Demonstrates real openness and willingness to change

Specific information from the group who are most aware of messages

Cons: Requires real discipline not to get defensive, which would be highly counter-productive

Unlikely to elicit the really juicy bits

5. From an external consultant or coach

Pros: May have professional experience in giving feedback constructively

Can link feedback to culture and performance impact

More of an impartial observer than your people

Cons: Will not see you in action in all circumstances

May have a commercial agenda

Listening to feedback

Your enemy here is defensiveness. In fact defensiveness is the enemy of all personal growth and transformation. Defensiveness is the ego squawking and fighting off a perceived threat. And from the ego's perspective, the feedback is a threat. It is a threat to the comfortable arrangement you and your ego have established over the years. This arrangement goes something like this:

You: The world can be a bit of a tough place, and it's best not to appear too vulnerable lest someone hurts me. I have been hurt that way in the past (especially as a kid) and it is not a pleasant experience. I'm afraid it may happen again.

Ego: Right, so let me build a protective shield so that next time someone tries to hurt you, you will have a defence. There are a number of shields we could use – 'tough, attacking', 'intellectual and detached', 'joking and deflecting', for example.

You: Pick whichever you think will do the job best.

Ego: (Following many successful rebuttals) I'm doing well here, and there seem to be many more potential threats than we first thought. In fact this seems to be a pretty good way to live our life.

You: (Some years later) The world is not responding the way I want it to. Couldn't have anything to do with me could it?

Others: This person is so hard to give feedback to; I don't think I'll bother.

The ego shield, the defensive response, becomes a habit, and often used when the threat is perceived, not real. These responses are commonly grouped in two categories: FIGHT or FLIGHT. Otherwise know as (from our animal roots) 'Will I eat him or will he eat me?'

Examples include:

Fight	Turning the tables, verbally putting down or attacking the other person Interrupting, preventing the other from speaking Damaging or removing the individual at a later date Avoiding tough or negative situations and conversations
Flight	Leaving the room, cancelling meetings Deflections, including humour at key moments Invalidating the data

We all have areas about which we are very sensitive. They are the parts of ourselves we cannot accept and therefore feel vulnerable about. The defensive ego response is natural. Your challenge in this situation is to feel the response rising (most people feel it in their body somewhere, usually their stomach or their throat) and STAY PRESENT with the feedback.

I once facilitated a very challenging feedback session between a top team and some of their direct reports. We had a practice drill beforehand. They each had a list of questions in front of them. They were enquiring questions, which are great for receiving feedback, because they move you into an open position, and your colleague feels heard. Enquiring questions include:

- Tell me more about what has brought you to have this belief?
- How does this play out in day-to-day life?

Forbidden was:

- Any sentence beginning with 'BUT'
- Justifications
- Counter-attacks
- Condescending remarks 'Ah, but you see you don't under-stand . . .'

I would have provided masking tape to seal up the mouths, but we thought that might be a little obvious! By the end I thought one or two of them were going to burst a blood vessel. But the trans-formation in the relationship was extraordinary. The group felt heard, I think, for the first time. Just that act defused all the negative energy built up over months, and cleared the air for new exploration of possibilities about how to do things differently in the future.

Selecting behaviours to change

Pick one or two behaviours to work on that will have the most impact. An easy mistake is to expect yourself to change everything all at once. Working on your problem behaviours one by one will give focus, a greater sense of accomplishment.

Since you have a clear idea of the culture you want to create, and the values which underpin it, you can focus feedback on the behaviours which are sending damaging messages.

Below is some feedback that would hold back the cultures defined earlier. It comes in many guises, using many words, and may be specific examples of behaviours or more generalised descriptions:

Achievement	Avoiding tough action on non-performers Lack of discipline Avoiding decisions Inconsistent, lacking purposefulness
Customer-Centric	No empathy with the impact of decisions on customers Telling, not listening Arrogance, knows all the answers
One-Team	Speaking badly of colleagues and their initiatives Isolating oneself Seeking to be the star Backstabbing and politics Closed and secretive
Innovative	Rigid views, dismissive Unwillingness to admit mistakes Acceptance of *status quo*
People-First	Lack of interest in others Overly controlling Lack of delegation

You will notice I have worded these in the negative. I find sometimes feedback instruments are too constructive. We need a bit of a jolt here, if your ego can take it. Knowing that you score 2.56 on 'Delegates Appropriately' can sometimes be a little bland for our purposes. Hearing that you are a control freak has a bigger impact!

Dealing with your own justifications

Whatever you hear, your mind will almost certainly build an impressive set of reasons why you need to behave in this way. These justifications are the ego's way of keeping you as you are now. Most of us have minds that have become complete masters of this technique. One of the early lessons of such a master is that any good justification has to be true.

John was seeking to lead his construction company to becoming a more customer-focussed business. The feedback he received was that in all major decisions, cost containment took precedence over customers. When the chips were down, his people did not see him put his money where his mouth was. His justification was a good one. The shareholders expected a profit quarter on quarter, and he could not jeopardise this. Whilst he was committed to customers, the failure of the business to hit revenue targets meant that costs had to be cut to meet profit. This is an outstandingly good justification. Really one cannot argue with it. The trick lies in the AND. To be seen to be truly customer-focussed John needs to find a way to deliver profit AND continue making decisions with the customer in mind. Only when he achieves that will he find ways of fulfilling profit AND customer.

There are many answers available to him. Better budgeting in the first place. Choosing other cuts which do not affect the customer. Rethinking the way customers are dealt with during the lifespan of a project. This creativity comes when he does not use delivering short-term profit as a justification for non-customer-focussed decision-making. Until this moment he will not even see these options.

Here are some of the best justifications that you will hear from yourself (and others):

- I didn't have time
- I didn't mean it that way
- My intentions were quite different
- They'll never be satisfied
- They were behaving in the same way
- Everyone's doing it
- How can I trust them when they are untrustworthy?
- It's just good management practice
- The market is down
- They took what I said the wrong way
- You don't understand
- We don't have enough information, we need more research
- It's the nature of my role

Some of these may hold up for one or two occasions. But if you are getting your feedback from a variety of good sources, you need to stop your mind jumping to justifications. Your culture will not change until there is the perception that you are changing. Your challenge is to find a way to do this and fulfil the other obligations you have in your job.

Understanding the link between your feedback and the culture
As you collect feedback from various sources, you are best served by engaging in conversations with people about what you are hearing. In addition to giving you a clearer picture of what is occurring, they will be able to help you see some of the implications of this further down the track. Your focus must be on those elements of your behaviour that have the greatest impact on the culture. If you find these, quite small changes can have a big impact.

The best culture change initiatives consist of a large number of small changes to behaviour. Imagine you are sitting at the centre of a huge wheel, looking out to the rim. If you turn your head a few degrees your vista embraces a large new section of the horizon. Small changes at the centre produce large results.

TECHNIQUES FOR CHANGING YOUR BEHAVIOUR

At the beginning of this chapter I explained briefly that your behaviour (what you DO) emerges from one or more of five drivers at the BE-level.

Some mind-sets are easier to change than others. Let's do a little test. We have mounted a fairly strong argument here that some behaviours are less conducive to culture change than others. Behaviours that display arrogance, for example the belief that your opinion holds more water than others', do not encourage the views of others, particular those more junior than you who are closest to the customer.

I imagine you are convinced by this argument. So stop doing it. Now, this minute. No more arrogance, no more interrupting, no more dominating the room with your views, no more not listening. Come back next week and tell me how you did. Class over. Process over. Culture changed.

Did it work? Did you forget? Did the situation just absolutely drive you to be arrogant? But didn't we agree that it wasn't useful? Why did you do it then?

Guess what? We have just established that you are not the rational, intellectual being that your company is paying you to be. You have an emotional being too. You have an ego. You are irrational. Welcome to the human race. And by the way, everyone in your organisation is an emotional being too, which is why just telling them to change their behaviour will have only limited impact.

This is the point at which self-help books get stuck. If it were this easy we would all be doing it. What we can achieve here is to build a strong enough case for change that you will take the steps that are necessary to explore and shift some of these deeper emotional motivations. I will point you in the direction of how to change mind-sets, and you will then need to organise a range of help to support you through that change. This is the journey.

1. Changing your rational, intellectually held beliefs
Beliefs of this nature are developed through learning. Learning occurs in several ways:

- Experiences you have had from which you have drawn conclusions about what works and what does not work, which you then project on to future situations
- Experiences of other people which have been described to you
- Views you have formed through deduction or intuition which may not be directly linked to anyone's experience, but drawn from a range of data
- Persuasive views other people offer you, which you adopt (consciously or subconsciously)

Changing your intellectually held beliefs is reasonably easy and is done by exposing yourself to new beliefs that come from credible sources. Or by drawing new conclusions from new experiences.

Common sources of new, useful beliefs
- Reading books, particularly studies of high performing companies
- Well-researched data from a source you trust
- Watching people you respect achieve results using an approach different to the one you would have used
- Receiving advice from a trusted source, or support from a respected leader

For example, you may hold a set of beliefs about individual motivation being linked to individual reward. This belief would lead you to the conclusion that an individual should be rewarded even if the team of which he is a member fails. You might then have the opportunity to watch a number of teams working with a high team bonus. This team appears to you to be very motivated, and when you speak to individual members they assure you that the motivation of not letting down the team works just as well, if not better, than their personal motivation to win as an individual. Your opinion on team bonus could change based on this one experience.

The culture you live in influences your beliefs about appropriate behaviour. Moving to a more constructive culture changes those beliefs, and this will serve you well further down the track. But if you are a pioneer in your organisation, you cannot depend on the culture around you to influence your beliefs about behaviour. You need reinforcement from some of the other sources listed above.

2. Changing beliefs with an emotional underpinning

Beliefs with an emotional underpinning are more challenging to change. Many are not even seen as beliefs, but that is in fact what they are. They are usually formed as a result of an experience (or number of experiences) which were painful, and which we do not want to expose ourselves to again. Some of these experiences may have come from childhood. We draw sweeping conclusions as a result of these experiences that may not rationally be true of the current situation. Because the original experiences were painful, we have a defence mechanism at play, and cling to the belief as a protection. Here are three very different examples:

1. I have a very old friend, Margie, who is absolutely brilliant at what she does. She is one of the world's best market researchers, accredited with some breakthrough insights which have turned around a brand. Ever since I have known her, she has been unhappy about her team. She fundamentally does not trust them, and often tries to do their job for them. Whilst others agree there may be one or two members who are not great performers, for the most part they are good and proven contributors. As a result of her continual interference the team gets less motivated, and high potential individuals have left. It's not much fun working for someone who will not trust you no matter what you

do. Meanwhile my friend is very overworked and overlooking some key customer relationships which only she can really fulfil. Her friends and family worry about her, but, from the sidelines, it is hard to help.

Her mistrust clearly stems from beliefs she holds about the trustworthiness of others, which pre-date the current situation. Her core belief is that people inevitably let her down.

2. Many years ago we worked on a merger assignment with a leader who avoided making decisions. When the situation got tough, he procrastinated, focussing attention on other issues. He allowed team discussions to continue for a long time, and in the end, if there was no agreement, he moved on to the next topic. He hated having to make the call if his team held differing views. Sometimes this went on for several months, which was disastrous for achieving the merger synergies, and as a result performance suffered. He drove his team nuts with this behaviour.

Tim's avoidance was not rational; everyone could see that situations got to the point where any decision would have been better than no decision. Tim's emotionally-based belief was that if he did not please everybody he would provoke their anger, and he hated conflict. Sadly in his case, he denied he had a problem, and was therefore not 'coachable'. Eventually he was 'moved on'.

3. Elaine is a young consultant we hired in her mid-20's. She has a good mind and is very perceptive. She often sees the solution to problems, but rarely speaks her mind. In the first couple of years with our company, which is full of people who tend to be very confident in putting their ideas forward, she developed an attitude of resignation, and acceptance of the *status quo*. As a result she was not seen as a major contributor, and her career stalled. Elaine holds the irrational belief that she doesn't make a difference, and is therefore unimportant. Elaine holds this belief at the BE-level and it causes her to hold back her comments at the DO-level, so that as a result, at the HAVE-level her career has

come to a stand-still. BE-DO-HAVE. Fortunately, Elaine chose as an employer an organisation full of people who were prepared to help her through this. Recently a couple of our consultants have been working with her to help her see the relationship between her 'self-talk' and the outcomes she was getting in her career. She is gradually starting to be more forceful in expressing herself.

As you can see, these beliefs are not lightweight. Acknowledging them, even to yourself, may not be easy. Changing them requires a real willingness to explore yourself and realign emotional areas most of us are more comfortable avoiding. If you want to take action here, you will probably need help. Because of the sensitive nature of this work, most people undertake it outside of work or through one-on-one coaching. There are many personal development programmes available or counsellors and therapists who work with people who have realised there are a couple of emotionally-based beliefs they hold at the BE-level which are holding them back in terms of what they HAVE.

However, there are many things that can be done in the work environment. The first step is simply to acknowledge that this is not an easy area for you, and ask for support. Some phrases take the heat out of the situation, and allow your colleagues to provide assistance:

'This is not my strong suit; I will need you to remind me about this'

Practise recognising when you become caught up in an emotionally-based defensive reaction. You can usually tell because there is a physical sensation attached to it, such as tightness in the throat or the stomach. Even if you cannot pinpoint the underlying belief, just knowing you are operating in the realm of irrational, emotion-based behaviour is a huge step forward.

In many cases this recognition is enough to enable you to substitute a more appropriate behaviour. Changing behaviour patterns is a step-by-step process, and every time you act in a manner that is uncomfortable to you, you are making progress.

When you see the positive impact that this has on your environment, this gives you confidence to try it again.

Your deep emotional make-up may never change completely. However, your self-awareness can increase dramatically through a deliberate path of personal development. A year of exposure to such work will ensure that you see many of your behaviour patterns as they occur. This ability to witness loosens the hold the emotional pattern has over you, and thus behaviour changes.

Emotionally-based behaviours are also changed by further emotionally-based events. If an emotional experience embedded the belief in the first place, it makes sense that it would take a further emotional experience to change it.

This is the reason why people do learn and change from adversity. A life-changing experience, whether it be a near-death, or near-bankruptcy, for example, will change how you behave in the future. Your beliefs about what is important have changed. Similarly a very uplifting and trusting relationship – personal or professional – can rebuild trust where it had been shattered before.

So, whilst you may not be able to plan them, very threatening or very uplifting experiences will change your behaviour in the future.

3. Changing behaviour driven by values

Values are a rich area for exploration for all culture leaders. You may be quite unaware of the values that shape your behaviour today. We often make values-based decisions without realising that this is what they are. Sometimes it takes us getting into a situation of conflict with another person to realise how strongly held some of our views are.

One of the most inspiring discussions I ever took part in was introduced by Simon Longstaff, who was the director of the St James Ethics Society in Australia. He facilitated a discussion for a group of us over dinner. He started with a fairly provocative question – I think it was associated with the use of human body parts for medical research – and asked individuals to express their views. He then followed the logic of their argument to present further, more challenging, values dilemmas to them, and asked for a judgment about what should be done. The more he pressed and provoked, the more we all realised that our first response revealed a value-set we did not necessarily aspire to, or that we were inconsistent in the application of our values. This suggested we were not as values-driven as we might have wished. Everyone left in deep self-reflection concerning their own values.

At the end of a most thought-provoking evening, he said that he saw his role as one of helping individuals ask themselves the right questions. He defined values-based organisations as ones that asked themselves these questions. Ones that did not take the first easy option that came to mind. He was saying, in effect, that he could not impose his values on us, but he could try to make us conscious of our own values, and force us to examine our choices more deeply than we normally did.

As with organisations, individuals are values-driven to varying degrees. Remember there are two sets of values – those which are more selfless in nature, and those more centred on you getting what you want, potentially at the expense of the greater good.

Honesty, for example, is a value. Being liked is also a value. Appreciation is important. So is performance. Avoiding conflict may matter a lot to you. Put these five ingredients together and see how you behave in the performance review of a non-performing member of your team who has been with the company a long time.

Here's how it might play out:

Value hierarchy

1. Appreciation
2. Avoidance of conflict
3. Need to be liked
4. Honesty
5. Performance

Individual is given a 'satisfactory' rating and thanked for their contribution

1. Performance 2. Honesty 3. Appreciation 4. Need to be liked 5. Avoidance of conflict	Individual is given an 'unsatisfactory' ranking and a performance warning
1. Performance 2. Avoidance of conflict 3. Appreciation 4. Need to be liked 5. Honesty	Individual is retrenched and given a great reference and a payout

These situations, as you know, are all playing in an office near you at this very moment. (And in your office as well.)

To change your values hierarchy, you have to first recognise it. Writing lists like the ones above is a great way to start. Refer to the longer lists in Chapter 1. This alone produces some fascinating dilemmas – for example, the old chestnut, 'is customer satisfaction more important than profit?' In answering this one you go to the heart of your real belief about customers. Do you really, really believe the service profit chain theory that satisfied customers deliver profit? (The service profit chain, which links employee satisfaction to customer satisfaction to profit is explained in the book of the same name by Heskitt, Sasser and Schlesinger.)

Here is a great exercise I learnt from Dr John Demartini, which tests how honest you are being with yourself about your list. Write your values hierarchy on one side of the page. On the other side list the same set of words, ordered in terms of how well they are working in your life. Score how well they are working out of ten based on past performance.

Stated Values Hierarchy		Performance	/10
Year on year profit	1st	Year on year profit	9
Satisfied staff	2nd	Growth	5
Satisfied customers	3rd	Innovation	3
Teamwork	4th	Teamwork	3
Growth	5th	Satisfied staff	3
Innovation	6th	Satisfied customers	2

Are the lists identical? No? The one on the right is probably your real values hierarchy. We place our attention on what we value. And what we place our attention on gets resolved and works well. What we neglect suffers. To get the scores of your lower items up, you need to lift them up your values hierarchy. Really, truly. This means making decisions in their favour ahead of others that are higher on the list right now, as well as ahead of the self-centred values list.

Becoming a more values-driven person

Some people have a stronger sense of their own values than others. They hold a set of altruistic beliefs about what is important in life, and they hold to these at difficult times, when the temptation to succumb is high. A values-driven person will more often hold to their values when the more attractive option would be to take the easy way out. They stay true to themselves more often. Their actions are more often guided by an inner set of principles about right and wrong, than by external circumstances or the influence of others.

The strength of your values only really becomes obvious when times are tough, and when there is a temptation to take an expedient path. Imagine you find a wallet in the street. If you are a fairly well-off person, you will probably hand this wallet in to the police station. But what if you are starving and have three children at home? The likelihood that you keep the money is greatly increased. Your need to feed yourself and your children may override a value you might have about respecting the property of others. It is then that the strength of your values is tested.

The same is true in business. It is easy to be helpful to your teammates when everything is going swimmingly in your area. But what if you are under tremendous pressure, your sales are down, and it looks like you might not meet targets? Will you still find the time to attend a meeting at which one of your colleagues is seeking input from your people in making a key decision? She has to implement a process improvement. It will not succeed if you and your people do not support it. But if it were to fail it would be her, not you, who would be held accountable. What do you do? My experience is that many people do not attend that meeting, even though teamwork is one of their values. They justify not attending by the challenges they are facing in their business. What they are saying is that teamwork is only a value for me when I am doing OK my end. If this organisation, and this individual, strengthened their value of teamwork, the behaviour would change.

We have a client who has teamwork very strongly embedded. In this instance, the cultural norm would have expected attendance at the meeting. The individual would have gone, and would have found ways to still address the issues in his own camp. The benefits of such a culture – for both the individuals and the organisation – is that when the shoe was on the other foot, when help was required in the other direction, it would always be given.

Values-driven people will tend to have a greater ability to direct their behaviour at will, rather than to behave in a knee-jerk way in response to pressure from others or external events. Consequently, when you really value what your desired culture stands for, you will find it easier to change your behaviour in-line with that culture.

Let's say your culture values the development and empowerment of people. Intellectually, you support this position; you can see the benefits of pushing decisions downwards, and freeing senior people, including yourself, to focus on bigger picture issues. Then, let's imagine you receive feedback from your people that you are very controlling, interfere with every detail, and do not allow them to make decisions. Now clearly there is a conflict between these two. On the one hand, the value of empowerment, on the other, the behaviour of interference.

This behaviour is probably a long-term habit, arising from a mistrust of others and their ability to perform. Perhaps there is also a belief that you are better than others, and that if you want a job doing you'd better do it yourself. You may just be able to stop this behaviour immediately, the day after you and the team defined empowerment as one of the values you wanted in your organisation. If you can, great. However, most of us do not find it that easy. In this instance, you could undertake some personal development work to lessen your mistrust of others. This path will produce big changes, but it does take time.

The other, complimentary path is to strengthen your value of empowerment. Become a more values-driven person. Become so passionate about valuing people and giving them room to learn and grow and make their own decisions, that you have a greater discipline around your own behaviour in this area. It is possible to make this choice, assuming your level of awareness is high enough to allow you some degree of self-reflection. You will still have the impulse to interfere. But you will be able to check this impulse more often. You will be open to feedback from others when the impulse gets the better of you, because the strengthened value causes you to be less defensive.

People trust value-driven people. They can see that they uphold a set of principles which benefit others, as well as themselves, and that they will not drop these principles for personal gain. If people believe you are only doing or saying something to further your own ambitions, they do not trust you. And people have an uncanny ability to smell this out. This is the reason why many people do not trust politicians. If it feels that a politician is only doing something as a vote-catching strategy, and that he or she does not inherently believe that it is the right thing to do, then we distrust their motives. We want our leaders to do what is right, not just what will win the popularity contest.

Strengthening your own values is assisted through exposure to others who embody such values more strongly than you do. Find these people and ask them lots of questions. Ask them:

• Why do they value certain things so strongly?
• What have been the benefits for them personally?
• How specifically do they deal with pressure that could tempt them to behave differently?

One of the great benefits of embarking on the culture journey is that you suddenly become surrounded by others who are struggling with the same issues as you. As people start to find solutions to the values dilemmas you all face, these solutions can be shared and copied by others.

4. Changing behaviours by changing your feelings

Everybody knows that feeling good predisposes us towards behaving better towards other people, being organised in relation to how we use our time, and making well-thought through decisions. You know the conditions that make you feel happy, energetic and positive. I will focus here on feelings, as they are associated with working effectively on culture.

From a work perspective, people feel good when they are respected, listened to, valued, supported and given meaningful work that allows them a sense of achieving and contributing. These are covered more extensively on pages 186–191. Many of you will be working in organisations with cultures that do not provide these features. This is one reason that you are seeking to build a better culture. If you are championing a culture change, you have to accept that you are unlikely to be provided with the environmental features to make you feel good. In fact, you may well find yourself attacked or ridiculed for your efforts, because early culture work often receives a defensive response.

You will have to find alternative ways to keep your feeling-state sufficiently positive to enable you to do this work

To my surprise we have, from time to time, found that teams who are supposedly leading or championing a culture initiative are, in fact, displaying behaviours of their own which are amongst the least constructive in the organisation. In particular, we have found these teams to indulge in blaming others. 'The culture is in the state it is because of all of you. You are the problem.'

This attitude does nothing for the credibility of the culture effort. I believe this happens in part because the culture pioneer is a difficult role to play, and does require considerable tenacity. When we have been asked by clients to help them select culture champions to play a special role in the culture work, we look for people who are able to live *above the line*. The job is to deal with *below the line* behaviour and that is why there is a culture plan to be implemented. Culture champions need to have an inner resourcefulness which enables them to remain constructive within an environment where others are being defensive. They have to walk the talk.

Your inner resourcefulness may come from a sense of purpose that building a great culture is the contribution you want to make. You came here to do this job, and you will stay until it is done. Or it may come from activities you do outside work which keep you balanced. Or it may come from building a small, tight and supportive team around you, with whom you can relax after a day doing battle with the culture. Whatever means you choose make sure you dedicate time to it: you simply cannot lead this culture work if your own feelings are as negative as those you are seeking to lead.

5. Changing behaviour by changing your level of awareness
Self-awareness operates at the base of the BE-DO-HAVE model. Changes to it will impact both your BE (values and beliefs and feelings) and what you DO (behaviour).

Your level of awareness determines the extent to which you can watch what you are doing at any moment, and choose different responses. It is an experience of watching yourself. There is a part of your mind that is witnessing the other parts thinking and behaving in their normal way. To truly explore levels of awareness we need to go down the spiritual and philosophical path that is beyond the scope of this book. Buddhists, for example, refer to this as mindfulness. However, the definition above is sufficient for the task at hand, which is to align your behaviour to the culture to which you are aspiring.

It follows that if I can observe, I will be able to choose the behaviour most appropriate to the situation. Since 'most appropriate' has now been defined as that which aligns to our values and desired culture, the result will be an alignment of behaviour to culture. This alignment will, in turn, act as a role model for others, and thus the culture process is accelerated.

Awareness is lifted by exercises that still the mind. At its most basic, any opportunity to take yourself out of the normal frantic pace of life will help you connect with this part of yourself.

- Walking or running on a beach or through the streets in the very early morning
- Taking your team away to a remote spot to think creatively, rather than trying to do it in the office
- Sitting quietly listening to classical music that transports you to another place
- Yoga, Tai Chi and other forms of physical activity that have been designed with awareness-raising in mind
- Meditation and all forms of contemplative techniques

In essence, all pursuits that still the mind and reduce its chatter will help you become more aware. Pursuits and situations which add to your stress will make you less aware and more likely to behave inappropriately.

Such pursuits carry a wide range of additional benefits, such as physical well-being and a more finely tuned intuition, which make them a most worthwhile investment of time. If you wish to explore this yourself, you may have to start by finding teachers outside of the work environment. There are encouraging early signs that some organisations are seeing the business benefits to such activity, and sponsoring them internally.

Your level of awareness will also be heightened by any experience which allows you to see yourself from the outside in. This includes feedback from customers, employees and friends. These all serve to make you more aware of your own behaviour. However, unless you have made some kind of shift away from defensiveness, you will find it difficult to really allow these inputs to influence you. You will be unable to let them in.

The best path to raising your level of awareness combines exercises to still the mind with good access to feedback.

SUMMARY: CHANGING YOURSELF IS THE TICKET TO THE GAME

I have been quite deliberate in starting the section on how to build a great culture with you personally. If you are not prepared to change yourself, you should not commence this journey.

> *'For things to change first I must change'*

This applies even if you are new to the organisation and can therefore justifiably state that you were not a part of the behaviours, values and mind-sets that created the culture as it currently is. Even as a new leader in the organisation you will have a number of behaviours and ways of thinking which still do not meet the standards set by your desired culture.

Never set yourself apart from others in this process, even if you are the CEO. The example you set through visibly addressing your own personal change encourages others. It is not an easy journey on a personal level. Dealing with a reputation crisis, technology failures, budget over-runs and downsizing is often described to us by our clients as easier than what we are encouraging them to do on the culture front. The reason culture is one of the last untapped areas for competitive advantage to be recognised and addressed is because it is so hard on a personal level.

The rest of this book addresses everything else that has to be done to build the culture you want. Never forget though, your personal development must continue throughout.

8

How to Change the
Behaviour of Others

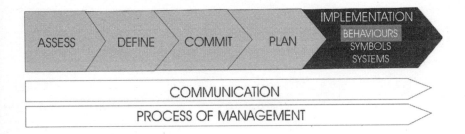

THE **BE-DO-HAVE** model describes how a change in behaviour will follow a change in mind-set. Your Culture Development Plan must contain a significant section on how you intend to modify the mind-sets of enough people to create the momentum for change. You will by now have a good sense of what the mind-sets are that you need, and ideas for this have been covered earlier in this book. There are three categories of mind-set, the three described components of the BE-level:

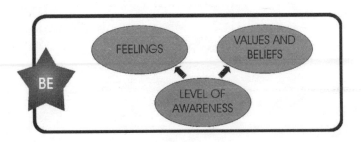

LEADERSHIP

Leaders drive culture

Leaders influence the beliefs and values, as well the feelings of their people. Every leadership action and style affects people at the BE-level in some way. For example, if a leader is encouraging or inspirational, people will feel excited and supported. If a leader continually emphasises the importance of understanding customers, this will, over time, influence the beliefs and values of those people who report to him or her. It is the goal of leadership to stimulate people to move along a certain path. It will be through good leadership that your people will be willing to change their behaviour, take a new approach to their work, and build new mind-sets. Just telling people to do these things rarely works; they need to be led along this path. Your leaders are therefore your critical tool for building the culture you want. They are with their people every day; they influence them through their words, actions, decisions and interactions. They set standards, hold people to those standards and enact consequences. The most important part of your Culture Development Plan is the part which covers leadership.

Leadership behaviours

The first step is to define the leadership behaviours which you expect your leaders to display. Once you have a draft set, involve your top team heavily in refining them. The more engaged the top team are in their development, the easier it will be for them to lead the process of building this capability in the organisation.

The behaviours expand your description of a desired culture into specific expectations you have of those who wish to have a leadership role in the organisation. Ideally, you will have picked a culture assessment tool that also allows you to assess leadership behaviours within the same framework, because this will help you define the leadership behaviour you want. Some assess team behaviours in the same way. This consistency is really useful to help your people see the link between each.

These behaviours become the standards, drawing the lines of the court within which you will play your particular game. Play outside these lines too often, and you find yourself losing the match. Without the lines, there is no game.

Leadership development programme

You can design and/or import programmes for your leaders which build their skill to walk the talk of your desired culture. The content of this programme will depend in part on the focus of your desired culture. For example, if your focus is People-First, you may decide that mentoring and coaching is the most important leadership competency for your first year, and build a programme which is centred on this. If it is Achievement, you may consider holding people to account is your priority. Or you can run a leadership programme which contains elements across the whole range of leadership attributes.

This programme will become synonymous with your culture development. It is a symbol, as well as a tool. It is worth taking considerable time to be sure it really is the flagship of your plan. Design, pilot, measure effectiveness, maintain trainer standards, do not accept anything except outstanding quality.

Most organisations expect all of their leaders to attend this programme – or set of programmes. Everybody experiencing the same development opportunity provides common language and reinforcement, and gives you the confidence that every leader has been provided with the opportunity to step up and lead their people through this process.

Leadership self-reflection

To lift the level of awareness of your leaders, you must provide them with the facility to observe their own behaviour. There are many techniques of leadership development design which help this to happen, and your programme designers should demonstrate the ability to do this. For example, experiential exercises ask participants to undertake an activity in which leadership skill is required – either alone or in teams – and then debrief what occurred in the activity. During the debrief, leaders have the opportunity to see the relationship between how they behaved in the exercise to the way they behave at work and their mind-sets which cause these behaviours. Such activities use BE-DO-HAVE to show the link between outcomes produced, behaviours displayed and thinking styles.

Some of these exercises take place inside a course room, and others in a structured manner in the workplace itself, in what are called 'action-learning' activities.

Measurement of leadership behaviour
It is essential that you select a tool to regularly measure the behaviour of your leaders, against the criteria defined for your desired culture. We have found that the best approach is to use tools which link together, so that your measurement of culture, of team effectiveness and of leadership all use the same framework, thus reinforcing each other. Having worked with clients whose tools did not link on many occasions, we invested in developing tools that had this capacity, because of the exponential benefits of this approach.

Having found or developed a tool you like, stick with it, so that leaders build year-on-year data about their own behaviour. Initially, these measurements will be for the purposes of self-development. Later, once your culture journey is well underway, they can also be used for leadership assessment, and ultimately reward.

PLANNING FOR CHANGING THE BEHAVIOUR OF OTHERS
The rest of this chapter shows a range of techniques for changing the behaviour of others. Some of these will be used by leaders as a part of their day-to-day leadership approach; others can form part

of the more formal Culture Development Plan. Some or all of them combined will cause change over a one-to-two year period. For both everyday leadership, and planned initiatives, there are three avenues of focus:

1. Ways to influence people's beliefs and values
2. Ways to influence people's feelings
3. Ways to influence people's level of awareness

1. Ways to influence people's beliefs and values

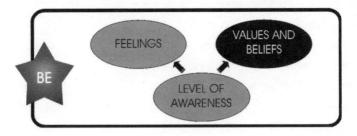

Your Culture Development Plan must include a range of initiatives which will influence the beliefs and values of your people so that they are closely aligned to those which will deliver to you the culture you need to enhance your performance.

Influence forums

Plan for a regular programme of forums in which target groups have open dialogue with yourself or others you are confident hold the values you want the organisation to adopt, and who would be seen by others as walking the talk. Dialogue is the key word here; these exercises are more successful when conducted in a manner in which everyone can participate than in forums when one person stands up on stage or on video, and talks. However, in larger organisations this is not always possible, and any opportunity should be taken.

As a line manager, you obviously do not need to wait for a culture team to design a calendar of forums at which you can influence your people. Consider every meeting to be a chance to lead the beliefs and values of your people towards those which you consider are important to underpin the behaviours your performance targets require. You are always influencing through what you say. Become more explicit in expressing your own beliefs and values, and labelling them as such.

'The reason I think this is important for us to do is because I believe that we should never feel satisfied that our standards are high enough' (Belief associated with Innovative Culture)

or

'However much pressure we are under to perform, we cannot chew our people up and spit them out' (Values hierarchy – performance and valuing people)

Tips for leading forums

1. Many people in your audience may already hold the values and beliefs you are seeking, but perhaps not with the degree of passion that is required to change behaviour within a culture that has not appeared to support such a mind-set. Assume the best of your people, and work with them on that level. Do not talk as if customer focus is an idea that they have not thought about before. This approach then makes the leader an equal and companion, one who is also on a journey

2. Be specific in the detail of why you believe what is being put forward is different from what is occurring now. This may be through lifting certain values up the hierarchy, which can best be explained using examples of how decisions have been made in the past, and how you want them to be made in the future

3. Provide the business logic for what you want – the market share gains possible through increased customer satisfaction or amount spent in duplication of effort through operating in silos

4. Do not berate actions and decision from the past. The past culture has had a values hierarchy that supported past decisions – it is the change in values, and the strength with which they are believed in, which will create new decision patterns in the future

5. Play to your personal style, or, if you are planning these events for others, to the style of your leader. One of the key pieces of advice we have to give is to help a particular CEO place themselves in situations where they appear authentic, so that their value-set comes through as real. A leader who is very stilted in large groups will end up seeming incongruent even if in fact the mind-set is right. Such an individual is better working with small groups or using other mechanisms

Exposure to others who have been successful

Seek out books which demonstrate the relationship between culture and performance, and describe successful culture journeys. Examples can be found in the reading list at the back of this book. Distribute copies to all your leaders, and encourage discussion on what they read. Find organisations whose success in this field would have credibility with your people. Invite their CEOs to come and speak to your people. Invite their HR people, their CFO, anyone who is prepared to give you the time. We have found that organisations who have gained performance success through culture are usually very passionate about the subject, and they love to talk about what they are doing.

We have several clients who deliberately use their measured improvement in culture as a marketing tool. The CEOs and HR directors undertake a very careful and well-planned series of public engagements each year. Their PR companies profile the CEO and how he or she has changed as an individual. This strategy of developing an employment brand around culture has given these organisations the edge to attract and keep the best people. Other organisations we know in the same market have told us they have tried to lure people away to transfer what they achieved, but these people are hard to lure. When you work in a great culture it is hard to walk away!

When embarking on a culture change process of continuous improvement, the CEO of another of our clients took their whole top team on a quality tour of five top companies in their field. At each place they met half a dozen key people, and were shown how they had achieved what they had. The tour was organised by a company specialising in such trips. Some of the large consultancies will offer a similar service. Our client visited five companies in six days. Every evening they would sit in hotel rooms, and debrief what they had learnt and how it could be applied. By the end of the week the team had a completely new mind-set about what was possible. They never went back to their old beliefs. The credibility of their peers in these companies was indisputable. Finally they experienced it together, so their power on returning home was much greater than it would have been if they had been one by one.

Values workshops for individuals and teams

The opportunity to work through what all of the intended change means for an individual is an essential piece to your Culture Development Plan. Most successful culture change processes contain some form of workshop-based intervention specially designed to bring your people along the values path, and influence their mind-set.

Your long-term goal is that everyone in your organisation holds the same interpretation of what your values mean, and the same strength of view that they really matter. If you were to achieve this (perhaps a little idealistic, but certainly a good stretch goal) you would know that you could put anyone in your organisation in the same difficult situation, a values dilemma, and they would all make the same choices about what was most important in the circumstances. When you achieve this, your need for rules diminishes – people hold the rules inside them.

Values workshops have particular power because they provide the opportunity to build critical mass. When a significant number of people go through the same experience in a short period of time, they reinforce each other's learning and change process. This provides an incremental benefit not received if individuals go off and have similar experiences on their own. For all of us, holding to a new set of beliefs when surrounded by others who do not is a tough process. Sharing a mind-changing experience with others is exciting and supportive.

The workshops need to cover:

- The values and beliefs that underpin your culture
- The values hierarchy and the values dilemmas encountered every day in your business
- Personal values and beliefs and the link for each individual between these and the organisation's intent
- The relationship between values and culture (behaviours, symbols and systems)
- The current culture (from the diagnostic)
- The business case for changing your culture
- The culture plan and process

The design of such workshops is a specialist activity, and one for which you may need external help. As an example, there are some great exercises which can be put together to explore values dilemmas within the framework of your values hierarchy. These pose challenging questions for which there are no clear-cut answers, such as:

> You are a professional services firm. You need to provide opportunities to your younger, less experienced people to stand on their own in front of clients. For a new assignment you have to select between a high potential person who needs the experience, and a more solid pair of hands. Which do you choose? Does your decision change if the assignment is one with a new, and potentially important, client, as opposed to a long-term client with less potential for future on-sell?

This scenario raises the dilemma between developing people, satisfying customers, making sales, and differentiating between customers. Debating possible solutions helps people to learn how the values hierarchy should play out.

Facilitation of the workshops must be of the highest quality, because you are seeking to probe and influence people at a profound level in order to bring about real change. If you use external facilitators, often essential to get the quality you need, you must be sure they are positioned in the facilitation only role, and that your own leaders play a key role throughout and are taking the appropriate leadership position with their people.

The workshops become one of the most visible early signs of the culture process in action. If carefully designed, they can achieve a number of different objectives, and certainly provide the opportunity to increase engagement and trust as well as develop shared values. They must be at least two days in length, and preferably residential. You need to create an opportunity to change at the BE-level. This is not achieved in a hurried one day session conducted in the office, with distractions pulling people back to their normal mind-set at every break. This is a significant investment of both time and money. To generate maximum return on this investment requires a quality approach in design, facilitation and follow-up. It also requires absolute commitment from your senior team.

Their timing in your plan should sit at the point where you are confident that the top team is making sufficient progress to be in a position to credibly lead such a process. This probably places them somewhere towards the end of year one or beginning of year two.

Having once started, it is best to involve as many people as you can over a short period of time. Spreading the process out too much decreases the value-add gained from critical mass.

Groups need to be small enough for everyone to have the opportunity to talk through what they are being asked to take on board. 15-20 seems a good number. It is possible to bring large groups together and then split them into syndicates, but this requires very high quality facilitation of the syndicates as well as the front-of-room roles.

Gathering intact teams together with their leaders creates a different dynamic, and, of course, requires everyone to participate twice, once with the team of which they are a member, and one in their team leadership role. We have experimented with both approaches with different clients, and incline towards mixing individuals up in groups of people they do not work with every day, which delivered a number of benefits:

- New networks are formed through the organisation as people bond with each other through a meaningful experience, and keep these bonds into the future
- Different perspectives are gained by seeing how other functions in the organisation work through the change challenges from their viewpoint
- The impact of a team leader who is not on board is removed at least for the workshop itself and thus individuals disadvantaged in this way get the opportunity to learn and grow more easily
- Taking mixed groups out of the business is easier from a business-as-usual perspective

The intact team dynamic is also an incredibly important one, and your plan should include mechanisms for team leaders to take what has been learnt in these workshops and other culture change forums, and lead their teams through what it means for their performance objectives and priorities.

Make the experience a model for the intended culture. Everything participants experience must give them the notion of what is possible. For example, in selecting facilitators, ask yourself: do these people give me the sense that they live this value? Will they be congruent? Do they display emotional intelligence?

In designing the programme, have you factored in your values? If you are driving for a performance culture, do you have ways of measuring effectiveness, which demonstrate that you want to know whether you are achieving your goals for the workshop? If you have a customer-focus objective, are the participants being treated as customers? Did the invitation process give them that impression or were they given too little notice and commanded to attend?

Your leaders must play an important role in this initiative, by facilitating sections of the sessions, participating in design, or undertaking pre- and post-workshop sessions with their people. Set your leaders up for success by having them participate at a time and in a manner which allows them to be at their best. Tearing in for a half-hour slot in the dead time after lunch, for example, will not give them the best chance.

Bringing in new people

You may have heard the expression: 'Change the people or change the people'. Help your people to change, or bring in different people. The introduction of some new faces forms a part of almost all culture change processes. However, it should never be your principle strategy. Cultures have a powerful effect on new people, and many of these new faces end up adapting to the culture, or being ejected by it.

As your culture starts to change, on the other hand, you will find that a number of people will end up leaving, either voluntarily or because it becomes obvious to the organisation that they are not going to be able to make the changes required. For example, if you start to build a strong Achievement Culture, where expectations of performance lift considerably, employees will become visible who have been out of their depth for a while, but within a framework where their non-contribution was masked.

In the early stages of a culture change, we have found the most effective course of action is to bring in just a few new people into carefully selected roles. However, don't expect miracles from them on the culture front. Their real contribution comes from their ability to role model certain behaviours within teams, and thus start some new trends.

A client of ours brought an individual in who had come from an organisation where challenging the *status quo* was an accepted, and expected, norm. This person had no fear of speaking up in meetings. The story of his first couple of years gives insight into the typical way in which this plays out.

The organisation had a very polite culture. People said what they thought others wanted to hear. They agreed in meetings and then afterwards often went off and did what they wanted anyway. The discussion during meetings was fairly superficial, and decisions that were made were at a high enough level that one could say yes and not necessarily act. For example a planning workshop would agree a fairly long list of priorities that had to be tackled in the following year. Everyone would agree to the list. Simon would start challenging them, and say that he could not agree because they had not been thought through in enough detail, they were not costed, the implications and trade offs had not been covered.

Fairly quickly he became branded as 'negative', and 'aggressive'. Following advice, he toned his style down somewhat, but continued to push for precision and rigour in decision making. When he had a win, the nature of the decision made became much more difficult for others to then ignore. Thus more effective. Over time some of the team came to appreciate the value that Simon's insistence on rigour added. The team gradually became more rigorous themselves. But the toll on Simon was high. He feels now that he often gives up, and that he picks only the really important battles to fight. He lets many things just pass. Emotionally he has withdrawn. He is less engaged in the larger group, with a stronger tendency to focus on his own piece of the business, where his style has had some success.

Simon – at the time of writing – has survived. He came with a very strong reputation, and a proven track record of success which was well known. He had some early performance wins. He found a couple of allies in the team, in particular another fairly new person with whom he formed an alliance which gave them both strength. And he was prepared to adapt his behaviour to meet the culture halfway.

Because he has survived, and the organisation is on the move culturally and has many other pieces of culture work underway, his appointment has definitely been a key piece of this organisation's culture development plan. Other new appointees are not so successful.

An alternative approach, which can often be effective, is to make some bold appointments from within. People already inside the culture know how it operates. We will cover this in depth in the section describing symbols, because unexpected and courageous internal hires are a very strong cultural symbol.

So, in planning your new appointee strategy, these tips will help:

- Find the organisations in your market that have the culture you want, and select people from there. For example, if you want to become more customer focussed, bring in someone from a good retailer. If you want to build performance culture, find one of the best global companies, and bring in a local person. People who know what your target culture feels and looks like will be a tremendous asset
- Pick individuals whose references assure you have the characteristics you want. A great team member, a strong challenger, a track record of good performance management
- Be honest with the individual about the culture you have, the culture you want, and the role you want them to play in helping you achieve it. Bring them in with this as a part of their mission
- Consider bringing in two or three people with similar behavioural and cultural background. Perhaps even from the same company. This allows them to form a beachhead, a firm unit who share the desired values and can back each other up to take a stand on what matters

2. Ways to influence people's feelings

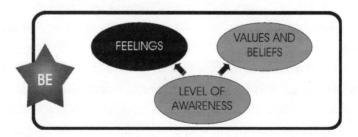

In addition to their beliefs and values, people operate in the world according to how they feel. Influencing this becomes the second major plank of your Culture Development Plan.

On the feelings side, our behaviour can be motivated by:

- A desire to move towards something which we perceive to be potentially pleasurable ('positive motivation') *or*
- A desire to protect ourselves from situations which may cause us pain ('negative motivation')

Increasing positive motivation

Natural human motivation to move towards pleasure, positive motivation, in the business environment, leads to behaviour associated with moving towards:

1. Making a difference – a worthwhile contribution to a cause, purpose or vision
2. Achievement – the satisfaction of achieving a goal
3. Being valued – receiving recognition (including reward) for a contribution
4. Helping others – supporting, developing or assisting another person

Increasing positive motivation increases the amount of discretionary energy of the individual. It is sometimes referred to as 'engagement', or extent to which someone's heart is in what they are doing. We feel engaged. We don't think engaged! It is the difference between 'want to' and 'have to' and we all know what that difference feels like. The motivation caused by moving towards pleasure will provide the state of mind that considerably helps the process of change. Change beyond the most mundane (changing your socks, walking a new way to work) involves some level of emotional engagement. The type of personal change covered in this book is not easy. It becomes ten times more difficult, and in many instances will simply not occur, if the individual is also in an apathetic, distrustful or fearful state of mind.

1. Making a difference – a worthwhile contribution to a cause, purpose or vision

The human being's desire to make a difference is an often starved component of our business lives. One only has to watch the outstanding contribution individuals make outside of work – coaching their local football team, contributing to charities, helping a friend – to know that there is a motivation in people which is often lost inside organisational life. One of the great benefits of your push to become a values-driven organisation is that it will create an environment where people feel this part of them is valued. It is no coincidence that so many managers who can afford it talk about retiring as early as they can so that they can start to live the life they really want. Many people feel they have to check a large part of themselves at the door when they arrive at work. They are searching for meaning; to contribute something meaningful, and believe they cannot do this at work. Tapping into this transforms how people feel.

Key here is the word 'meaningful'. Most statements of vision or purpose do not motivate in this way. Let me let you in to a secret. 'We will provide high quality service and value-for-money products and thus meet our shareholder demands and become number one in our market' will not unleash the motivational power of your people. In fact nothing written on a piece of paper will. Making a difference means just that. People's lives are different because of me. 'Putting a computer on everyone's desk,' (Apple), makes a difference. 'Glorifying the beauty of ordinary women,' (The Body Shop) does that too.

Defining the statement is of course just the very first step. Framing people's work so that they see it as meaningful, as adding value in a real way, is the real task here.

Undertaking work which is not directly related to the organisation's performance targets can provide a balance. When an organisation chooses to give to the community in which it exists, it taps into a motivation which is beyond making a profit or meeting targets. The role of organisations in the broader community, and their responsibilities to facilitate the broader social agenda, has the potential to tap into the motivation of employees to make a difference. This factor is not always taken into account in calculating the cost benefit of such activity. Linking the effort with the product can also strengthen employees' belief in the value of your product. A hardware chain, for example, built tremendous employee, customer and community goodwill through its activities in using its products and its people to help build and repair homes for the benefits of the underprivileged.

2. Achievement – The satisfaction of achieving a goal

David McClelland's work on achievement motivation, covered in his book *The Achieving Society*, found that, even within good teams, individuals need to be linked to the outcomes of their own efforts. Satisfaction comes from seeing the outcome, and knowing it has been caused, in part, by my efforts and that I can see that link.

A secret to facilitating this is to make outcomes much more short-term. Normal performance objectives are usually measured annually. That's a long time. We worked with geologists whose job it was to find the next big discovery. A new copper seam or unknown source of oil. To find one in a lifetime is a big achievement. Many never do. That's a long time between drinks. The key for this organisation was to find many small wins along the way, and train their people to define them and recognise these wins as they occurred.

Breaking achievements down by milestones, achievements by a certain date or hitting weekly targets, is a good way to increase the motivation to achieve.

Most efforts at measuring people's achievements are undertaken in order to plan for reward or bonuses or to identify poor per-formers. That is they are designed for the evaluation of one person by another. Here we are talking about doing this for a different purpose. Our purpose is to tap into the internal, constructive motivation which comes from seeing the relationship between effort and outcome. Think about that moment when you have worked all afternoon in the garden, and finally look up to see a bed of freshly planted seedlings and no weeds. That's the feeling you are looking to generate.

In a large organisation, creating this feeling for every job is no small task. Required is:

- Clarity about what success will look like
- A reasonably strong relationship (that the individual can see) between individual effort and outcome
- A means of measuring that success was reached
- Feedback of this measurement to the individual either instantaneously or within a short timeframe

3. Being valued – Receiving recognition (including reward) for a contribution

When you think about making people feel valued, consider it on three levels:

- Being valued for what I have achieved (outcomes)
- Being valued for what I think (ideas)
- Being valued for what I feel and who I am (being)

All people thrive on receiving some of these. Even those big tough ones who say they don't care! In creating opportunities for these to occur, it is useful to break it into these three categories, because strategies for each are quite different.

Some of your leadership development work will be well-served in educating your people in the differences between each. Different styles of people naturally incline towards one or the other. If you have adopted People-First as one of your values you must explore this in detail, because within these three lie the answers to some of the values dilemmas associated with people. For example, someone who is not achieving outcomes cannot be permitted to continue to remain in this situation (they will need to be moved to a new role, coached or exited). However, even when they are not achieving outcomes they can still be valued for what they think and for who they are. In fact they are more likely to lift their performance game if they are feeling valued on other levels, because their positive motivation is stronger.

Valuing outcomes

Financial reward, of course, must be lined up as closely as possible to outcomes. If you are confident the cause and effect relationship between an individual and their outcomes can be measured, then higher variable pay will motivate.

Other forms of recognition of contribution are important, through both formal and informal channels. Your plan must include mechanisms for recognition, such as contributor of the month awards and other such devices. These have the secondary benefit of sending a cultural message about what is important.

Valuing ideas

Set up forums to listen to those who are closest to the customer. Have lunches between your leaders and more junior staff. Ask your new employees how they find the culture and what could be done differently. Invite cross sections of people to strategy sessions. Design problem-solving groups. Create rituals for learning from each other, testing ideas with peers.

Valuing feelings

Ask questions and listen with empathy. If I have empathy with you it does not mean I have to agree with you, but I have to make it my job to understand you. What are your feelings, values, beliefs and experiences? Set up forums with this in mind. Bring leaders together with people for the purpose of listening and valuing someone else and how they feel. Remember what we talked about earlier about non-defensiveness!

Some of this can become part of your Culture Development Plan. Some of it comes naturally when your leaders increase the extent to which they really value people. Increasing their value of people occurs through the strategies described under the sections of changing values and beliefs.

4. Helping others – Supporting, developing or assisting another person

Under the right circumstances people will become highly motivated through opportunities to help each other. The satisfaction comes from seeing another person grow and develop, or solve a difficult problem, as a result of one's input. This approach can be hard to get going in the early stages of culture change in certain organisations, particularly those which are very internally competitive.

These opportunities can be set up formally, through some kind of mentoring programme, team-to-team learning arrangements or informally through leadership.

Decreasing negative motivation

Positive motivation is driven by the desire to move towards pleasure. Negative motivation is driven through a desire to move away from pain. It thus produces defensive behaviours.

The seven most common negative feelings which produce defensive behaviours that impact on business performance are:

1. Mistrust
2. Avoidance of responsibility, blaming others
3. A need to win over others, and never be seen to lose
4. A need to be liked
5. Fear of making a mistake and being punished
6. Bullying
7. Fear of change

When we are feeling defensive we are much less likely to change. In fact we retreat into a shell and become rigid. As you create opportunities to help people in your organisation become less defensive, you will notice the whole culture start to feel more positive. For some people being defensive is a very deep-seated behaviour pattern. For others, it has become a habit. The second group will find it easier to change than the first. There will be people in your organisation that just can't change these defensive patterns. There will come a point where you may have to ask some of these people to leave. But there are many others whose defensive orientation can be adjusted. The errant behaviours will still pop out when the individual is under a lot of stress, but these occasions become less frequent. It is certainly worth trying some or all of the techniques and tactics I will show you. You will be surprised at what a difference they will make.

1. Mistrust

Creating a trusting environment reduces defensive behaviours. We are all more open and constructive when we feel we can trust those round us. A definition of trust I like is:

> *A belief that another's intentions are good*

It is true that trust is something than has to be earned; you cannot mandate that people start trusting each other. However, you can, through your Culture Development Plan, facilitate the building of trust.

Familiarity and exposure

In many cultures, there is a tendency to mistrust management and those in other divisions who we do not know. The default position seems to be that 'they' are the reason things are not working the way we want them to. Not everyone feels this way, but it is easy for the peer norm to default to this. If we don't know somebody, we are more likely to interpret negatively what we see of them from a distance – his or her decisions or performance. If a report is not delivered, we may assume they have not written it, while it might have been hiding on our desk. If someone is promoted over another individual with whom we had allegiance, we may assume it is cronyism, and not give the benefit of the doubt that this person has talents we do not know about.

Part of your trust building strategies should be to expose people to one another. When you get to know someone, you come to understand their motivations better and as a result are more likely to see the positive reason behind their actions. Familiarity is more likely to allow us to give someone the benefit of the doubt, to assume his or her intentions are good.

A client of ours was trying to build a single technology community made up of the heads of technology from each of their businesses. The organisation had deliberately created a very business-focussed organisation, and the majority of the technology people's time was, in line with this, dedicated to the business within which they sat. However, there were issues where the technology community needed to come together as a whole and take a stand on behalf of the whole business. The technology head from one of these businesses never showed up to meetings. Other priorities took over. Over time the rest of the team became very frustrated and mistrusting of this individual. Finally time was put aside to build the team. Together they talked through the challenges of their businesses. It became obvious that this individual was under the most incredible pressure. He had been given another role in addition to technology that was taking up half his time. He had been unsuccessful in hiring an individual who would have taken much of the load. He needed help but had been unable to ask. As the discussions continued, the mistrust disappeared. The team was still unhappy about not having this person's attention and commitment of time. But their behaviour was not destructive. The situation ceased to escalate beyond what it actually was. In this atmosphere, a way was found to ensure that the broader organisation's needs were met and this business stayed in-line with common standards and policies.

Trust building initiatives can include any forum where people are given the time to understand each other and what drives them and their businesses.

- In conferences, set up small booths where people move from place to place and get to sit and talk with people from other parts of the business

- Organise lunches with a range of different people
- Arrange out of work activities such as community activity, drinks and dinners

Trust building in teams

Intact teams are a special category when it comes to trust building. Teams are the backbone of your culture, and a key opportunity to send messages about your expected behaviour.

In teams the issue is not usually one of unfamiliarity, but rather of unclear expectations with regard to purpose, roles and process. Curiously, whilst we mostly acknowledge that organisational development and individual development are activities that one would expect to evolve over an extended period of time, team development is not usually considered in this manner.

In our work we treat a team like a mini-version of an organisation, and in doing so, have been able to eliminate many of the causes of mistrust, and ineffectiveness, within teams. If you are intending to use One-Team or Customer-Centric as one of the platforms of your culture, you will need to put particular attention here.

Effective teams need:

- Clear goals and purpose
- Clear roles and accountabilities
- Clear team process
- Good relationships

In undertaking our diagnosis phase with a team, we often find that it is one of the first three that is the root cause of the issues within the team. The relationships may have deteriorated and trust may not be high, but usually the cause of this is misaligned expectations about the purpose of the team, conflicting views about individual roles or accountabilities, or frustration that meetings and other team processes do not line up with the team's purpose.

Talk to a team about their meetings. If they say they are a waste of time, take too long, do not reach conclusions, get into minutia, you can be sure the problem lies in the team not being clear about its purpose. 'What are we here to do?' Without this it is not surprising that meetings are not valuable, since their potential for value has not been defined and shared.

From this position, trust and relationships can deteriorate very quickly. Building trust in a team is firstly about defining expectations and purpose, and ensuring everyone understands these. Once behaviour can be defined as breaking the team charter, and thus untrustworthy, it can be dealt with more easily.

Different types of trust

As you work on forums for familiarity and team, you will be in a position to understand more deeply the meaning of trust, and how to build it across your organisation. Efforts at trust building are often impeded by the ambiguity in the word itself, and the different meanings people attribute to it. When someone says they trust you, they may be meaning several different things:

I trust you to do your job	you are competent
I trust you to deliver on your promises	you are reliable
I trust you to support me as a person	you will not betray me, you have integrity

If you invest enough time in team-building activity, you will create an environment where behaviours which jeopardise trust can be discussed and resolved either one-on-one or with the team together.

Role of the team leader

The willingness of the team leader to open themselves up to feedback of this nature is key to building this level of trust in a team. The team leader has to initiate such conversations, set the standards of team membership and be prepared to act if those standards are not met. This does not remove responsibility for upholding these standards from all team members, simply that there are some decisions that can only be made by the team leader, particular those associated with long-term tolerance of untrustworthy behaviour.

Important trust relationships

There are a number of other key relationships in addition to the team which must contain trust to set the environment for removing defensive behaviour. All of these relationships can be targeted by interventions specifically designed to increase trust. Key relationships include:

- Individuals across the value chain who depend on each other
- One division with another
- CEO/executive team and groups of individuals throughout the organisation
- Head office roles traditionally seen as controlling (for example finance, audit, risk) and business lines
- Major providers of service (for example IT) and business lines

Clearing the air

Frustration and mistrust builds up over time, and will often reach a point where every action by the other party is seen through a negative frame, ensuring that the other's intentions are seen as malicious, when in most cases this is not the case.

Rebuilding trust in such cases requires opportunities to listen to another's point of view, and find ways to see the world through their eyes. Such opportunities usually have to be engineered, since most individuals do not have the skill to work their way through the emotional mind-field that a long period of mistrust generates.

Engineering these opportunities can occur through any forum where individuals are brought together with a structured agenda involving listening, discussing and clearing the air. Sometimes such sessions can be set up with strict rules for communication and deliberate exercises.

We use one called BIG-SMALL where each team member is given feedback in this format:

- One thing about you that makes you BIG in my eyes
- One thing that makes you SMALL

BIG-SMALL is useful because it shows people how the behaviours and attitudes they display cause others to see them at less than their full potential.

Being in the same room together is important. Whilst such trust-building can be done long distance, it always seems to be much harder because the visual sense is cut off, and so much human communication is non-verbal.

Learning trust-enhancing communication skills
There are many basic communication skills that should be a part of your programme to build trust. Some techniques are essential for these sessions to make progress, and often have to be taught or structured into the rules for the exercises and team charters They include:

- 'I' statements
- Being specific, rather than generalising ('you are always late for meetings' versus 'the last three meetings you have been late')
- Active listening and inquiry
- Making specific requests

2. Avoidance of responsibility, blaming others

At the beginning of all of our programmes and workshops we introduce a core concept, encapsulated on a single flipchart. The chart looks like this:

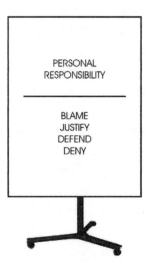

It is a chart I learnt from my friend Robert Kiyosaki, before he became famous through his *Rich Dad, Poor Dad* books. It contains a way of looking at the world that changed my life, and I am indebted to Robert for introducing me to it. Whenever we use evaluation forms in our programmes, and ask participants what had the most impact on them, this concept almost always ranks the number one. Above all others, this is the concept from my professional life I have tried to teach my children. It is such a profound idea that almost every consultant, facilitator and manager who has been introduced to it by our company still uses it as the basis for their work.

With such a fanfare, let me explain it.

Let us imagine you are faced with a situation which did not work out the way you wanted. You have a choice in the way you respond. You can go *above the line*, and take personal responsibility or you can go *below the line* and blame, justify, defend or deny. The path you choose will determine the outcomes you get in your life. Some people live *below the line*. (Let's face it, all of us go and visit there from time to time!) Everything is someone else's fault. Or there is a good reason why things did not work out. Or everything is just fine (even when it clearly is not). The language in each of these tends to be THEY or YOU. *Above the line* language is I or WE.

Warren Buffet, the US investor, was quoted as saying after September 11th: 'I apologise to our investors. In evaluating insurance stocks I did not anticipate an event with a combination of factors like loss of life, loss of building, loss of business, loss of aircraft'. Note the key phrase: I DID NOT ANTICIPATE. In making a statement of this nature, Buffet is going *above the line*. He is taking personal responsibility. As a result, we can be sure that he will have learnt something, and that next time he will take a different approach and thus get a different outcome.

It is this mind-set of personal responsibility, or ownership, which is the one you are seeking to establish in your organisation in order to move away from defensive behaviour and thinking. Such an approach embraces mistakes, successes, failures, unanticipated events, and learns from them. This mind-set is key if you are looking for an Achievement Culture, and is an astounding asset for every culture.

Putting an end to justification

Teaching people to *act above the line* who do not already do it instinctively, involves the continued push-back when justifications and blame are offered in response to unwanted outcomes. It is a management technique that lies at the heart of the skill of holding people to account, and can be taught in a leadership programme centred on accountability. You will find that a commitment by a small group of people to stay *above the line* and help others to do likewise can spread an epidemic of similar behaviour. However, watch yourself. Going *below the line* is a habit for us all – it is 20 years since I was first introduced to this powerful concept, and I still find myself slipping down into justification and blame at times.

You get what you settle for, justifications are often accepted in organisations.

A re-forecast, for example, can represent the acceptance of a justified reason why the original budget will not now be achieved. 'The market was down,' 'everyone's in the same boat,' the government changed the rules or the union or management. Everyone knows the best justifications are true. September 11th was true, but notice the different mind-set behind Buffet's statement about not anticipating such an event. We call these 'reasonable' reasons. They may be true, and very well-articulated, but they are also excuses.

If these factors fall in people's favour notice how quickly they take credit for the upside benefits. This is a useful technique to determine whether you are dealing with a reasonable reason you are prepared to settle for!

Introduce a discipline of not accepting blame and justification. This one change in mind-set will transform your culture and your performance.

3. A need to win over others, and never be seen to lose

There is a common mind-set in organisations which I will call the need to win over others or never appear to lose. It produces a competitive streak which many managers would consider to be an asset. There is a subtle, but crucial difference between a desire to win, and the defensiveness associated with never being prepared to lose. The behaviours associated with the latter can include:

- Self-sufficiency to the point of never sharing information or asking for help
- The use of meetings as an opportunity to 'show off' and look good
- A conviction that one is right and closing off other options.

A client of ours recently told me a story that horrified me, but which I suspect is more common than I realised. We had done a piece of work for him which involved undertaking a diagnostic to find out the root causes of poor service being delivered from his division to the rest of the company. We had charged him a reasonable, but not large, sum for the work, and presented some good insights which would enable him to target where he put his focus to lift performance levels.

At the same time, he had commissioned one of the big consulting firms to undertake another piece of work related to a proposed restructure. Their fee had been four times ours. Over a drink one evening, I asked him why he had asked the big firm to take on this other piece of work that we were equally capable of doing. 'Oh,' he said, 'when I want to find out something I don't know, I use you. When I have already decided on the answer, and want to add weight to my argument, I use one of the big firms. They know the answer I want, and what they give me is increased credibility and someone to blame if it doesn't work out.' This man is strongly driven by the need to win and never appear to loose. His saving grace is the humour with which he acknowledges this trait! Nevertheless, he will spend whatever it takes to win over others in the organisation who might try to stand in his way. Competitive cultures operate this way all the time, and consultants, with their beautiful packs and weighty arguments, sometimes feed this defensive drive and profit from it.

The need to always look like a winner is possibly the most subtle mind-set and cultural trait in terms of its cost to the business performance. A CEO I know well who had done great things to the culture of his organisation, had this as his Achilles heel. He saw an acquisition opportunity. He waded in very deep and the situation became hostile. Emotionally he just could not back down. The result was the beginning of the demise of a well-respected corporate icon.

These 'heroes' – I refer to them as such because there is a 'lone ranger' quality to the mind-set that can be quite engaging and inspiring for the people they manage – have mind-sets that can be difficult to shift, because individuals will have experienced many rewards associated with the behaviour. To some extent, it will be the very attitude that got them where they are in the organisation today.

The defensiveness in this behaviour is the inability to admit to weakness. We have found many cultures which seem to encourage this trait, perhaps influenced by the large egos of those who have reached its highest echelons. There has recently been more written on the usefulness of humility as a characteristic of a CEO, and thus perhaps the interest in building cultures which discourage this one-upmanship will increase. Jim Collins refers to this as one of the traits of Level 5 Leadership in his book *Good to Great*.

It is a key to building a One-Team and Customer-Centric Culture. Both of these require the willingness to be guided by the needs of others.

The pursuit of excellence – redefining what it means to win
Shifting this mind-set in your quest to shift your culture requires you to redefine what winning means in your organisation. Looking good must come to mean winning as a team, helping others succeed, admitting mistakes and learning. The pursuit of excellence, which always involves the need to critically examine current performance and acknowledge weakness, is another useful goal in changing this mind-set.

Shifting this trait in your culture and this mind-set in key individuals, requires structured opportunities to learn what it feels like to acknowledge weakness, and to make mistakes in an environment where doing so in fact is the 'new winning'. We have found this to be the easiest path to shifting this particular mind-set. Finding instant humility is just too big a leap! When people with this mindset get what we are trying to achieve with our clients, they actually become the greatest advocates for our work. They jump in and work at being the best culture builders in the business. Look, we'll take help from wherever it is offered – we're not proud.

So, people with this mind-set become a valuable asset in your quest to build the culture you want. And in the process, many of them learn the wisdom of humility, and, above all, the sense of connection that it gives them to others. Underneath all the bluster, this mind-set often covers a sense of loneliness and isolation.

However, the star quality does produce some cultural barriers, in particular, in relation to teamwork and learning.

If you can structure, through activities in your Culture Development Plan, opportunities for these people to connect with others on an equal-to-equal basis, you will find they become the leaders and drivers of your cultural aspirations. Ways of doing this include:

- Mentoring programmes
- Post-implementation reviews
- Learning and support forums
- Project teams

4. A need to be liked

The need to be liked sits behind much of the unwillingness to take tough decisions, give feedback on poor performance, tackle poor behaviour and confront unsatisfactory situations. People who are strongly driven by this trait find it difficult to take a stand in these situations, knowing that, as a result, they will become unpopular with the individuals concerned.

Clearly this trait will hold back your culture efforts, because it will limit leaders' ability to hold the line on the standards which define the culture you want. Their desire to keep everyone happy flies in the face of these aspirations. You have to find a way to help those who want to be liked, channel this need to the benefit of your culture plan.

On the surface, this trait may not appear to be as defensive as some of the other more aggressive defensive styles. The defensiveness displays itself in a FLIGHT mechanism, not a FIGHT one. Individuals avoid difficult situations where they will have to confront others, and thus turn a blind eye to situations which require a more direct response. Light-heartedness and bantering is a common trait of individuals and teams who have a strong need to be liked by each other.

Most of us never really reach a point where we are completely comfortable with giving others difficult feedback or holding the line on high standards or making an unpopular decision. However, it is possible to make the experience easier.

Ritualise the difficult moments

Awkwardness is reduced by ritual. A structured format is easier to cope with than one which has to occur spontaneously.

In team-building events, structure ritualised feedback sessions:

> 'One thing I notice about you which I would like to see more of is . . .'
> 'One thing I notice about you which I would like to see less of is . . .'

Use scoring systems to vote on ideas being discussed: on a scale of one to ten, everyone write down their score for:

- The likelihood we will achieve this goal
- The attractiveness of this idea

In performance feedback sessions ensure the format used requires both positive and negative feedback.

Work with the desire to be popular by rewarding and recognising those individuals who do take an unpopular stand in order to uphold the standards you need. Such an approach can make being unpopular the 'right' thing to be, and therefore the thing that will elicit praise from others. In this way you feed the need to be liked by setting up new criteria.

When a manager knows that he or she will be praised for taking an unpopular position, it makes it easier for them to step into that uncomfortable position. The awkwardness is still there, but it comes with its own reward. The manager finds that he is liked. Not by some individuals, but by the broader group of people who are important to him.

Teach people about saying 'no'. Make it one of the beliefs of your organisation that it is better to say 'no' than to say 'yes' and then not deliver.

5. Fear of making a mistake and being punished

A fear of making mistakes feels very different from a drive for excellence. It feels different on the inside, and it certainly feels different for those around you. Defensive behaviour arising from the fear of making mistakes includes working incredibly long hours, taking much longer on tasks than is necessary, and being unable to distinguish between things which really do need to be perfect, and those where reasonable standards are sufficient.

If your manager is driven by this fear, you will find yourself on the receiving end of micro-management. The impact on the business is that two people are then doing the same job, and the broader overview role to be played by a manager is not carried out. Time is not used effectively, too much being spent on elements of very little value, while other, more important items get overlooked.

The fear of making a mistake may not be linked to any recent experience that individuals have had of being punished. Like most emotional responses, this defensive reaction is not logical, and this makes it all the more powerful.

This response will certainly limit a drive towards an Innovative Culture. When it is important to understand and manage risks, and take action with confidence that you can correct when mistakes are made, individuals with this drive will definitely inhibit progress. Their obsession with getting it right is rewarded in so many organisations, and the defensive response is quite subtle. Many reading this will not perceive this behaviour as being defensive at all. It is only defensive because it is obsessive. Any behaviour over which we have no choice is a reactive response, and thus a defensive mechanism.

Individuals have to learn to accommodate mistakes within the framework of achieving the larger goal. Managers learn to temper their range of responses so that a typing error does not incur the same level of response as losing a major customer. The shift is a subtle one, but tremendously important for both the individual and those who are building a new culture. To be comfortable with mistakes, but to always succeed is a paradox which is exciting, once grasped.

To help individuals make this shift you have to show that making mistakes can be acceptable. Those in role-model positions help this by acknowledging their own mistakes often and publicly. Using the phase 'I don't know' is powerful role-modelling (perfectionists always feel they must know!).

Training and coaching can help these individuals to distinguish between the outcome required and the steps along the way. They can learn to hold others to account to deliver outcomes, rather than jumping in to fix every mistake they see their people making, thus never really allowing them to learn and grow. Allowing others to make mistakes and watching the benefits that arise from the experience is a great learning opportunity for those with a fear of making mistakes themselves.

6. Bullying

Bullying is a strong word. It does however describe behaviours that are prevalent in some organisations, and often unseen by those in senior leadership positions. A common characteristic of bullies is that they are tough with those who are smaller than they are, and sweet with those who they perceive as stronger than they are. In an organisational context, this means being nice to the boss and brutal with subordinates or those in other teams. I have a wonderful client called Vanessa who is one of half a dozen people I have met in my career who are 100 per cent role-models for valuing people. She runs a large utility, and has transformed the place through her disarming simplicity when it comes to the importance of people. I like to sit with her and listen to her talk because I learn so much about how this value works.

She was talking one day about one of her team, a man who had recently come into the organisation, and was performing reason-ably well. But Vanessa had heard of some incidents of him bullying his people. Shouting at them, throwing papers around. She was beside herself with anger. There was simply none of the intellectual debate around how to balance results with behaviour in evaluating his contribution. She has always seen her role as having to protect people from this type of behaviour. It is completely unacceptable, and she knows others cannot easily protect themselves from the impact of this behaviour from their boss. This man was marked. Vanessa was on to him like a ton of bricks, performance warnings were issued, and she had managed to get him out within three months.

Tough, bully-type behaviour is a defensive response to being attacked or hurt themselves. These individuals have learned that attack is the best form of defence. Over the years they have built up a shield which ensures they are not left vulnerable themselves, and their mistrust of close contact means that they avoid interactions where they engage on an equal basis with others.

From a cultural perspective, this behaviour produces fear in others, and shuts down communication. One of biggest business risks is that such individuals are not told bad news. They are closed off from input. They do not hear (or are not told) information about customer's views, problems with deadlines, budget over-runs or illegal activities, and lack of buy-in to plans. Over time they therefore form an ungrounded view about what is really going on. Their behaviour can cause others to fudge or bury problems, causing long-term organisational risk. Bullying represents a major risk to efforts to encourage whistle-blowing. A goal of People-First Culture is to tackle bullying head-on.

The global divisional head of a large listed company set extremely stretching targets. He slammed anyone who suggested that these targets were not achievable. The business was a cyclical one, and the downturn merely spurred him to more unreasonable demands. His company missed their targets for three years in a row. In the third year the Board removed him from his position. In interviewing managers in the organisation afterwards, the response was universal. 'Tom blasted anyone who challenged his thinking. He got rid of several non-believers,' his managers told us. 'In the end we just stepped back and watched it happen. We were completely disengaged. The sport became whether one could look as if one was performing whilst really just moving figures around to please him.'

Aggressive defence patterns – FIGHT responses – can seem harder to deal with than the softer FLIGHT ones. Aggressive defensiveness has to be met with an equal force. Not an aggressive response, but an extremely strong, assertive one. Aggressive individuals do respect people who stand up to them. Your plan must be to continue to hold your line no matter what is thrown at you. Any weakness in your position will be attacked. To achieve this goal you have to be very clear about what you believe and what you stand for as a culture champion. You do also need some authority. The occasional shock does work well as a tactic in these circumstances.

Being strong yourself, and designing interventions which are uncompromising in their standards, will build respect from individuals with these tendencies. In this way you can achieve some tacit support for the culture process. However, you are still left with the issues of the bully's behaviour with subordinates, which will clearly undermine the role-modelling required to achieve the change you seek. You have to find ways to make this behaviour visible to those who can act to stop it. Quantitative feedback tools will achieve this because they provide some anonymity. The data will provide you with the evidence to start the process of giving feedback. Because of the bully's failure to listen, this is one of the more difficult defensive responses to correct. If correction is not possible, you have to remove these people from the team. The damage to the culture by keeping them in the team is too great.

7. Fear of change

The fear of change paralyses individuals and companies. In an attempt to stay away from the unknown, which feels too vast, too unstructured, individuals cling to what they know. In the past, individuals with this fear gravitated towards career positions which they felt offered security and a certain future. In the past few years, downsizing and restructuring have taken away some of these options. There are few jobs today which fulfil the need for certainty and security. But the fear remains, and some individuals in your organisation will be seeking to build themselves a secure structure within which they can live with a degree of comfort.

A culture leader is unlikely to be seen as a benefactor to such individuals. Yet their drive for structure and certainty can provide some benefits. Their sharp nose for chaos will drive them to build order and process into your plans. If you can bring these people with you, they actually put substance around initial ideas and aspirations. The challenge is to move past their primary defensive reaction.

This reaction will be presented in rational ways:

- We did this before and it didn't help
- It is time to settle down what we are already doing, rather than start a whole lot of new initiatives

The defensive response is polite stonewalling, rather than anything too aggressive or obvious. You may be lulled into believing that you are being supported in your efforts to change. The words may be supportive, but it is by their actions that you must identify these individuals in order to work with them and bring them with you.

Your primary strategy should be to provide as much certainty as you can. Fear of change is, at its root, a fear of the unknown. Looking at change feels to some people like standing at the edge of a high cliff and being asked to jump. The fear is almost as palpable as that felt by people with a fear of heights, but rarely expressed or acknowledged in that way. Their response is to move away from the edge. Your job is to build a stairway.

Small steps are less frightening than big leaps. The vision only comes alive when it has form and substance. Filling out your view of the future with as much detail of the steps along the way will give some structure which makes it feel more comfortable. Because of their fear of the unknown, these people will often be quite conservative and anxious to do the right thing. If you can lead them step-by-step they often follow more willingly.

- Provide detailed descriptions of the expectations of the target culture. Lists of behaviours, rules of engagement
- Be specific about the tasks in your Culture Development Plan you expect individuals to carry out
- Describe how the target culture looks and feels in as much detail as possible

3. Ways to influence people's level of awareness

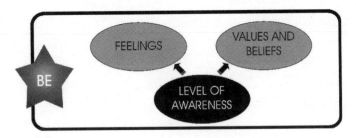

Composure and balance were, until very recently, considered outside of the realm of organisational change. Even the most enlightened HR manager would have thought long and hard before introducing such pursuits into the workplace. However, in the last few years, such ideas are gradually beginning to hold greater business benefits than was previously understood.

Some of this change can be traced to the increase in the number of women in management positions. As companies realised (or were forced to realise through equal opportunity laws) that by making the workplace friendly to women they doubled the size of their employment pool, the concept of work-life balance came into the corporate lexicon. Women with children had requirements in relation to work hours and flexibility which men had not previously demanded.

As organisations came to terms with what this meant, they

moved towards a more general understanding of work-life balance. Men as well as women started appreciating that being a complete workaholic did not necessarily produce the best outcomes for the organisation, never mind the personal life.

Being very stressed will lower your level of awareness. When we are stressed we lose perspective, develop tunnel vision, become defensive in our interactions with others, and are rigid in our approach and lose good judgment. All of these are characteristics of someone who is unable to step back and be conscious of their own behaviour.

To change the level of awareness of people in your organisation, you need to design opportunities which will give them balance, restful quietness and perspective.

Balance is achieved by:

- Changes to working hours – shorter, more flexible
- Ensuring people take their annual leave
- Softening the lines between work and home
- Work environments which are different

Restful quietness is achieved by:

- Meditation
- Religious practice such as prayer
- Yoga
- Some sporting activity, especially those with a rhythm carried alone – running, swimming
- Some forms of travel – driving on empty roads, cycling
- Music

Perspective is achieved by:

- Time away from the office in teams, workshops, conferences
- Opportunities to move around the organisation
- Feedback tools

- Coaching and therapy
- Personal development programmes
- Opportunities to learn from others
- Exposure to others whose problems are greater than one's own

SUMMARY

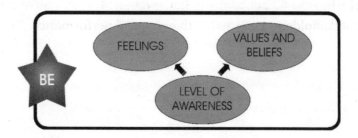

Changing others is one of the most difficult tasks for a culture champion. But it can be done and it is the most rewarding task. To watch colleagues change, who have for their entire career been driven by whichever defensive demon dominates their style, is a tremendously satisfying experience. A life of defensiveness is most exhausting. It keeps one separate from other people, and disconnected from the best parts of oneself. It leads to every manner of disease, some of them life-threatening. When an individual sees their own defensiveness and its impact on their lives, and is able to stand apart and choose a different set of responses, they feel exhilarated. Fear is crippling, and in most cases people are not even aware that it is fear which causes them to react a certain way. If you can help people take this step, you will be rewarded with watching this change.

Seeing it as a personal challenge is more useful than becoming angry with them. It is easy to blame people for holding back your culture goal. But people are the cultural journey. The culture champion's job is to find ways to facilitate the changes I have described. The first group is always the hardest. Once you get some momentum up, people become engaged with the new way of behaving, are able to adjust their knee-jerk responses and substitute others more suited to the emerging culture norms.

It is at this point that it becomes more obvious which of your people have simply got into defensive habits, and which are driven by demons which they will not be able to shift. At this point you will need to filter some of the latter group out of your organisation. In my experience it may end up being around 20 per cent of your people. But the 80 per cent will be enriched for the experience, and your stakeholders rewarded with enhanced performance.

9

Cultural Enablers

SYMBOLS AND SYSTEMS TO UNDERPIN YOUR CULTURE

SYMBOLS are visible decisions or artefacts to which people attribute meaning, such as titles, office-layout, how the budget is allocated. Systems are underlying mechanisms by which the organisation is managed, such as the planning system or the remuneration policy. Culture is sustained by behaviours, symbols and systems because each one sends messages about what is valued and thus set the behavioural norms for all who belong to your organisation.

We have discussed that to achieve change you have to change the mind-sets which sit behind the behaviours and the decisions about systems and symbols. (BE-DO-HAVE.) As these mind-sets change, your own people will start to make a different set of decisions, and start to display a different set of behaviours. For example, if your CFO develops a strong belief in the importance of customer delight, she will ensure that reporting requirements from the front line are streamlined. This will ensure the customer-facing staff spend as much time as possible interacting with customers rather than feeding data up the line.

If one of your managers starts to really value the opinions of her people, she may choose to remove the walls of her office, and sit somewhere where she is more in the thick of conversations about what is happening with the business.

If you get it right at the BE-level, then everything else will eventually fall into place because all decisions at the DO-level are made by people with the right mind-sets. This is what actually occurred in the early stages of your organisation's history. A bunch of likeminded people set it up, agreed what was really important and designed the organisation according to these values. Your systems therefore will be legacies from the values held by previous leaders. They will have been designed to fulfil a slightly different values hierarchy, and will now be reinforcing this values hierarchy, even if the values of the current leaders have moved on. This can be very frustrating for those championing change, because they seem to hold the organisation back.

You should accelerate making changes to the systems and symbols which have reinforced your culture up until this date. If well-planned they can stimulate individuals to behave in a new way, even if they are not very comfortable with it. Changing systems and symbols takes time, and you will need it completed further down the track, so it is best to start early, whilst working on their mindsets too. Otherwise your people will gradually change the symbols and systems back to ones which support the current mind-set. Perhaps you want a culture of transparency and seek to introduce measurement systems which provide this and thus enable accountability. If there is not a mind-set that believes accountability is important, your people will gradually distort these systems. First they will make them very complicated, thus distorting the numbers and making it hard to see what is really happening and who is doing what. Or they might, over time, stop using these new dashboards in the manner which you intended. Or there will be a budget cut and the IT project which would have facilitated the entry of the data gets cut. You get the picture. Like weeds taking over an untended garden, it takes two-to-three years for the natural state to re-exert itself.

A lot of money is spent on changing systems without changing mind-sets. The original business-case value is often not delivered because all of the work is focussed on changing what people DO in order to HAVE the outcome described in the business case. But those who work on these projects often lack the understanding of how to change people at the BE-level. So the benefits are lost.

For example, a new performance management system will gradually become a mechanistic activity in which a number of boxes are ticked, and everyone ends up being ranked a three or a four on a five-point scale. If people do not hold in their hearts a belief in meritocracy, and some of the other values required for an achievement culture, they will not use a new performance management system in the manner in which it was intended. And skill training alone will not overcome this. There are only a few skills required to give someone feedback. By far the greatest requirement is that the one giving the feedback believes that the benefit of doing so outweighs the discomfort almost everyone feels whilst actually doing it. I have to hold meritocracy and honesty higher up my values hierarchy than being liked, in order to go through that discomfort.

Another example we frequently see is the use of measurement. A client of ours had known that it was important to begin to measure customer satisfaction if they were to make progress along the path of becoming more customer-focussed. By the time we met them, they had spent three years debating the best way of measuring this satisfaction. Each business unit was using a wide range of methods. They were not able to agree whether their goal was to score higher than the competition or to improve against their own previous score (and these tended to be interchanged depending on how their rankings stacked up). As a result, a large amount of money was spent on research, with little effect. We helped the top team realise that they had not changed as much as they thought they had with regard to their value of customer-focus. Once they shifted their thinking and mind-set, they made decisions very quickly on future measurement. Because now they *really* wanted to know.

When you are on an active path of mind-set change, then supporting this by accelerating changes to systems and symbols is very valuable. Systems and symbols touch everyone in the organisation, so they are a good way of sending new messages to everyone simultaneously. Your Culture Development Plan should include a large section on this topic.

Tackling the systems
There are five main areas which act as culture levers:

1. People systems
2. Planning
3. Measurement
4. Work processes
5. Structure

When you complete your diagnostic you will discover what messages these systems are sending about what is really valued in your organisation. Armed with this information, and your description of the culture you want, you can then develop a prioritisation process for which systems you are going to tackle first. How to redesign each system requires a depth of knowledge which individuals in your organisation will either have or you can recruit. Here I will describe what you should be looking for as you make the decision to introduce changes to any of the major systems which underpin the human dynamics of your business. Changes to these systems take some time, and often considerable investment, so prioritising is important. A good approach is to pick:

• Some quick wins
• A few big circuit breakers

You will have to address each of the areas listed above to some degree. Your approach to each will depend on the type of culture you have chosen to adopt.

What if you cannot access your systems?

Many culture leaders cannot access the key systems which run their organisation. For example, if you work in a global business, many of the systems lie outside of your control. This will change the nature of the work you do on systems, but should not eliminate it from your thinking. There is a lot that can still be achieved by changing the *way* in which a system is used. In the example above, you can change the way your performance management is used, without changing the system itself.

1. People systems

Selection

Selecting people according to their values will become an important criterion, and one which your recruitment agency must thoroughly understand if they are to help you. You will need to introduce an interview process designed to uncover mind-sets, which are linked to, but not the same as, competencies and previous experience. The more traditional selection processes are strongly based on what the individual can and has DONE, rather than at the BE-level of their beliefs, values and attitudes.

Promotion

It is easier to establish what an individual's mind-sets are if you promote from within, because you have a more extensive experience of them. You must conduct internal reference checking with the same amount of rigour that you would expect from your recruitment agency when they recommend people from outside. You are seeking evidence of the mind-sets and behaviours you have defined as being important, as well as the normal performance criteria.

Your talent evaluation process must enable you to identify and categorise your people based on the values and behaviours of your desired culture. Results plus values should be your mantra, and your succession planning and career development decisions be based on both. Every time you compromise the values dimension for the sake of outstanding performance on the results axis, you undermine your cultural process.

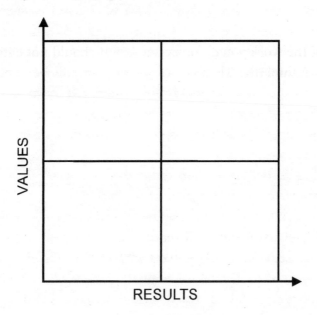

Organisations with great cultures tend to promote from within, because it gives them the opportunity to watch staff over a long period of time to ensure that individuals display the behaviours they want. They can be more confident that the person promoted will sustain the culture they have built.

Leaders who are passionate about culture will often make promotions and appointments which others would see as risky. This is because they believe that promoting on values is safer than promoting on performance. They reckon that you can take someone with the right attitude and train them in the technical skills required to ensure their business performs, and that this is an easier task than instilling the right values in someone who does not have them.

Talent management

Many organisations have a process which plans the development of people's careers. Such a process combines the importance of providing a future path for people, so that they choose to stay, with the organisation's need to build a solid succession pool. This process must line up very closely with your Culture Development Plan.

For example, if you have a special programme for high potential people, those selected for this programme must already be demonstrating that they hold the values you have selected to underpin your culture. This gives you the opportunity to accelerate the careers within your organisation of a group of people who will become beacons of the values you are seeking to embed.

If, on the other hand, high potentials are selected on performance criteria only, this opportunity is missed.

Individual goal-setting

Objectives form the basis of the contract between the employer and the employee. It follows then that there is an opportunity within this framework to clearly articulate what is expected of the individual within the new culture. Any cultural driver can be translated into an individual performance contract. You should aim to have each element of your cultural expectations appear in some way.

For example, customer-centricity might appear as a customer satisfaction metric or alternatively, as the delivery of certain customer service standards or completion of a project which will improve the experience of the customer.

One-Team Culture might be represented by cross-sell numbers, by outputs delivered to another team or work undertaken on their behalf or perhaps by an evaluation by a peer with the individual's co-operation.

Achievement requires very rigorous performance targets, since these form the basis of the accountability contract.

For every culture, clarity and simplicity will assist your process.

A list of objectives which spread over two or three pages with long lists of measures will only serve to achieve a culture of bureaucracy!

Evaluation

Performance management systems are the formal mechanism for sending messages about what is expected from individuals in your organisation, and whether they are meeting those expectations. Simplicity is the mantra here. Complexity dilutes the messages. Some performance management systems become too bureaucratic, measuring on too many behavioural and results dimensions. The system must enable people to be held to account – if it is difficult to measure whether they have or have not met expectations, then this tool is lost. Ask your people what messages they received from their performance management process – if they cannot answer that question clearly, then it is not providing cultural value.

Your system must include both behavioural and results measures if you are going to achieve behavioural change. Comments about an individual's behaviour should be collected throughout the year, from multiple sources – peers, boss, direct reports and customers. A simple multi-rater, completely electronic system, with recipients agreed upfront will provide the quantitative component.

Honest performance evaluation will be essential for you to reinforce your culture and encourage the behaviours you want. It will also identify those values and behaviours that are misaligned with what you want. Finding ways to ensure managers carry out such evaluations is very important, and this can be achieved through reporting systems which require rigorous performance conversations to be carried out with each employee. If you are looking for behaviour change, these are best completed more frequently than the traditional once a year, because behaviour adjustment requires lots of feedback.

Remuneration

Financial reward can be a powerful mechanism for supporting the behaviour you want to build your new culture. However, it does require measures that are absolutely rigorous and not subjective. Use a balanced scorecard which includes metrics based on financial, customer and people dimensions to demonstrate that your performance means both the 'What' and the 'How'.

Using financial reward to change cultures can be hazardous, as the pursuit of money can cause quite distorted behaviour. In some organisations, financial rewards in the form of bonuses are not a highly effective driver of cultural change. However, if your organisation is in an industry that attracts people who value money very highly, then reward will work as a lever for change.

Many organisations have bonuses that are linked to the achievement of the whole team or organisation, and yet individuals in those teams still behave in individualistic, siloed ways. However, you do not want financial reward schemes which actively force people into counter-cultural behaviours.

Dismissal

Your processes for dismissal can be a strong driver of cultural change. A good game must have clear rules, a process for umpiring and penalties for breaking the rules. If the penalties are not enforced, the rules lose any power and the game loses its effectiveness and also its fun. Although it is easy to try and bend the rules, and to resent it when a penalty is handed out, we often forget that the power of rules and their penalties actually make a game great.

Establishing the rules for dismissal acknowledges and values the 99 per cent of your people who play by the rules, thus strengthening the tribe and game you are playing. You can design processes which help your managers enforce these rules, and help individuals to blow the whistle if they see behaviour which breaks the rules.

Dismissal for misconduct is much easier than dismissal for poor behaviour. Sometimes you have to find other ways of removing individuals whose behaviour is holding back the culture programme.

Both reward and dismissal are consequences. If there are no consequences linked to behaviour, the motive to change is weak.

Policies

Review all of your HR policies through the filter of values you have chosen and your desired culture. Do they reflect what you are trying to achieve? Look at the places where they are written down – the intranet, the manuals. Often the language of policies undermines their intent. Language that is autocratic, cold or bureaucratic sends a signal that is as strong as the content of the policy. Try to word policies in the positive – 'managing for superior performance' rather than 'consequence management'. Watch the balance. It is how you manage the 85-90 per cent of people who are performing that will impact most on the culture. Policies are often worded in a way that focuses on the 10-15 per cent of poor performers.

Key people metrics

HR can provide some key metrics which will be indicators of cultural change. Resignation rates, sick leave, employee satisfaction, ratio of internal and external hires; whichever metrics you decide are important should be provided to each manager, so that the indictors of a good culture become a part of their performance targets. Chapter 11 covers more on how to pick metrics to measure improvements in culture.

2. Planning

Budget-setting

The process of deciding how we allocate money is one of the most powerful symbols of an organisation's culture. Because spending money is such a reflection of what we value, the process for choosing how we do it must be designed to allow the values to be expressed and argued in a constructive and invigorating manner. Too often the budget process is painful and drawn out, disempowering to all, occupying a part of the brain far removed from the uplifting areas of values and culture. Most organisations, in fact, would not see the link between the two. However, because in for-profit organisations, the financials are often a more important value than the people, the budget process provides a great opportunity to play out what we intend to value through our most precious process.

In seeking to redesign your budget process to align it more closely to the values, ask yourself:

- Are targets built up from the bottom (valuing the involvement and opinions of people) or from the top (signalling a stronger drive and Achievement Culture) Or do they come from the bottom and then get over-ridden from the top without consultation, resulting in disempowerment and the practice of holding something back to meet these demands? (Which supports neither Achievement nor People-First Cultures.)
- Is the process very divided, with budgeting occurring in isolation from other divisions or units (individualistic), or does it involve negotiation and discussions between units (One-Team)?
- Where in the process does the voice of the customer appear?
- Is the process quite rigid; does it allow for innovation? Once signed-off, does the budget facilitate or inhibit flexibility and entrepreneurship?
- Is accountability embedded in the process in an on-going manner? How are the budgets treated after they are created? Do they live or remain in a drawer? How do you deal with non-performance in the early months? What does re-forecasting do to the organisation's beliefs that justification for non-delivery is acceptable?

Review your budget process with your values in mind. Put your most fervent culture champions on to the task. It teaches the art of the 'and'. How do we hold true to our values *and* deliver our numbers?

Strategic planning
Considering and planning for the future provides an opportunity to demonstrate both your customer-centricity and your willingness to

really listen to and involve your people. The process for making key decisions about what you will and won't do is always a demonstration of your culture in action. Conservative cultures will make conservative choices; gung-ho cultures risky choices.

A culturally aware organisation can test its decision-making processes against its values, and become more conscious of how emotionally-based behaviours influence strategic choices.

Consider your strategic planning processes. What strategic choices align with your values? How does holding these values change the way the organisation thinks about the future? A water utility is under continual pressure from its minister in government to deliver funds to support other government requirements. They are also aware of their responsibility to ensure they consider the needs of future generations, and encourage water management practices which take this into consideration. Sustainability is a value they hold dear. Their strategic planning process has to find ways to fulfil the needs of the future, which requires less water consumption, with the demand for revenue now, which is most easily achieved by encouraging greater consumption. The path they plot becomes their values in action, and the process they use builds a culture where their people understand sustainability and how to balance a triple bottom line.

Experiment with different approaches to strategic planning and ensure that your values are a part of the decision-making.

Project planning

A client of ours had its company roots in the building industry. Their core business was the construction of large office buildings, public works buildings and residential developments. These disciplines require excellent project management, and this had developed as a core competency within the organisation. They had mastered project management at both the DO and the BE-level – their people held the values and beliefs required, such as the importance of anticipating risk, and breaking large goals into measurable milestones. Their cultural breakthrough came when they realised that they could treat life as a project. Most of what they did in their organisation could be turned into a project. They spread the disciplines across the whole organisation, and these became one of the major planks of their Achievement Culture. When new people come into the organisation, they are taught the techniques, rituals and processes the organisation uses in projects. Their HR systems support them pulling people off their jobs and putting them on to a project for six months. This is considered an honour, and there are always volunteers. This also provides a career development opportunity, because people get exposure to new parts of the business. As soon as a new idea or initiative emerges – whether it is negotiating a new agreement with the unions, planning a merger, moving offices or addressing a series of customer complaints – teams determine whether this can be designed as a project. If possible, and in most cases this is so, the project management discipline swings in, and everybody knows how to play. The team is selected, roles are defined, a steering committee established, and the process commences. As with all projects, completion is defined at the start, and everyone has the added satisfaction of a successful outcome. Then they move on.

This has been one of the most effective examples of using a system to drive culture change that we have seen. It contains all of the ingredients for success. It is tied to business outcomes, not off to the side. It causes behaviours and mind-sets which are important to every part of business-life. It aligns to the values of account-ability, transparency and lack of hierarchy. It is backed up by other systems (induction, training, selection, career development) which make it work for people. Every division at every level uses the same ritual. It has been used for a long time. It is led by leaders who believe in its value.

Linking individual and team goals to the overall
Alignment must be a goal of all great organisations. When each of your employees has a line of sight between what they do and the

overall goals of the organisation, their action will fall more closely into alignment. The process for achieving this builds cultural muscle because it brings different people and units closer together and feeling more closely bound to the tribe.

Whilst this process does not strongly embed any particular value, it provides the glue which holds your overall culture together. When identification with the organisation increases, people care more about the values of the organisation, and push more strongly to become a values-driven organisation. When individuals feel isolated in what they do, they care less about these things and more about their own self-interest.

Interdependencies between divisions

Your planning processes can enhance the horizontal, as well as the vertical alignment. In almost every desired culture, the awareness and consideration of the needs of others is a useful mind-set to cultivate. Horizontal interdependencies are the needs and obligations that exist between one unit and another, in a peer-to-peer relationship. You can encourage conversations, which formalise these relationships through processes in your planning cycle. For example, you can require one area to be involved in, and then sign-off on, the budgets and plans of another, signalling that they have been consulted and that the plans seem to have taken their needs into account. It is surprising how many organisations miss this step in the process

A client of ours undertook this process in a formal way with the top three layers of the organisation. The organisation had seven layers in total, but they felt that to tackle the first three was a big enough stretch to start with. Individual units set a range of objectives for each of their teams. These covered financial, customer, project, people and behavioural. They used the same template for this process. HR then took all of these, and laid them all out. If one person was intending to achieve a lift in sales figures, they checked that the product people had goals related to new products that would facilitate this achievement. If product managers had targets, they checked that sales were expecting people to sell to this product. If one person was intending to lift culture scores, they checked that HR had some initiatives that would assist. Where there were gaps, they went back to the individuals involved and asked them to sit down and work out the issues.

As a result some targets were changed, and the frustration of feeling your peers are working against, rather with you, was removed at the beginning of the year. They are now working through how to take the process down through the next couple of layers, which exponentially increases its complexity, but the value delivered is worth the effort. The process has opened up an entirely new way of setting goals, with peers now working closely with their counterparts in other divisions. In the past they had either actively competed with them, or simply worked against them unconsciously. Collaboration benefited both the customer, who started to receive a more coherent offering, and the shareholder.

3. Measurement

What gets measured gets done. To this I will add: what gets measured is deemed to be important, and therefore gets done.

In organisational life, measurement has a far higher profile than it does in our personal life. It is not measurement in itself which causes action, but the interest that people place on the data generated by measurement, and its ability to make people look good or bad in the eyes of the tribe. Measurement in organisational life is a strong symbol of what is valued, and therefore your measurement systems must form a part of your Culture Development Plan.

The right metrics

Many organisations have huge amounts of data about everything. What matters to the culture champion are the measures that are actually used. For example, all organisations will have data on sales, on profit, on repeat business, on margins. Some organisations, however, use the sales volume measurement as their primary driver. When you ask them how big they are, or how much they have grown, they answer in sales numbers. This drives their culture. Others are entirely focussed on profit. Some use service measures strongly; others argue that service will result in sales so sales are the important metric.

Thus the selection of the right metrics to have as your high-profile measures is a strong signal of what is valued. Changes to this measurement system will change behaviour, and over time changes the way people think as well. I have found that unless you have the mind-set absolutely aligned to what you want to achieve, having the right metrics is an essential piece to corralling those whose values are not yet the way you want them.

Use of data – speed, accountability, accessibility

An organisation I know used a transparent and easily accessible Management Information System as the powerful tool to make everyone in the organisation feel equal. Accessibility was very high, everybody could see all the numbers, and as a result transparency was assured. Investing in the technology and processes to provide this quality of data facilitated a range of cultural changes:

- Transparency increases accountability and reduced power games
- Accessibility taught individuals about the performance and mechanics of other businesses and thus increased a One-Team Culture
- Management was able to hold on to the one piece of information they really needed to feel secure – which was the performance data, and then let go of how individuals went about their day-to-day jobs

Who gets to see what information, which report gets on to the CEO's desk, are strong cultural signals, and you should consider these processes as a part of your plan. On the whole, greater transparency will improve your culture because it increases the fact-base of the business, and leaves less room for emotional game playing and defensiveness.

How data is used has a cultural impact too. If data is to be used for correction and improvement, it needs to be accessible quickly and within a timeframe where correction will make a difference. It also needs to be accessible to the people whose actions can cause it to change next time it is measured. It needs to be specific enough that action can result.

Measuring once a year is likely to be less relevant than measuring it every month, especially if individuals are being held to account to deliver certain targets. Data is at its most useful when it is seen as a tool to facilitate decision-making and correction. It is least useful when it is used for punishment.

Review your reporting and accessibility mechanisms with these thoughts in mind and you will find flow-on benefits to your performance, your culture and your mind-sets.

4. Work processes

The behaviour of people in your organisation is shaped in part by the processes within which they are required to operate. For example, if you are a bank, and your lending process is very complex, with numerous hand-offs and a focus on accuracy and credit-worthiness, but not on speed for the customer, then over time your people's thinking and behaviour will be influenced. They will stop thinking of what they do as serving the customer, and see success as ticking the boxes and following each step that they have been asked to do. The process discourages them from taking a balcony view, stepping back and seeing the whole picture. They become narrow in their thinking, and their behaviour reflects a lack of awareness of other people. If you simplify the process, with an emphasis on customer measures as well as credit ones, and design roles so they have a broader view on the whole, your people will change their behaviour. If they have been working in the process for a long time, you will also have to change their mind-sets through education, because some of them will have embedded a narrow, bureaucratic view as a part of their standard mind-set. In fact, the process may have actually attracted employees with that view of the world.

Using naturally occurring changes

Your organisation has many processes which form the framework within which work occurs. Most organisations review these on a regular basis anyway because they are seeking to improve efficiency and service levels. It is useful to hook into these reviews, and to implant the cultural perspective. In so doing you will assist in the effective implementation of the change, by considering the required education components to support behaviour change. You will also ensure the changes to processes that support the culture you are targeting.

If you can find events or processes that occur naturally in your organisation, and couple your culture work to them, it is also possible to use a process change as a culture change initiative. This works well because it embeds culture into the regular improvement process of the organisation, rather than it being off to the side. You can pick particular processes and ask teams to recommend and then implement changes which specifically ensure they will reflect your values. Eventually this will have to be done with all of the processes in your organisation, because they will all be operating according to the values of the past. This will become clear through your Culture Diagnostic.

5. Structure

Structure can be useful to culture change, but less so than is often thought. A structure change can often be the first approach that comes to mind when a leader is seeking to change some behaviours that are holding back performance. Structure highlights certain elements of the organisational mix, and, when lined up with strategy, sends messages about what is important.

Customer-centric

A change from a product-focussed strategy to one lined up behind customer segments, groups together those people the organisation most wants to make decisions together. A customer-aligned structure is more likely to ensure that its decisions look at the customer as a whole person rather than as a series of products.

Often organisations grow up with a product-focus because that is where they started. Telecommunications businesses, for example, had a focus on fixed-line products long before mobiles arrived on the scene. They set mobiles up as a new division in the early days of the development of mobile technology. Years down the track they discovered they couldn't send one bill to a customer for both their home phone and their mobile. Their systems did not allow them to view the customer as one person. This makes it more difficult for them to implement strategies to retain the customer by, for example, offering price discounts for the use of multiple products. To address this problem many have now moved to a customer-focussed structure.

However, in this instance the structure change alone will not centre customer-focussed culture which sees the customer as a person with a range of telecommunications needs which fit into a broader life. This change will require change at the BE-level. But structure will put the right people in the room together.

Achievement

Structure has a strong influence on accountability. Clear delineation of roles makes it easier to hold people to account. A structure which gives more people authority, as well as accountability, will increase the ease with which they deliver. Interdependencies make accountability harder, because people are more comfortable when they control what they are being held to account to deliver. On the other hand, this also makes them more likely to be one-eyed, seeing only their piece of the world.

One-Team

Structures which are organised by product line or by function (such as marketing, sales, operations) will require a One-Team Culture to be really successful.

Most structures today create some form of matrix, where many individuals report to more than one individual. These structures facilitate a One-Team Culture, as well as providing the checks and balances important to ensure compliance and profitability. However, they only work if people have learnt how to think and behave in a matrix environment. They have to learn how to negotiate priorities between two bosses, how to be an advocate for each in the other team of which they are a member, how to work their way through so they can find ways to achieve both sets of objectives.

People-First

The number of layers in your organisation impacts your People-First Culture. The closer the front line is to senior management, the more likely their voice will be heard, and they will be given the authority to make real decisions. But a flat structure will not guarantee that this occurs. Structure can help empowerment by creating meaningful jobs with real decision-making authority.

Innovative

A more fluid structure, with cells and resource pools that move from project to project works well for an Innovative Culture. Innovation and learning requires change at a faster rate than major structural changes can allow, and some fluidity allows people to move around according to the development of opportunities.

Review your structure in-line with what your cultural aspirations are, and change it if necessary. When you do implement change, ensure you simultaneously put in place the supporting programmes to change the mind-sets and teach the new skills to make the structure work.

Achieving change through systems change

As your eye becomes attuned to seeing systems as cultural levers, you will find many others which you may wish to include in your cultural plan. The criteria for their selection would be that they corral your people into a set of behaviours and habits, and, over time a mind-set, which sustains your culture.

As you progress down your cultural path, you will find that the natural owners of every system will start to review it from the viewpoint of their new mind-set, and then you as a culture leader can start to relax on this issue. In the early days, however, tackling some of these big sacred cows will be a great boost to the culture shift. You will be involving people who might not have seen themselves as central to culture work – such as your finance people – but because of this, the impact of change has all the more credibility in the organisation.

System change is complex and takes time to implement, but is no more complex than the human mind, which is your other big focus area. System changes are harder to undo, so once one has really become established, they are quite resilient, at least in the short-term. Once in place, they can pull a good culture through a difficult patch. I have seen a great culture, belonging to an organisation acquired by another with a weak culture, held up by strong systems during the merger. Their financial reporting, communication approach and employee benefits were particularly innovative. By the time the acquirer got around to wanting to change the systems – which acquirers are wont to do – they had seen and understood the value of the culture they had acquired and were able to assimilate much of it into their own approach.

In another instance, the rigorous and honest application of the feedback cycle enabled a company to hold to its cultural values during a time of sudden, catastrophic downturn in their market. Lay-offs and quick changes to product lines were necessary. At a time when many organisations throw all cultural aspirations out the window, this company was upheld by its great cultural systems, which literally propelled it into its next era of growth, stronger than before.

CREATING NEW SYMBOLS

Symbols offer a very creative way to influence culture, and new symbols can be introduced in quite a short time-frame. The overall goal when working on symbols is to produce the response, 'Wow, that's different'. To be effective, a symbol has to be visible, preferably to a large number of people, and clearly show that the values of the leaders of the organisation are changing. As more leaders embrace the new culture, they will initiate their own symbolic changes. As part of your Culture Development Plan, however, you can pick some high-profile ones and use these to give hope to a broad number of people, to bypass the managers that are not on board and provide role-modelling for your people. A good symbolic change will tell people that they too can do something similar, and it will be supported.

Some powerful ways to demonstrate values change through symbols include:

- Changing how time is spent
- Changing how money is spent
- Changing what gets priority in times of pressure
- Giving key roles to people who live the values, especially if these choices are unconventional
- Changing where people sit, with whom they sit or office layout
- Changing titles, car park policy or other status signs
- Introducing new rituals such as employee gatherings, feedback techniques or problem-solving approaches
- Publicly recognising people for culture-supporting behaviour
- Changing how you use external consultants
- Lining up you external advertising to your cultural goals

Rather than going through these one by one, I will tell you a number of stories of people who have used symbols powerfully. Once you start to think in terms of symbols, you will find thousands of ways in which you can use them to send new messages about what is valued.

Symbols stories

1. The family football club

The New York Giants, one of the leading football teams in the USA, has a very strong culture based on being a club with family values as its cornerstone. They are one of only two clubs in the NFL that don't have cheerleaders supporting their team at games. They have been put under pressure many times to change this policy, but have not because they believe there is sexual undertone to the cheerleader ritual which they believe is not in-line with their family values. Each time they restate this decision, they send a message to their whole organisation – players, fans, administrators, that this is the value-set they have, and this is what they expect of their people. This position has stood them in a good light at a time when the sexual behaviour of players has tainted the reputation of sporting codes.

2. Bending the rules

A government department did not have the same freedom to use financial incentives to cause behaviour change that was available in the private sector. For most employees, a bonus is only 5 per cent, or nothing at all, and this is focussed on performance, not behaviour. They used this situation to their advantage, building a strong belief that they were seeking intrinsic, not extrinsic motivation, as the basis for the behaviour change they were seeking. By building a strong inner belief that exceptional service was what they stood for, they found their people were going the extra mile for customers, sometimes working longer hours, going over and beyond the expectations laid out in their employment terms.

But they supported this by having very high expectations of their managers in terms of how they treated their people. Managers frequently encouraged staff to take time to go to their children's sports events or to work from home if they needed to be there. They took special care to support staff moving to new roles when the opportunity arose. The intrinsic motivation was supported by a relaxation in policies and a strongly supportive management approach. This strengthened their value of customer service, and the system was not abused by employees, because everyone believed in the values.

3. Burn-out

An organisation of about 400 people, which valued its people strongly, ran a big upgrade to its IT systems. The project was challenging, and a couple of people were 'chewed up' in the words of the managing director. But the project did come in on time and on budget. However the project director did not get the recognition he expected. His failure to manage the stress overload on these two people was considered to represent failure. One, who had been put on the project for the experience, and was considered a high potential individual, had resigned. The other became completely stressed and started to behave in ways which were very out of character. Bill, the managing director, spoke openly that it was not acceptable to damage people as a tactic for achieving the on time, on budget goals. The message was loud and clear. Achieve on time, on budget *and* look after the well-being of your people.

4. Tenacious Rose

Rose, the woman responsible for building a culture programme in her organisation, decided to take one team and help them become a role model for the approach she wanted the whole organisation to take. Believing in the tactic of taking naturally occurring opportunities, she seized the moment thrown up by setting cost targets for the customer service group responsible for dealing with claims on life insurance policies made by the families of customers who had died. She asked to take the team away for three days. These were not sophisticated university graduates. This was a rag-tag group of clerical staff. Together she helped them write a business plan, starting with the core question of 'who is the customer?'

Rose has a passionate belief in people and their capacity to excel if given a chance. Her organisation's culture journey has been based on this belief, and their culture measurement scores are as good at the front line as they are at more senior levels. She used her belief in these people to allow them to build their own plan. When it was built, she brought in the head of the operation and the team presented their plan to him. He was so impressed he suggested they should present to the Board. This team of clerical staff presented their business plan to the Board, to show directors what could be achieved if people were allowed the dignity of setting their own goals. The numbers they believed they could deliver were more than the targets that had been cascaded down to them the previous year.

The team changed from being a group of clock-watchers to an innovative group who were focussed on improving their piece of the process. From this point, Rose used her influence, plus the profile of Board support, to gradually spread this methodology for business planning across the whole organisation. She had bypassed the head of customer service to do the first piece of work, and bypassed many more middle managers on the way through. She was not popular. What was achieved was a revolution which was both top-down and bottom-up. The symbol was, 'the front line matter, their ideas are the best.'

5. Road-shows

The senior team of an organisation made the decision to dedicate six weeks of every year to travelling around the country speaking to large groups of staff. This process started five years ago and continues today. It represents a huge commitment of time, but the decision was made that this investment was worth it, because it provided the opportunity to educate staff in what was really important to the organisation – the customer – and to hear directly from them the issues they have, and barriers they face. Question and answer sessions are open and challenging, responses, if incomplete, are followed through later, and action is taken.

Whilst cynical at first, the organisation has now received the message that communication matters, and that their opinion is valued, and managers are expected to dedicate time to talking with their people, rather than being shut in their offices. Such a big allocation of time, in an organisation that had not previously seen the senior team outside of head office, sent big signals.

6. Wallabies

The Australian Rugby Union team that won the World Cup, I have been told, had a ritual which was highly effective at embedding cultural values. They called the ritual Happy Hour. The team met alone – none of the coaches or managers were present. Each team member had the opportunity to talk about incidents where they believed a colleague had broken one of the rules the team had about how the game was to be played. The colleague, if he acknowledged this was the case, had to down a schooner of beer as a punishment.

By the end of the evening a good few beers had been consumed. The air had been cleared. A self-regulatory system implemented. The rules re-established. The incidents acknowledged. A punishment administered which worked for everyone. When John first told me this story, I wasn't sure the punishment quite fitted my idea of how a feedback process of this type should work. But then I'm from a different culture. For them, he assured me, it worked just fine!

7. A gay promotion

A CEO comes in and within six months promotes a gay man to run one of the organisation's largest divisions. Before the leader's arrival nobody in the organisation even knew the man was gay. The organisation was very conservative, and for all of his years of employment this man had hidden his sexual preference. In the six-month period, the CEO had firstly established a good enough relationship with this man that he trusted him enough to disclose his secret. Then he had determined his skills were right for the job. Then he had promoted him. Then he supported him gradually coming out, eventually inviting his partner to the 'partner functions' so prevalent in large organisations.

Through this move he achieved a number of cultural objectives. First of all he got the best person in the job – meritocracy at work. Secondly he sent a huge signal of support for many other people who felt they were discriminated against – women, gays, people of other nationalities. His organisation attracted many of these people, and therefore got a talent advantage over competitors, because he was trawling the whole talent pool rather than the white, male, heterosexual part of it. Third, he showed what it meant to support your people to the hilt. To have them feel the protection of your support. This single move, backed by his broader approach with people, inspired tremendous loyalty. His people were prepared to follow his lead, and together they achieved a great turn-around of the company.

8. Indonesian drivers

The company had a large office in Indonesia. Outside the office, sitting beneath a tree, could always be found a group of drivers waiting for the next call by an executive to use their services. There were quite a number of them, and they often spent all day there in the hope of one fare.

The company was redesigning its offices. The team came up with an innovative idea, one which was in-line with its values of wanting to contribute to the community in which they operated. They allocated one room on the ground floor to these drivers, who were not employees of the company. In this large room they put a number of computers with Internet connections. The drivers were free to use the computers while they waited for fares. Employees volunteered to teach the drivers the computer skills they needed to use the computers. Sometimes the drivers would bring in one of their family members, and pass these skills on to them.

In a manner which was costing hardly anything the company sent a strong message to its people. All people matter. Learning matters. Coaching matters. Our relationships with the country in which we are operating matter. Simple and powerful.

The power of symbolic acts

The most powerful symbols of all will be the decisions that are made to exit those who do not live by your values, and to promote those who do. Because people know these decisions take courage, they are viewed as particularly symbolic that the organisation is serious about its culture.

All symbolic acts achieve big results. They become a part of your organisation's mythology. People are still talking about them years later. In terms of 'bang for buck' they are an incredibly good investment! One bold move, if it is genuine, and indicative of a larger trend in changes to the values hierarchy in your organisation, sends a message to everyone in your organisation, either directly or indirectly.

The opportunities for these are everywhere. Get your team on to them, because they can usually be implemented quickly, and offer the opportunity for quick wins. Select opportunities which will be visible to large numbers of employees.

You will meet some resistance to these ideas, because they may be counter-cultural right now. Those who do not hold the values you are building, will not like them. You need the support of a leader with clout, if you are not in that position yourself. But often you can find this by jumping around the hierarchy until you find a leader who will support some of these ideas which may still feel radical to others.

SUMMARY

Systems and symbols are enablers for your culture. They accelerate the process, and provide the opportunity for a culture team to put in place initiatives that will touch large numbers of people, thus bypassing the normal chain of command. Even if people are reporting to a manager who is stuck in the past, they will start to realise that the broader organisation is changing. This creates a ground swell of support for your work, and enables behaviour change to occur all over the organisation. This is a much quicker approach than relying on a purely top-down cascade of mind-set change.

Behaviours, symbols and systems together send messages about what is expected in the work place. When you pull all three levers simultaneously you gain an exponential benefit. All this needs to be communicated, and this is the topic for the next chapter.

10

Communication

W̲ᴇ know that most cultural communication occurs through behaviours, symbols and systems, which are much stronger than words. However, direct communication still plays an important part in your process, and one which must form a part of your Culture Development Plan. I have, unfortunately, seen many organisations undertake communication believing that it actually *is* their Culture Development Plan. Develop some values, design brochures on the new credo, do a few road-shows with PowerPoint presentations and the culture plan is complete. Tweak the remuneration system to back all this up. If these people took the time to think through what they were doing, they would realise that these actions were not going to produce the required result. The truth is probably that they don't really want to do culture at all. But everyone else is doing it, so they feel the safest option is to follow the crowd.

Such superficial attempts at culture change are more damaging than nothing at all, and in particular will damage the reputation of communication in your organisation. In designing your communication process to support your culture plan, you will find you have to undo a number of communication initiatives, and the leaders of these initiatives may resist your efforts strongly. Glitzy communication is a great strategy for looking like you're leading when you're really not.

By this stage in your journey you will no doubt have learnt some tactics for dealing with such resistance, so let's take a look at what you need to consider in regards to communication.

THE IMPORTANCE OF COMMUNICATING YOUR INTENT

Culture changes when messages about what is important change. Messages received are not usually the same as messages sent. The purpose of your cultural communication strategy is to create the environment where people will recognise the changed messages when they receive them.

Our brain leads us to hear and see primarily what we are expecting to hear and see. We sort information according to sensors which tell our brain what to look for. If I have just bought a new model of car, I suddenly notice other models of this car on the road. They stand out from the mass of cars I see.

Our mind-set causes us to give a different meaning to any particular situation than the one given by a colleague who has a different set of values. If I believe this organisation values people, then when a colleague is transferred to another area I will assume this has been done for her own good. If on the other hand I believe it does not care about people, I will see this as a plot to reduce staff numbers in my area without letting us know.

The purpose of your communication strategy is to increase the likelihood that every message sent is received in the manner it is intended. In this way you prepare a fertile soil. Good communication will multiply the positive impact of your actions in behaviours, symbols, and systems. This multiplier significantly speeds up your change process, especially in the early stages when mind-sets are against you. Let's look at some specific examples.

Communication reinforcing behaviour change

You decide that listening more and interrupting less is an important change for you in your quest to value people and their opinions. Tell your team this is your aim, and ask for their support. Ask them to give you feedback when they experience you doing this more, and to point out when you slip into old habits. Enrol them in your efforts to succeed. This communication makes them a part of your support team. They will start to notice your efforts, and be more tolerant of your relapses. They become pre-disposed to receiving the message that valuing people matters. Similar efforts on your part, without the communication element, may simply go unnoticed.

The communication will not work on its own. There has to be accompanying change. But it will multiply the cultural benefits of the change by reinforcing the message of valuing people.

Communication reinforcing symbols change

Somebody is asked to leave the organisation. After they leave you explain that it was their lack of team play which made it impossible for them to remain, even though they had been hitting their sales targets. Without the communication, people may have believed he left for some other reason. As he was in the process of leaving, he may have told everyone that he had chosen to go because his boss was such a pig. With careful communication you could counter this claim. Reinforce the teamwork value and have people realise that financial performance will not be sufficient in the future. Very powerful.

Communication reinforcing system change

You introduce a policy of paternity leave and encourage new dads to take it up. This change will be appreciated by the new fathers in your organisation. A good communication process which links this new policy to your values and desire to support work/life balance will have people talking about what a great policy it is and how it's an example of what the organisation is trying to become. Next time one of your male employees is talking to a mate whose partner is having a baby, he may start to talk about the policy, further reinforcing in his mind that the company values people. Same policy. But the benefit is multiplied because you have encouraged people to link it to one of your values.

COMMUNICATION CONTENT

Communicate everything that you know and want about culture:

- Your desired culture, its description
- The business case for building this culture, how it will support your strategy and performance, the benefits for customers
- The benefits of this journey for employees
- The values and beliefs that will underpin the culture
- The behaviours you expect
- How you will measure your progress
- Your culture plan, the specific initiatives you will put in place to build the culture – behaviours, symbols, systems
- Your expectations of leaders as role models of the culture
- Your personal motivation and feelings, and those of the top team

Obviously you would not cram all of this into one presentation! Your plan should consider how and when each group of employees receives information about each of these topics.

The content of your communication describes what you expect of people in your organisation. This element becomes stronger as time goes on. At the beginning, you are talking mostly about what you intend to do. As your culture process accelerates, the message becomes one of setting standards. Much of the standard setting must occur in small groups, and is best done by leaders with their immediate teams. Leaders have to hold their people to account to uphold these standards of behaviour and values – over time it will become less and less acceptable to not meet these standards.

THE IMPORTANCE OF ENGAGING YOUR PEOPLE

Your communication process must be designed to engage others. When someone is engaged, they will follow your lead. Engagement is a primary purpose of leadership, because without followers there are no leaders. Engagement does not automatically occur as a result of somebody being told of a new direction or given an instruction. If you tell me to become more entrepreneurial, nothing very much would change as a result. But if you engage me in your quest for entrepreneurship, I will support your efforts by seeking to contribute in whatever way I can. The difference between these two responses is fundamental to your communication strategy.

When a person is engaged they are emotionally involved. Engagement is an emotional response. It is a pre-requisite to commitment. When you engage me you touch my heart as well as my mind. I am moved. I may be excited, apprehensive, touched, inspired; sometimes uncomfortable, fearful, edgy and frustrated. But I am not bored and disengaged. Once I have an emotional response to what you say, I am in a position to react. Remember emotion, movement and motivation come from the same root.

Communication which is simply delivering information does not require people to take action. On these occasions you do not need to emotionally engage your audience. However, culture communication requires not only action, in the form of changing behaviour at the DO-level, but considerable change at the BE-level too. So your communication first needs to engage people on an emotional level, and work on turning any negative emotions into positive ones through building trust. Focus on those with whom you are communicating. Trust is built when people feel you are congruent. Congruence occurs when what you are saying, thinking and feeling is all aligned. It is this that others pick up on and respond to.

Geoff is a polished speaker. He would score well on most criteria for evaluating public speaking. But people leave sessions with him feeling cynical – even those who do not know him and cannot judge whether he walks the talk outside of the room. Just based on what they experience in the room, they don't trust him. I feel the same way when I watch him speak. It is, I believe, because he uses his polished technique to mask his own fears. He speaks of being excited about what he and his staff are going to achieve together. But his body language, his tone of voice – the best indicators of what someone is really feeling – tell a different story. I think he is terrified of what might happen if his business doesn't perform. I don't think he has the answers, and he is worried sick about that. I am trained to observe what is going on under the surface. Most of the audience would not be able to put a label on what they observe in Geoff, but their gut tells them his story doesn't quite add up. His lack of congruence prompts them to distrust his message.

For similar reasons reading speeches or giving PowerPoint presentations rarely engage the audience. The speech and the presentation cause the speaker to disengage from their own feelings, and concentrate on the written page or the projected image. It is possible to do both simultaneously, but difficult. For those who are uncomfortable with their feelings, the slide projector or the written speech provide a comfortable barrier. If your message is a lot of facts, your audience will probably receive most of these. But if your message requires engagement to be effective, you will fail.

Being yourself means simply being present with your own feelings. People trust this, and therefore believe the message. A great exercise to test this is to get a coach, colleague or, if you are really brave, a whole team, to give you feedback as to whether they feel engaged by you. On one of our workshops, we have individuals give presentations from the front of the room, and ask the audience to stand up at the moment in the presentation when they feel engaged for the first time. Quite a confronting exercise for both speaker and audience, but one in which both learn that engagement inevitably accompanies presence. When the speaker becomes present, speaks from the heart, puts their whole self into what they are saying, the audience responds. Some speakers get a real jolt, because they cannot cause the audience to stand in the first round of this exercise. It becomes apparent to them why their people are not following their lead.

People become engaged when they are involved, so two-way communication is always more engaging. When forums provide the opportunity for the audience to work their way through what is being proposed, they start to articulate it in their own words. We all believe our own words and our own voice more than anyone else's! Question and answer sessions do this to some extent, but small group discussions are better. Question and answer sessions, almost by definition, address the doubts an audience has. This is an important part of engagement, but not the only part.

Sessions where the participants work through particular elements of the presentation, and then have a chance to comment in an open forum, are best for engagement. For example, you could ask your audience to work through what the benefits of the culture you are proposing would be for their area and to consider what the barriers to it happening would be. These tasks engage through involvement.

As you consider the engagement process, it always pays to remember that you, and the team you are involved with, have been focussed on this culture journey much longer than any audience. During the past few weeks or months, you have been working on this issue extensively. During this time you went through the process you now want your people to go through. Engagement does take time. Your communication plan must accommodate this.

I have had teams shoot out highly motivated from workshops I have facilitated where we have been working on culture. We have spent two days thinking through every angle. Unless I issue dire warning to this effect (and sometimes even when I do!), individuals arrive back in the office on Monday morning, hold a communication meeting, and are surprised when their team doesn't immediately respond positively to their enthusiasm about the culture journey.

Emotional engagement in your cultural aspirations is easiest to achieve face-to-face. It must become a priority for all of your leaders. You can use other forms of communication to back up the job done by your leadership group, but there is no substitute for good, trustworthy communication by this group.

FOUR-FOLD PURPOSE OF YOUR CULTURAL COMMUNICATION

In summary, design your communication plan with four goals in mind:

1. To show your intent and link the changes that are occurring to this
2. To engage others and have them want to come with you
3. To receive input for further progress
4. To set expectations and standards

BUILDING YOUR COMMUNICATION PLAN

Your Culture Development Plan should have a communication section, designed for a year in advance. The major pieces of this can be co-ordinated through your core Culture Team (described in Chapter 11), and will be supplemented by local leadership who will see communication as a part of their regular leadership activity.

Changing the style of your communication systems or the mix, will send messages that new values are being established. Communication provides the opportunity to profile emerging role-model behaviours and leaders, to reinforce messages of change. Above all it provides forums for listening – to customers, employees, ideas, complaints, emerging trends.

There is no cookie cutter formula for how you should build your communication plan. I recommend experimenting with a number of different approaches, and being rigorous in measuring how effective each is. This can be done through questionnaires, telephone interviews and asking local leadership their views on how their people are responding to the communication approach you are using.

Channels of communication

Formal communication road-shows, meetings, informal get-togethers, one-to-ones, workshops, email, newsletters, telephone, chat-rooms. Each channel provides the opportunity to send new cultural messages or reinforce the old. Communication systems need to be very strong during times of change, and their priorities must be established if you are intending to increase the amount of communication flow as a part of your change.

Communication mechanisms are a crucial piece of building a strong and effective tribe. Good systems become automatic, and therefore stand the test of time-pressure. Every organisation has mechanisms unique to its approach. Here are some I have found to be particularly effective in changing culture.

Communication calendar

Use an annual calendar for communication which creates a pattern of face-to-face interactions. Unless these are put in place and become sacrosanct and part of the ritual they will get bumped for other pressures. The more people who have diarised key communication events, the harder it becomes for them to get cancelled. Into this calendar go:

- Team meetings
- Team off-sites
- Big road-shows
- Feedback lunches with groups of employees
- Feedback lunches with groups of customers
- One-on-one coaching to set behavioural standards
- Meetings between interdependent teams
- Project meetings
- Planning meetings
- Blue sky innovation sessions

They may be face-to-face, by telephone or in a chat-room. The wider spread your people are, the more important it becomes to get this calendar in place. It requires effort at the start of the year, and determination to hold meetings in place. Upholding this discipline for more senior players is a great contribution that can be made by a strong team of personal assistants.

The process of human engagement requires mechanisms which enrol the mind as well as the heart. If you want change you must design mechanisms which consider both of these.

Once the face-to-face calendar is in place, add to it a schedule of electronic and paper based updates, and assign accountability for implementing these.

Communication options

Beyond this calendar you have a wide range of options. In considering your options, think about your media in four categories each of which suits particular needs:

- Same time, same place
- Same time, different place
- Different time, different place
- Different time, same place

Same time, same place
Here the sender and the receiver are in the same room at the same time, for example in a meeting.

This can send messages that people are important, because the person who set up the meeting is saying, 'I want to talk to you; I have something I want to say to you or hear from you.' Because it is an investment in time, it demonstrates that the receiver is important.

Face-to-face is also the most personal medium through which to engage in dialogue. It is the most complete, because the receiver picks up messages from the words, the tone of voice and the body language. In fact research has shown that we pick up 55 per cent of our messages from body language. It is therefore the most revealing, because the true feelings are likely to be communicated. It is most effective if you truly believe what you are saying, and your feelings for the other person or people are genuine and line up with your thoughts. They 'get' your message on many levels.

Same time, same place allows a good leader, one with a

reasonable level of awareness and empathy, to see whether people are receiving the communication. Many leaders stand up and give pep talks in which the words say, 'You are a great team and I encourage us all to strive to succeed,' but the body language says 'You'd better perform because my job is on the line here and my boss is on my back and I don't really know what else to do except stand up here and try and drive you to do more.' Here there is incongruence between the words and the feelings, and this will show through in the body and be picked up by the audience, often subconsciously.

This experience can be marred if the communicator is nervous, which can sometimes occur simply because of the public speaking environment, rather than because they do not value the people in the audience or do not believe in what they are saying. Establishing a communication system which puts people who are not comfortable in front of groups in a key speaking role will not enhance your culture. Your communication choices should be tailored to the capacity of your communicators.

As a leader, find the environment where you are most yourself. Many leaders are better in smaller groups talking informally, and this is therefore a better vehicle for them. Some are better answering questions than delivering talks. Cultures which encourage the traditional path often send completely the wrong message through believing that road-shows and other large group environments are a crucial part of the picture.

The one-on-one and small team sessions are essential parts of your cultural communication mix. Establish these opportunities through your calendar system, and then design them so that they are fit for your purpose.

Same time, different place
The sender and receiver are communicating in real time, but are in different locations. For example, the telephone, a chat-room, video-conferencing.

These media are an expedient use of time and overcome issues of geography. The aim of such communication is to have as meaningful an interaction as you would have had face-to-face, but this needs careful work. Because face-to-face is unrealistic in so many circumstances, developing good systems of *same time, different place* communication can make or break your ability to build unity across distance, and engage with people in a personal way. To be engaged requires the use of the emotions. Engagement is an emotional state, and emotions are harder to convey accurately in *same time, different place* situations than they are face-to-face.

Look very carefully at the habits and disciplines used around the telephone and how they reinforce your current culture and can be used to build the one you want. Some teams, for example, will communicate with each other by phone almost every day. Others never do. I find that to check whether team members have their colleague's phone numbers in their speed dial can be indicative of the health of the team! Emailing, whilst often the most useful and convenient approach for facts, is often used as a means of avoiding the personal, emotional risk of the real conversation.

Chat-rooms, video-conferences and team phone hook-ups require good structure and good facilitation, as well as important rules such as using one's name if others on the phone would not recognise your voice. Developing common telephone phone hook-up habits unites a disparate group, and can be used to reinforce cultural values and behaviours. It is worth investing time to train groups on how to lead and participant in *same time, different place* meetings, because, if well done, they greatly expand your communication options.

Connecting by telephone is helped when you are fully 'present' – not multi-tasking (answering emails whilst also on the phone) or having side conversations out of view of the video-conference. The real you is communicated through your voice!

Different time, different place
The sending and the receiving occur separately. For example email, community sites, letters, newsletters.

Different time, different place allows you to reach a large number of people very easily. The medium therefore offers the opportunity to delight, bore or frustrate large numbers of people at the push of a button. Its wide reach means it is a strong and consistent cultural driver, and one which you must include as a part of your Culture Development Plan.

Different time, different place is ideal for sending messages that you want the other person to consider at their leisure, and which do not need a lot of discussion for full understanding. They allow a message to be crafted by the sender, and for the receiver to consider their response. For this reason they are useful when the right message and response is more important than the more free-flowing experience of other mediums.

Of the *different time, different place* options, email has become the dominant medium in organisational life. The sense of remoteness that it provides causes many to become quite rude and abrupt. Orders are issued in a manner which most would not dream of adopting in face-to-face conversation and with the assumption they will be carried out. The receiver interprets those missives as a reflection of the behaviour of the sender, and when carried-out en masse, this becomes a cultural norm. Email is a great tool for the assistance of those who are seeking to raise their level of awareness. It is called the 'Save as draft' button. Reading emails after they have been written enables you to see the tone – the under the surface expressions of the feelings and values that the words express. Rewording them helps to send a different message.

Small amounts of attention to put the human touch back into emails send strong cultural messages. In this manner they can become a very powerful tool to engage and personalise your organisation. A weekly email, truly engaging from the CEO or any leader, can make the whole organisation feel personally involved. A strong word of advice. These must be written by the leader his or herself. Everyone can tell when it is written by someone else and sent under the leader's name. The best ones are chatty, personal, amusing, showing something of the real person, and include little stories. They are always carefully created to reinforce certain key cultural messages within the normal information update. If your leader takes up this habit, give them immediate feedback if the emails come across as pompous, condescending, bombastic or boring. Yes, all of these may happen, and as a culture champion you cannot allow that to continue. It takes practice to use email well after years of careless habits. Reading your own emails with the cultural messages in mind can be very revealing and lead to immediate change in approach.

Sadly email has become a tremendous frustration to many people, and an indicator of a range of cultural traits: disrespect, covering one's ass (the 'cc'), laziness, status seeking, and unwillingness to take decisions. Introducing new rules for your email use is a strong cultural signal.

Different time, same place

A single communication is posted in one place and a number of people receive it over a period of time. For example, notice boards, posters, and exhibitions.

This approach is used for communication which is unique (such as a work of art) or where repeated viewing in a low impact way will embed the message (such as a billboard). The communication vehicle stays in one place, and people walk by and see it many times.

Unless the work is beautiful or very amusing there is unlikely to be an emotional response. Some advertising copywriters are able to engage an audience through this medium. But most of what is pinned to walls is very uninspiring. I am fairly unenthusiastic about the use of posters and plaques to communicate values statements and other corporate slogans. This may be useful as a reinforcement. I believe there are so many other ways to achieve this goal more effectively. As a statement of intent they could be useful, but they would need to form a very small part of a very large communication plan.

Systems for gathering feedback

Almost every type of desired culture requires better listening.

- To achieve, we must know whether we are succeeding or failing.
- To become customer-centric, we must deeply understand our customers' needs
- To participate in a team we must know what our team members need from us
- To be innovative we must listen for the whispers of a new trend
- To value people we must hear what they are thinking, and value their opinions

The complete feedback process is a five-stage cycle:

Information	What was said or written by the communicator
Knowledge	What we extract from the information, what we actually hear
Learning	The conclusions we reach from applying our knowledge
Response	The action we take from our learning
Result	What occurs as a result of our action, which we find out through a new set of information

Observe how this cycle works in your organisation, because it will tell you a great deal about how the culture operates. Because organisations exist to produce results, the effectiveness of this cycle drives the performance outcomes. There are countless cycles occurring all over the organisation. Picking a few key ones to tackle in your Culture Development Plan can have some very quick performance benefits if you can move the mind-sets along at the same time. You could consider:

- Customer satisfaction data
- Stoppage or rework data
- Industry trends
- Employee satisfaction data
- Sales analysis
- Performance data

Of course all of this data is available somewhere in your organisation. You conclude rapidly that it is not the first stage of the cycle that is your problem. In fact, you probably have way too much data. You may consider changing the nature of the information so that it actually facilitates movement through the other five stages. Attendance at a customer focus group has much more impact on a manager than reading a set of customer satisfaction statistics. A close friend of mine is a market researcher and has an extraordinary ability to sort through pages of data collected and extract the main insights it gives. But she goes completely crazy because she is usually handled by a research manager buried three layers down in the marketing department. By the time the information gets to anyone who can make course-changing decisions, it has been so diluted that nothing happens. A customer-centric organisation would put her, uncensored, in front of the top team. When this finally occured, one particular client, a fast-food chain, introduced an entire new range of healthy options to bring mothers in to eat in their own right, rather than just with the kids. The turnaround in their declining revenue was substantial. This type of information is too often buried before it reaches this level, and so the feedback loop is not completed and no improved results achieved.

In building your Culture Development Plan, pick just one or two of these cycles. Perhaps just one element of one of them. Employees' understanding of a recent change in strategy, the relationship between the time of a sales call and the likelihood of a sale or a talk given at a conference on a topic which represents a new opportunity for you.

Bring together a group of people and design a new way of

working this information right through the five stages of the cycle. In doing so, you contribute to a number of good cultural messages:

- Involving people in work that will produce a satisfying result
- You are listening and responding and valuing the end user
- Learning and changing
- Confronting reality
- Treating mistakes constructively

Creating a methodology and embedding it as a system builds cultural momentum as well as producing improved results in the cycle you tackle.

Practical tips for building your communication plan

These tips are based on my experience of watching and helping many organisations work through their communication plans, with varying degree of success.

Start communicating widely once you are sure you will not turn back
Once your top team have committed to tackling culture seriously, the communication of intent should commence. Every employee can be touched.

Going public is a statement of intent. Your communication establishes a framework within which your people can then play. You are setting up the rules of the game you intend to play. As you design this game, the rules may be a bit fuzzy, and some of them may not quite produce the intended result, but over time you will be able to refine and thus sharpen your communication. Game designers know that the best games have simple rules which produce certain behaviours and make for a fun and exciting ride.

I often hear a debate about whether to go with a 'big bang' or 'softly softly' approach to communicating your cultural intent. The more important question is whether you are sure you will not turn back. Sometimes the softly softly argument is underpinned with a residual doubt about the journey as a whole, perhaps a desire to takes some initial steps to build confidence. If those concerns exist, then the softly softly approach will be the better one. Often voiced as a desire to get some wins under the belt to build the organisation's confidence that this journey is for real, I have found it to be as much about building the leadership team's confidence in their ability to do this thing. Both motives are good ones, and building confidence through action is always valuable.

There is, however, an advantage in signalling intent. It makes it harder to back away from. It's like telling friends that you intend to give up smoking. Sometimes embarrassment about being seen to fail spurs the individual on to success. Personally linking your name and reputation to the intent to change culture gives you increased skin in the game. This could be the difference between giving up when it gets particularly tough, and keeping going.

From the perspective of the receivers of the communication, a high-profile approach will work fine so long as you can demonstrate commitment through action within a reasonably short timeframe. Any individual who hears that the organisation is intending to build a better culture would expect to see some evidence of this within a couple of months.

A high-profile approach is one that involves leaders talking to their teams about what is intended, in groups of ten or a thousand. This would be backed up by written material: newsletters, intranet sites, mementos. A softly softly approach might use the language of the intended change in the course of day-to-day business, but not actually stand up with a list of values and explain what each meant.

I have found it risky to label your initial communication a launch. Modelled on a product launch, these involve supporting marketing material and a glitzy big bang style. Culture is fundamentally different from a new product. Elements of your desired culture will already be present in your team. You will have many people who hold these values dear and whose behaviour is exemplary. These people can become disenchanted to hear their leader announce teamwork as if he just invented the term. This tone can very easily come across in the big bang launch, even if it was not intended.

Build common language and be consistent with it

Language is a key uniting force in any tribe. Consider the challenge political leaders have when they are faced with uniting groups without a common language. How much easier would the development of the European Union be if everyone spoke the same language! Football crowds build unity through their songs. Teenage peer groups use shared slang. Language and identity are strongly linked. To build your culture you need to build a new language. One that unites different parts of your group.

The most successful language is one which is unique to you. Pick unusual words to describe your values, rituals and processes. In our organisation we schedule one day a month as a client-free day, where our team gets the chance to be together, discuss issues and have some social time. We call it Wonderful Wednesday. 'Brown bag lunches' is a phrase used for informal lunch sessions where groups get a chance to talk through concerns with a senior manager. 'Face reality' is punchier as a value than 'transparency' or 'honesty', because it's a bit unusual. Having picked them, stick with them for long enough for them to gain street-cred. Introduce new ones every year.

It is important to use common language as much as possible across your whole organisation. People find it very confusing to hear their CEO talk about learning, but their direct supervisor refer to it as initiation, unless the link between the two has been very clearly made.

The words you use to describe your cultural aspirations must be consistent. Their power builds as it becomes clear that this is not a fad and you intend to stay on this path. If you started with 'customer-centric', don't change to 'customer-focus' after six months. Although to you they mean much the same, others who hear them often see a casual change as a sign that the exercise lacks depth.

There will be times during the process where a change in language is important. This would emerge as you receive feedback from the whole organisation. Your own thinking will evolve. When you do decide to make a change, do it very publicly and use it as a way to reinforce certain messages.

Describe your intent through stories

Stories are the best way to describe a desired future. They encourage without patronising. Here is an example:

> A manager is talking to a large group in her division, 'When a client comes to us, we want him to leave with a positive emotional feeling about us and the experience he has just had. Last week I was at a dinner party and a woman was talking about this extraordinary thing one of our people had done for her. She did not know where I worked. The incident was quite small; she felt that our employee had gone out of their way to resolve a problem she had. Listening I knew precisely the amount of behind the scenes process re-engineering that had gone on last year to empower that employee with the information and authority she needed to fix the problem. Our customer touched one person, but one thousand had made the experience happen. And now she was telling another seven people around the table. A couple asked for more details because they had a similar problem and had not been able to find help. They said they intended to follow up and I believe they will.'

A million stories like this work better than lists of values because they engage the imagination and enable an individual to see how they would fit.

A simple framework woven into a million examples builds that picture, repeated and repeated through every available medium.

Do not confuse wishful intent with current reality

I often meet with leaders who want to communicate their values as if they were already alive and well or will be within a week or two. 'From this day forward we will stand for teamwork, and we expect all behaviour to line up behind this value.' This approach shows considerable ignorance of the process of human behaviour change. It also sets the leader up for ridicule. It is appropriate to say, 'these are our values,' but only if it is followed by an acknowledgement that right now we are not a strongly values-driven organisation, and we allow these lofty ideals to be compromised when it comes to making difficult decisions or behaving appropriately. 'We aspire to these values,' has more credibility and still drives home a desire to become a great organisation.

Values and other descriptors of culture are inevitably broad, generalised statements, which means there will inevitably be specific examples of non-compliant behaviour. If you describe a value as if it is completely true in all instances, the minds of your audience respond by thinking of an example where it was not the case. If I asked you to put the lid on the toothpaste each time you used it, I might (but only might) get what I wanted. If I ask you to be considerate of my feelings at all times, I am almost certainly doomed to be disappointed. So I might risk stating that 'we are a family who always uses toothpaste tops' but I would be very unwise to tell somebody that 'my family is always considerate'.

Balancing words with action

Hearing a leader speak on the topic of culture and values once or twice is a statement of intent. Hearing and seeing it too often without any sign of follow up action will lead to considerable cynicism. Your plan must pace communication with visible change.

For example, an initial series of communication meetings with the appropriate senior leader might then be followed by very low-key messages through stories in newsletters, until the timing of your plan has ensured that this group of employees will have seen a recent promotion of a culture champion leader, an increase in their authority levels to serve the customer (framed as an opportunity to better provide the speed the customer seeks) and an opportunity to participate in a new team process for using customer feedback, previously only accessible to managers. Now this employee will be listening. Further communication opportunities will become much more interactive, because trust is building.

Jump the middle layers – for a while

Communication allows the leadership group to access individuals whose immediate boss may not be sending the right cultural messages through their words and behaviour. It can validate the values and beliefs of more junior employees and give them hope that this organisation will support the aspirations they have. This is only a holding tactic while you sort out the middle layer. Research has shown that the most important influence on an employee's behaviour is their immediate supervisor. This is the person whose decisions will affect an individual's career, and whose behaviour will leave them feeling uplifted or demoralised at the end of every working day.

The greatest gift you can give to your most junior staff is to change their supervisors and managers. Change their behaviour or bring in (better still promote) better ones. Every change of this nature builds the credibility of your communication message.

Being honest about the present

When I talk to junior and middle level employees they often express doubt as to whether management really understands what the culture actually feels like to live in and how much it costs the organisation in terms of ineffectiveness. In their minds they find it hard to believe that their leaders would actually know this and do nothing, so they assume leaders do not know.

Just acknowledging that you have heard the feedback and are aware of the situation is a great step forward. Communicate the results of your Culture Diagnostic and other employee data you have, together with stories about what you have been told during walks about the organisation. Give it straight. This demonstrates honesty, transparency, respect – all values you will be wanting in your culture.

Reveal your own journey

Tell your people that as a leadership group this feedback is a reflection on you. If you have embarked on the personal change process, talk about what you have learnt about yourself and the feedback you personally received. This level of openness is extremely powerful. It puts you on a level with those you lead in relation to the need to change mind-sets and behaviours. It is nerve-racking because you are showing vulnerability. Some leaders believe this reduces their authority and position. Clearly you would not want to collapse on the floor a jabbering mess of self-doubt and flagellation. But acknowledging that you see that your behaviour has contributed to the current position is a wonderful role-model for your people. You are demonstrating that your level of aware-ness is high enough to give you an accurate picture of yourself. They know, probably far better than you, how your behaviour has led to cultural problems. Unless they see that you now know that too, their belief that any substantial change will occur will be very limited.

The leader of the organisation profiled in Chapter 15 frequently put up his own personal feedback results along with the culture results. As one improved the other did too. Profit improvement tracked the same path. What a story! It is pretty hard to mount an argument for why your own poor behaviour feedback results are justified when the leadership group talk about their own struggles, and emerging success, in changing their own behaviour.

Spread the communication responsibility

The immediate supervisor is the most important source of inform-ation for most employees. The more remote in the structure an individual is, the less relevant their message seems. Thus whilst large forums with the CEO can serve a purpose, they should never be a substitute for face-to-face communication between leaders and their teams.

Communication from peers is always very credible, so use individuals who have something special to say to teach and work with their own colleagues. Hearing the same message from many different leaders builds its credibility, and asking team colleagues to speak to your people shows unanimity amongst the team.

Join the dots: link every key decision to the desired culture
From where you sit it is easy to see how everything fits together. It may seem obvious to you that you are moving one unit and relocating them in a building with their key internal customers so as to increase the One-Team feeling in the company. But from where they sit, it may feel like a downgrading of their status and an inconvenience. They may not even appreciate that their customers are just down the corridor. They will almost certainly not link this move to the workshop they attended a couple of months ago where they were learning about the mind-sets required to be a One-Team Culture.

You have to constantly join up those dots. Every time you do so, you increase the number of co-ordinated, consistent messages your people are receiving about what is valued. Without making these links, many of the initiatives designed with positive intent will not send the powerful message they were designed to do.

Use the phrases and words that form a part of your cultural aspirations. Refer specifically to a particular value or cultural style which you have articulated in your statement of intent.

JUDGE YOUR COMMUNICATION BY THE RESPONSE YOU GET
We have a phrase we use in teaching communication, which we acquired from my friend Robert Kiyosaki:

> TRUE COMMUNICATION IS THE RESPONSE YOU GET

The measure of your communication effectiveness is the response you get. The response mirrors the message you are actually sending. If you are saying the right words and getting the wrong response, look inside yourself, not out to your audience. This is taking responsibility. I have found that when an individual 'gets it' at a BE-level, others respond positively. Much of your communication work needs to occur inside you. When your beliefs, values and feelings line up with what you are saying, others pick you as being congruent and having integrity. Body, mind, heart and words are aligned. This alignment will cause your actions to line up too. It then becomes automatic to walk the talk.

Watch a speaker preparing to give a talk. Are they fiddling with their papers and the technology? They spend the minutes before a presentation making changes to words on their slides. Many speakers believe it is what they say that matters most. This is not true. It is who you are, the BE-level that is most important. Being composed and centred on your team, making a connection with them, builds trust. Once your team trust you, they will come with you on this journey.

For example, if you are setting standards for behaviour, and you really mean it, people 'get' that you do. They just know that if they deviate from these standards, they will be in trouble. (Those of us with children may wish to experiment with this concept!) There is an authority behind the words, and a congruence, which commands support. On the other hand, if someone makes the same presentation, but would probably not follow through with consequences for non-compliance, and does not really believe in the standards anyway or does not live to them personally, the audience feels this. The power of the message is lost. Often audiences are not consciously aware of the difference, but it is demonstrated through their behaviour afterwards.

This is a personally challenging concept. The easy option is to blame your team for not 'getting it'. Acknowledging that you are not embodying what you are saying yet is much more difficult. If they are not receiving the essence of your communication, ask yourself, how and where am I sending contradictory messages? Where are my feelings or thoughts not lining up with what I am saying? If you can pinpoint this, you have two options to enable you to come into alignment:

1. Change your words so you say what you are feeling. If you have doubts, express them. 'I don't know how we can achieve this, I don't have the answers, I am looking for your help,' is more congruent and engaging than a pep talk about how great we are when your tone of voice or body language is betraying your doubts anyway
2. Change your feelings. Work with your coach or close colleagues to figure out why you don't trust your colleagues to deliver, and how you can change that feeling

The purpose of your communication is to engage with others so they want to come with you. Being engaged is an emotional state. It is not possible to engage with someone who is not engaged with themselves. When you are out of alignment you are covering your own feelings with words which are crafted to impress. People do not engage because on an emotional level they pick this up. They may not be able to articulate clearly that this is what is happening, but their response shows that it is. Engaging is the connection that occurs between two people. Once it has occurred, then it can be directed by the content of your words. But it is not your words which cause someone else to change their behaviours and attitudes. The impulse to do this comes from the emotional connection established. The words direct this impulse.

An emotional response can be anything across the whole range of: warmth, enthusiasm, being moved, excited, even apprehensive or frustrated. It is a feeling, usually accompanied by a sensation somewhere in the body outside of the head. This impulse engages the whole self, and takes you out of the intellectually curious state of the observer. It is this engagement that produces the energy to change.

SUMMARY: ESTABLISHING INTENT
Communication is an important first step, but it will not actually change the culture in itself. It must be used in conjunction with all of the other strategies to change behaviours, symbols and systems.

Some plans seem to contain a great deal on the engagement and communication front, and not enough on the other levers for culture change. For the most part I believe this comes from a lack of knowledge about what culture actually is and how it changes. Occasionally it stems from arrogance. 'I am so powerful that if I tell people how it is going to be, this will cause it to happen.' This is not true of many things, and it is certainly not true of changing the way people think and behave.

I like to think of communication as a statement of intent. Intent is a powerful force in organisational life. It cuts through the noise and builds momentum. Intent pits your own will against the forces of nature. It is your ability to turn an idea into reality and make it happen.

When communication is considered and used in this manner, it becomes a powerful force. Aside from the practical considerations of what and when, test your resolve before you embark on a communication exercise about your culture. How strong is your intent? Do you have a small band of people whose intent is equally strong and who you trust to link arms with you on this? If you cannot answer these questions with an unhesitating yes, then you should spend more time working your way through the business case and personal challenge considerations covered earlier in this book. Sit with the culture idea a little longer.

Communication lets people know what you are intending to do and gains their support. Places a stake in the ground. This is crucial because you cannot embark on this journey alone. You need a fair number (a third to a half) of your people to support you in your intentions. Interestingly, you will not find getting that number to support you to be as hard as you might expect. They will have been more frustrated with the culture than you, but powerless to take action without *your* support. This is an important step, and prepares the way.

11

The Process of Management

THE chapters up until this point contain all of the pieces required to design and implement a culture journey. This chapter shows you how to manage this process. The rest of the book then picks up special cultural circumstances which you incorporate into your plan if they apply to you, and rounds off with the description of one company's journey.

CREATING THE RIGHT MANAGEMENT FRAMEWORK

This chapter lays out a recommended governance structure for ensuring that your culture efforts deliver results in the timeframe, who to involve and how to use outside support. It acknowledges that, whilst some people would happily undertake culture work for the love of it, its purpose in this context is to deliver a return to the organisation's stakeholders, and as such it much be managed with the discipline afforded to any important investment. Some people are uncomfortable with managing culture as a project. They believe that giving it a framework makes it mechanistic and takes the spirit out of it. I disagree. Whilst you may not treat it as a project in the strictest sense, it absolutely needs the governance structures around it that ensure that activities happen within an agreed time-frame and deliver the benefits anticipated.

Using structure to create momentum

The right management discipline also speeds up the process. Left to its own devices, culture evolves slowly over generations. This is its natural pace. The journey you are on to change or build a culture within a time-frame required by competitive pressures is un-natural. This means it will not occur without processes that build momentum. To get the wheel turning at the pace you require, you have to apply a lot of force. Once it is spinning fast, this force can be eased off.

In organisational life, there are always competing priorities for a limited budget. There is a window of opportunity to get an initiative going, and if that window is missed, others fill the space. It is not that later the culture project is seen as unimportant, just that dynamics shift.

A plan and a governance structure puts your culture process on the map. It creates momentum. To get things moving you need to bulk your project. Without this it tends to get lost in the noise of organisational life. There is momentum already up around your budgeting and reporting processes, around the pressures on your sales activities, on the calendar of your board meetings, and your product promotions. These powerful forces will overcome your fledgling culture work unless you help it build up some real muscle.

Organisations respond well to the discipline of project govern-ance, because there are elements of it that you can do on automatic pilot. The project meetings occur the first Thursday of every month, the measurements are collected, the money is in the budget and individuals have the authority to spend it. The plan has deadlines and responsibilities, and the project team builds a persona of its own.

Most culture change work does not commence in the systematic manner described in this book. In the ideal world the CEO has the first big idea, the HR manager is right with them from the start, the business case stacks up, the top team buy in and everyone moves ahead in an orderly fashion. I actually know of very few change projects that actually occur this way, and in an area as emotionally challenging and initially nebulous as culture, this becomes even more unlikely.

Everyone reading this book will be in a different position. Your organisation will be at a different stage of the culture process, ranging from nothing at all, to a good way down the track, or started but lost your way. You will sit in a variety of roles in the organisation: CEO, a director, HR manager, line manager, frustrated but committed team leader and front line operator, advisor, coach or consultant. Your team may be one of ten people or a hundred thousand.

In considering how to structure this process so that it gains traction, design an approach which is a realistic starting point from where you are right now. There are so many great efforts which die because of an over-ambitious starting point or a belief that unless the CEO is totally on board, nothing can be achieved. In this book I have been describing an ideal path. Reality is a lot messier than this, but it stumbles along and gains momentum as it grows, and looking back you see a path which is straighter than it might feel while you are travelling.

The early stages

Let's start from the smallest possible point, which is one person wanting to make a difference and having a passion for this path. Your first stage must be to gather enough support to actually turn this into something which resembles a project. You know you have reached this stage when money and time is being dedicated to it, decisions are being made, and someone is being held accountable for certain deliverables.

In the influencing stage you can:

- Work on yourself – hold up the mirror and make changes to your values and behaviours
- Build circumstantial evidence that culture may be impacting performance
- Find allies and gradually build a network
- Hold each other to standards which align to the values you hold, and meet the challenge of not being dragged down to the lowest common denominator of your culture
- Target your influencing efforts to someone who has enough authority to make a piece of the culture process happen

Commencement of a proper journey

The journey commences in earnest when someone with some authority decides to take action. If you have this authority, you can move directly to this point. To take action in the cultural dimension, you need to be in a position to galvanise resources that are beyond those in your immediate team. If you can only make things happen within an immediate team, then the path you will most successfully embark on is team-building. A team is a mini-culture, and you can create team behavioural norms and habits following mini-versions of what is described in this book. The special conditions of small businesses, teams and changing from the middle are covered in Chapters 12 and 14.

Let us assume that you have this authority, or that you have been asked by someone who does to set up a culture change process.

Definition of desired culture, diagnostics and business case should always be considered by the largest group you can draw together. The smaller the organisational chunk who undertake this work, the more limited the business case will be. It is harder to understand the full benefits of a One-Team model if you are a tiny piece of the whole. Harder to become Customer-Centric if your team is only one isolated piece of the customer value chain.

There comes an important decision point when this first stage is complete and you are entering into the planning phase. You will inevitably find that some of the team are more enthusiastic about this work than others. Some may consider they have higher priorities. Some may want to implement a culture plan in their own manner, in-line with their managerial authority and approach.

There is no right answer to this one, although I do swing more towards the 'all in this together' approach in most circumstances. The topic is covered in more depth in Chapter 12. The issues for you to consider in making this decision are varied:

1. Your desired end state culture
One-Team and Customer-Centric really do require everyone to be on the same page and moving forward collaboratively. The nature of the culture you are seeking to create is defined by lateral relationships with peers across the business. The Achievement Culture, People-First and Innovative values are more easily built around smaller independent units.

2. Your structure and business model
A cultural journey is best managed by a natural work group. A natural work group operates fairly independently, and has authority over a large number of the behaviours, symbols and systems which drive their culture.

3. The motivation behind team members' desire to implement separately
Sometimes the reasons for fairly independent implementation are real and valid. One division has already committed to a work schedule, which simply makes this unrealistic for the next year, or is being lead by someone about to retire whose heart is not in it. Other times, the expressed reason is actually an excuse, and the motive is the desire to do my own thing, or do nothing. Clearly in the latter case you need to weigh up the risks of allowing this motivation to block a decision which could be for the greater good. On the other hand, forcing a key leader to implement a value to which they are not committed is unsustainable. Sometimes the lagging divisions follow as benefits are seen.

Often the best plans set a middle course, requiring common approach and initiatives, whilst encouraging individual areas to determine the timing and to put a strong leadership stamp on the process. If this is the case, you will need to consider which items are 'tight' and which are 'loose', covered in Chapter 12, and from here determine your process of management for the whole.

Selecting your core culture team

In the first stages, you will need to form a team who will take the change forward until such time as the leadership group is fully on board. Later your culture work becomes part of the normal responsibilities of leaders, and specific initiatives will be created and implemented by them. Some areas will already be doing this in the natural course of managing their unit.

There are a couple of criteria for determining who is on the core team:

1. Share a passion for this work

This is the most important qualification. You have a big task ahead of you: dealing with the resistance in the wider organisation. You are adding to your burden if you have people in your inner team who are not on board. You need a sanctuary, a place and a team where you know your colleagues share your vision. This builds strength to hold to this vision when it feels as if nothing is changing.

2. Are willing to personalise this journey

This is the way to become role-models for change. Being willing to acknowledge and work with your own behaviour, and remould your own thinking is more important than being a perfect behavioural icon from the start. Dirk was one of the best core team members I have ever seen. He was demanding and did not tolerate fools easily. When under pressure he became belligerent and pretty disempowering to be around. He had a turn-around moment when one of his star people left the organisation and, on the way out, found a way to tell Dirk how his leadership behaviour had gradually worn down her enthusiasm for the organisation. Something stuck a chord and Dirk got the link between behaviour and consequences. He became a passionate believer in this work. His honest personal story as to why this was so, was all the more powerful to others because of his previous reputation.

3. Display certain leadership capabilities

Desired capabilities	Less useful characteristics
Influencing skills to bring others with them	Tendency to preach or sound evangelical
A caring for others which enables them to give feedback with the intent to help	A self-righteous energy which seems to point score when giving feedback
Business savvy to describe the business benefits of each step	An approach which looks after people in isolation from business needs
A belief that they can always make a difference, a willingness to take responsibility and see their impact on situations	A tendency to become overwhelmed, feel a victim or blame others

Which positions must be on the team?

Organisational position does not seem to be as important a criterion for being in the core team as the criteria above. I have seen teams get culture work moving through a skunk-works approach, working steadily from the sidelines, grabbing the odd bit of money from various budgets to get some work underway, talking and influencing and building interest. Two or three people with a clear intent and plan for what they are doing can build extraordinary momentum. Their presence may be almost unnoticed to start with. Almost a secret society. But a group with a purpose, not a collection of people who get together to grumble about what is wrong with the culture.

Traditional wisdom would suggest that you need the CEO on this team, as well as other key line managers. Eventually you do, but not necessarily in the early stages. There seem to be no rules, because the characteristics described will not have been used in the past to fill certain positions in your organisation. Sometimes the HR team leads this work, on other occasions they are one of the greatest barriers to its success. Sometimes one division or team moves forward alone, and is able to influence other teams without being accused of arrogance. Sometimes a project team can get the ball rolling, or a change management group attached to a broader change; a strategy group; a group who find a way to bring the voice of the customer inside. Perhaps the culture work is started in response to a demand from the board, or a crisis, and thus CEO-led from the start. It is usually great to have one senior line leader closely involved who has some experience in this process, either through having moved ahead in their own area already, or implemented something similar in a previous organisation.

The stories I am told, and the journeys I have been a part of, have no common thread except a group of people who have the personal presence to hold a vision of a different reality, and cause it to happen through their leadership ability. Leadership is, after all, the ability to attract followers, and not associated with any particular position.

Building the team's identity

Your first step is to gather together these like-minded people. You could call them culture champions. Provide some training for them in the mind-sets required to be pioneers in this field. Build their sense of being special and valuable. Strengthen their resolve. Often people with these mind-sets and passions feel somewhat isolated in organisations, and forming them into a coalition gives them camaraderie and purpose. As this influencing power increases, you will reach a point when there are sufficient people in positions of authority enrolled in this vision that you can move to a more formal arrangement.

If those with the vision coincide from the start with those with the authority, then you can move more quickly to the next stage. However, you should still form these voluntary coalitions of like-minded people, because they are such a powerful mechanism for change.

The formal culture governance structure

Once your organisation has decided to invest seriously in culture, and has built a business case to support the implementation of a Culture Development Plan, you will be best served by a formal governance structure which gives it prominence and discipline.

Some organisations simply place their whole Culture Development Plan in the hands of the leadership team, with one member responsible for its day-to-day management. Others set up a project governance structure and have the leadership team as the steering committee. It depends on the scale of your plan. If you are linking culture change to other business change initiatives, you may find they are best managed together. However, in this case be careful that culture does not become a poor cousin to the initiatives with the more immediate financial return such as cost reduction, or with more tangible milestones, such as technology.

Your diagnostic results and content of your culture plan determine who should sit on your governing team. There are many parts of your plan which go beyond traditional HR activities, and so your culture management team must contain a broader scope of disciplines than HR. The selection of this team is itself a symbolic act.

If you have a Customer-Centric Culture vision, then include your marketing or sales leader. If part of your transformation includes the move to a new building, include the leader of that initiative. If you intend to drive an Achievement Culture through transparent dashboards, include your CFO. Balance line and functional roles. As far as possible, select people with the personal characteristics already outlined. The team should be led by the most senior person in the group in which the culture change is targeted. The CEO or leader of the division or unit involved. I have found that culture has to be championed by the leader. It cannot be delegated. You cannot delegate work which involves changing at the BE-level, only DO-ing tasks. Whilst the culture team is managing the DO part of the work, they are also role-modelling the BE part. They themselves will go through a transformation as the work progresses, and they need to be working on themselves whilst managing change in others. Such work needs leadership at the highest level.

The role of the culture management team
1. To build the Culture Development Plan
2. To manage those elements of a plan which are projects, using normal project governance disciplines
3. To capture activities and behaviours which take place as business-as-usual and link them to the cultural vision to demonstrate that culture is the way we do business, not some separate stream of activity
4. To communicate, reward and hold the line on cultural standards, starting with themselves
5. To measure and track progress
6. To walk the talk

The evolution of the culture management team
A team of the type I have described would be unlikely to stay in place for more than a couple of years beyond the start of implementation. By this stage you will have the majority of the leadership population on board. Many of the roles of the original culture management team will be picked up by the business leadership team. Once this transition has occurred, then management of on-going cultural

initiatives will fall to their natural business owners. Regular processes such as culture measurement will probably be conducted by HR, who will also maintain carriage of the behavioural training elements. HR are great leaders of the continued drive for culture. In some organisations they drive the process all the way through from the start. I have just found that in the earlier stages the savvy HR team plays a quieter behind-the-scenes role, recognising that credibility is gained by having the line leaders take the process forward.

MEASUREMENT OF PROGRESS

An investment of this importance needs solid processes for measuring its progress, and goals for which the team is held account-able. There are four methods available for the culture management team to consider in determining its measurement approach, and selecting the right combination in order to set appropriate goals:

1. Employee surveys

You will have the existing employee surveys used in your Culture Diagnostic or other tools used regularly such as an employee opinion survey. Obviously tools which specifically measure culture will be the most effective. Set realistic goals for the first year or two, with a big stretch for four or five years out. As you build your experience of how your culture responds to the various levers available to you, you will get to know the potential pace of change, and be able to set better targets.

2. External awards and league tables

The media, in conjunction with various privately and publicly owned organisations, are sponsoring several rigorous annual initiatives. 'Best Employer' lists are now developed in many countries, and results made available in the press. Methodology is scientific, and organisations are compared with others of similar type and size. There are others which cover 'Best Service Organisation', 'Most Environmentally Aware' and other awards related specifically to an industry. Pick the most suitable award for your cultural goals, and set yourself a long-term goal to be near the top, and some milestones along the way.

3. Business case realisation – key metrics

Each type of desired culture carries with it certain metrics which you would have identified in your business case. For example, People-First Culture might track a reduction in the number of 'regrettable' resignations. (The terms 'regrettable' and 'non-regrettable' being a good way to distinguish between those you want to lose, and those you don't.) One-Team might track the cost reduction associated with sharing resources rather than building empires, and Customer-Centric would pick some specific customer satisfaction metric. Each of these should have financial benefits calculated in the business case.

4. Lead indicators

Some organisations develop lead indicators which, whilst they cannot be immediately linked to financial benefits, once calculated will be indicators that their culture is moving in the right direction. For example, an organisation I know used the very rigorous Six Sigma statistical methodology to determine that there were two particular measures which, if improved, would indicate an improvement in People-First values, in particular work-life balance, on which they had focussed. One was the extent to which people were taking their allotted annual leave quota, the other how often they had to work (or travel for work purposes) on a weekend. They selected these as their key performance indicators of their work-life balance value.

A combination of these four types of measurement will work for you. Pick the approach, stick with it so you get year-on-year numbers, and publish findings as a part of the transparency associated with your emerging culture.

ADVICE FOR BOARDS OF DIRECTORS

As I write the last sections of this book, there has suddenly been a surge of interest in culture at the Board level. Corporate disasters in many countries brought about by dishonesty of one kind or another – ranging from overstating oil reserves to traders overstepping their limits and then covering this up – have been identified as having a cultural basis. You can see from the arguments put forward in this book, that not only dishonesty but also a wide range of other, less dramatic, contributions to performance emerge from a culture where certain behaviour, and mind-sets, are tolerated.

These recent events, coupled with the gradual arrival amongst the ranks of directors of more executives who themselves have participated in active cultural work during their recent years in management will result in Boards taking a more proactive interest in culture.

Until recently, it was extremely rare for us to find a Board of Directors of a publicly listed company requesting information on culture. A few of our clients have presented their culture progress to their Board, to analysts or to their ministers in the case of government departments, but, lacking an understanding of what they were seeing, these people have found it hard to ask the right questions. In many cases the CEO had to persuade apparently disinterested Board members that this work was even worth talking about at this level. However, this is changing very rapidly.

The purpose of this section of the chapter on governance is to provide directors with:

1. An understanding of what to look for to test whether your culture is an asset or a liability
2. How to put in place, from a risk management perspective, processes to ensure management is taking the necessary steps to address culture

Other key roles that Boards play – in particular the selection of the CEO, and strategic decisions related to mergers and acquisitions –

also have an important cultural component, and are covered in other parts of this book.

Key cultural traits to look for as a Board

No culture can completely eliminate the presence in its midst of a rogue – a dishonest and malicious individual with intent to harm. However, certain cultures dramatically reduce the possibility that such an individual would stay in employment with the company for any length of time, even without any criminal act having been committed. It is possible to create a culture where unethical intent or action would be dealt with by the immediate supervisor and, if undetected, reported by colleagues in a whistle-blowing environment. It is also possible to achieve transparency of reporting and a constructive relationship between departments, such as finance, risk and audit – traditionally the functions through which the Audit and Risk Committees gather their information. The presence of any of these cultural traits would have saved the companies whose demise has been reported by the media in recent times. From a perspective of a director, certain traits are crucial.

The first and foremost requirement is that the organisation is values-driven. From this position, there are then four particular values that, from a risk-management perspective, are crucial:

1. Transparency, a no-surprises culture
2. Listening, accessibility, lack of arrogance or bullying
3. Balanced partnership between line and functional roles
4. Accountability, being held to account for both performance and compliance

Being values-driven

Value-driven people and organisations make decisions just because they are the right things to do. They have other criteria for decision-making beyond that of profit performance and not breaking the law. They would continue to make certain decisions in the absence of a law, just because they are 'the right thing to do'. Building a values base to your organisation is the most reliable mechanism to protect yourself against future disaster.

Let's take the analogy of road safety. There are speed limits – they are the rules. Many drivers drive at about five-to-ten miles per hour above this figure. They know at this level the speed cameras will not catch them or that if they do, the fines are not prohibitive. There is a rule, and they bend that rule just as much as they think they will get away with. Other drivers go more slowly. They drive at a safer speed because they believe speed kills. They value safety. This is the difference between values-based and rules-based organisations. In rules-based organisations the sport is bending the rules. Values-based organisations don't do this – not because they are afraid they will get caught, but because they support the spirit of the rule.

You can test your organisation for values-based decisions by listening to the number of times management tells you that it cannot do something because, 'it would not be the right thing to do'. This might be associated with ethics regarding customers, keeping employees safe, going beyond the letter of the law. Consider, for example, their approach to tax. I recently heard a tax commissioner talk about how his office sees two types of companies from the approach they take – those who run the business they are in and seek to pay the right amount of tax that flows from it, and those who see themselves in the business of tax. Without getting into a discussion here about the motives of any tax administration, it seemed to me he was describing the difference between values-based organisations, and rules-based ones.

The Board plays an important role in helping management become more values-based. You are communicating your expectations through your questioning and your attitudes. Your role is to protect the interests of the shareholders. You determine the interpretation of that role. Are the interests of the shareholders best served by making the highest profit possible without breaking the law? Unquestionably it is possible to deliver in the short-term a profit which is at the expense of treating customers, the community and employees fairly. Are you happy if this occurs? Review the values hierarchy in Chapter 2. What does performance at any cost mean in your organisation? Can you define the boundaries of 'any cost'? These boundaries will be indicators of your values. If people are values-driven, they too apply this to every part of their life. You cannot expect your organisation to be values-driven with regard to not overstating a financial position but be content that its activities damage the communities in which it operates. Once employees realise the organisation is prepared to compromise what is right, to achieve the bottom line, they will spread this attitude from one sphere of organisational life to another.

If analysts want to build their confidence that a particular stock will not in the future suffer a catastrophic decline caused by the revelation of unethical behaviour, they would do well to probe and test for the strength of the organisation's general values. Values-based organisations are less likely to produce such an occurrence because everyone in the organisation knows that they will be supported in making values-based decisions, and that indeed they are expected to do so.

A CEO I know well recently stated at the Annual General Meeting, in front of shareholders and analysts, that he considered the company, 'had made a fair profit. To have made any more would have required practices I consider to be unfair.' He is in the insurance industry, and to have made any more profit would probably have involved taking a stand on the payment of claims which, whilst perhaps just within the bounds of the contract, would have been outside of what he considered fair and ethical. If he had been the CEO of your company, would he have been supported for this statement?

Performance pressure is intense, and the analysts' expectations push companies to the limits. As a Board, your role is to protect the interests of shareholders. This poses some challenging questions associated with values. The Board has the opportunity to lead the values in an organisation. But many CEOs do not feel supported to take a stand on a values decision that will negatively impact short-term profit. They may not tell you this, they may not even be aware of it themselves, but they have picked up the messages over a long period of time about what you value and what you expect.

In a different arena, there was media uproar recently when a top-level cricketer walked back to the dressing room from the crease. He knew he was out; even though the umpire had not given that call. He afterwards said it just felt like the right thing to do. In professional sport, this is a rare occurrence, and some of his teammates were not best pleased. This reflects on the change of values in sport from winning fairly to winning at all cost. What would be your position if your CEO took a parallel position on an issue of ethics?

An important piece of work for a Board is to test the messages sent to the organisation by its behaviours, symbols and systems. Include yourself in the Culture Diagnostic. Ask the organisation what messages they receive about what you, as a Board, value through the decisions they see you make, the metrics you request and the areas in which you show interest.

In line with the theme of this book, which is to look first to oneself and take responsibility for one's own role in culture in order to walk the talk, the first question to ask, as a Board of directors, is: 'Are we facilitating a values-driven organisation through our own behaviour?'

A turning point for values often comes with the realisation that being values-driven does actually also benefit performance. Companies do not realise how much of the bottom line they waste chasing it. How much money is poured into winning customers back – through branding, marketing, customer relationship management systems – because we lost them in the first place through not valuing them? How much money is wasted on recruitment and training because good people left out of sheer frustration with the culture and its one dimensional view of the world – short-term performance at any price? How much cost is tied up in relentlessly cutting costs and then having them grow back because we did not take the time to change the mind-sets that sat behind the costs in the first place?

In Chapter 5 of this book I have shown the bottom line cost of a poor culture. You can see how to build evidence from your organisation that will enable managers and Boards to stand up for this position in the face of a broader investment and business community which is only now starting to emerge from the era when 'all of this warm and fuzzy stuff' was seen as something separate from the real world of generating profits.

It is at times of such stress that the strength of values is tested. Management needs to hear from you that there are certain values you too uphold, as a part of the company, and your behaviours, symbols and systems need to reflect them. Decisions rejected by the Board on the basis of values ('this is not the right thing to do, despite being attractive financially'), will send a powerful signal. Just as the desired culture flows down from the role-modelling displayed by the senior leadership team, because messages from the top are the most powerful, so the Board sends messages to its CEO who sets the values standards for the whole company.

Testing for key values in you organisation

There are some values which give you confidence that the culture of the organisation is conducive to good risk-management practice. On the basis that your first priority is to build your organisation's overall strength on the values-driven dimension, the four values covered below will be your allies.

1. Transparency, a no-surprises culture

Transparency as a cultural trait will give you confidence that managers know that communicating bad news is better than covering it up in the hope that it will never surface. You will get a sense of this through both the papers and presentations you see. 'Look good' cultures will always put the best possible spin on a set of circumstances – not untruth, but a strong emphasis on the positive. Transparent cultures are comfortable, but realistic, with both good and bad news. In fact, a very sound way of testing the level of transparency in your culture is to observe the way management deals with good fortune. Truly transparent organisations do not take credit for upswings that were outside of their influence, such as an upturn in the market, and will present the difference between a contribution based on their skill, and one based on luck.

This realistic view, not based on the need to pump oneself up, is also displayed in the way management deals with bad news. They are not defensive in their response; they do not display the FIGHT or FLIGHT reactions described in Chapter 7. If they do not display them to you, chances are they will also not display them to their people, who therefore feel safe raising bad news. This trait encourages the behaviour you want.

2. Listening, accessible, lack of arrogance or bullying

A closely aligned value to transparency is that of management being open and accessible throughout the company. This ensures that people at the front line feel they can raise difficult issues, go around their boss if necessary, and do and say what they feel is right without fear of retribution.

Both arrogance and bullying would prevent this from occuring. Arrogance, because it assumes that I have all the answers, and there is nothing I could be told that I don't already know, so I won't listen. Bullying, because it instils fear in staff of their immediate manager, and they will not therefore blow the whistle.

In considering whether such traits exist in your organisation, look for evidence that senior management has a direct relationship with a broad cross-section of both employees and customers. Are they protected by an 'inner sanctum' who control the power and access, or do they have knowledge that comes directly from where the action is? Are they curious, learning, seeking information from everywhere? Do they seem to engender trust in others? How passionate are they about people? How strongly do they see their role as one of protecting their people from any bullying or inappropriate behaviour? Their passion for the policies of valuing people – safety, anti-discrimination, work/life balance – are likely to translate into an antipathy for bullying and an intention to drive it out of the organisation. This will serve you well for building the trust required for the communication of bad news.

3. Balanced partnership between line and functional roles
The functional roles traditionally are the keepers of the rules. Risk, compliance, legal and HR set the rules and the line managers try to deliver their numbers.

In very passive rule-based organisations, people are compliant, but blindly so, they comply because it is the rule, rather than because they understand or believe in the principle behind the rule. Thus whilst they may comply when the situations are clear, they are not able to think for themselves in situations which are not covered by an existing rule, because they are rules-based rather than values-based or principles-based. Studies by organisations seeking to improve safety standards, for example, have found that many accidents occurred in situations which required people to think for themselves around safety principles as well as follow safety standards.

In more aggressive rule-based organisations, line mangers bend the rules as much as possible, in-line with the idea of driving slightly above the speed limit. The keepers of the rules are the opposition, and the sport becomes finding ways around them in order to score the goal of performance. In these organisations, once in a while someone comes along with very low personal ethics, and they don't bother with just bending or finding ways around them, they break them altogether.

Good functional leaders see one of their roles as that of educating the organisation, especially the line roles, on why certain policies are important. In so doing they influence the values and beliefs of staff about what is important. This, in turn, changes their behaviour. Simultaneously they have to play some degree of the policeman role. This is a difficult combination to do well.

An insight into how to play this role well can be gained through watching good referees overseeing football matches. Since the television coverage has provided us with the benefits of the referee's voice, the duality of the role is easy to see. The referee is coaching, warning and advising players if they are getting close to a situation where some form of penalty will be imposed. A good referee will use this side of the role to prevent penalties and steer the game within the rules. The role of policing faults is there, but it is balanced by the role of educating. Good referees are trusted by players.

The quality of the relationship between line and functional managers lies at the heart of achieving both compliance to rules and an ability to work with the principles behind them. If the relationship is good, and trust and respect high, then both sides understand the importance of each other's role. Line management knows that they will always be pressing to drive harder on performance, but understand that the functional roles are there to help create, and strengthen, the boundaries they must not cross. They see them as allies to help keep them and their people, within these boundaries, which both groups acknowledge and respect.

The functional roles understand that the organisation is in the business of achieving the performance targets given to line management, and that they must try not to make it too arduous, through their practices and processes, for this to occur. They both understand the importance of the policies. The behaviour and attitudes of both groups determines the quality of your compliance culture.

As Board members, you observe the quality of this relationship, and encourage management to fill these roles with people who respect its importance. If you see signs of the policeman/cowboy stereotypes in either role, then you must assume this carries inherent risk. On the other hand, if the relationship becomes too chummy, there is a different risk. Through your own dealings with both groups, demonstrate your understanding of the importance of both roles, and the inevitable tensions the 'performance plus compliance' demands will place on their relationship. Encourage both to appreciate the challenges of the other. Seek evidence of good teamwork between the two.

4. Accountability, being held to account for both performance and compliance

Chapter 4 contains a lengthy description of the Achievement Culture, and the characteristics it upholds, in particular the belief that, 'my word is my bond'. Accountability requires two parties: one, who is delivering, and the other, who is holding them to account to deliver. To achieve accountability, senior management has to be good at holding people to account. There is a 'what' and a 'how' component to this. The 'what' are the performance outcomes, the goals to be scored. The 'how' are the values, principles, policies and rules which form the boundaries within which the game must be played. Step outside of these in a game of football, and the goal is disallowed. The same must hold true in an organisation.

There are several steps to the act of holding to account, and as a Board you should be seeking evidence that each occurs effectively.

- Communication of, and engagement in, the goals, values and rules. People need to be very clear of what is expected in each of these three categories. This requires a high quality of communication. For example, people understand things much better when they have a chance to ask questions and discuss, than when it arrives as an email. It also requires clear, simple content: 565 rules in a book, or performance metrics with so many sub-clauses that no one can work out what's required, do not help
- A clear 'sign-up' to the expectations, and the opportunity to raise concerns if staff believe they are not realistic. Unfortunately many managers feel their targets are not negotiable, and the policies are unworkable, but they live in a culture where they will get shot for saying so. When someone signs-up, they are more likely to feel that their word is a bond
- Good information about performance progress (both financial and others such as customer and employee satisfaction), with data that is not in dispute, and justifications and wriggling are not condoned. When people are given poor or no data about

what is happening, they cannot take corrective action, and therefore feel less accountable for what happens

• Fair and consistent consequence management. There has to be a visible cause-and-effect relationship between the extent to which individuals delivered both 'what and how' and their consequent treatment by the organisation. This includes who gets rewarded and how, as well as the consequences for non-performance or non-compliance. 'Consequence management' is often used to describe only negative consequences, but people read both positive and negative consequences as equally important signals about whether accountability matters

A Board can review the quality of each of these steps. A senior management team who holds the value of accountability strongly, will demonstrate evidence of this through the rigour with which they apply each step. Sometimes it is easy to assume that accountability is a value in an organisation because the organisation is currently performing. It is true that *sustainable* performance will inevitably be an outcome of an accountable culture. However, as is explored in other parts of this book, it is possible to perform in the short-term at the expense of values, even the value of accountability. Testing for evidence of the steps outlined above is a more reliable mechanism than assuming that because we are performing we must be accountable.

Putting culture on the agenda

All of the above show the specifics that, as a director, you can do to ensure your organisation has a culture that will enable sustainable success. In a more general sense, the most important contribution is to demonstrate that culture is actually important to you. This means asking for culture metrics and evidence that management is focussing on culture, and participating yourself in the culture process management is supporting.

Each of us demonstrates what we value by how we spend our time, where we express our interest, and what we expect of ourselves and others. Boards must show that they value culture if they want it to deliver for them. In the governance required to achieve a successful cultural outcome, the role of the Board is paramount.

USING EXTERNAL CONSULTANTS

The culture has to be owned and driven by you and your people. Whilst you can delegate many DO-ing activities to others – internally and externally – you cannot delegate BE work. No one but you can change what goes on inside of your head. Consultants cannot do the personal work that has to occur internally for each individual in your organisation, as they come to terms with the emerging expectations, and determine whether they have the courage and will to change. However, often an outside party can provide just the right jolt or insight to help make an internal shift. And over time there are a number of practical elements, particularly in the systems component of the behaviour, symbols and systems model, which you can outsource.

Every advisor has his or her own methodology, language and style. Your role is to ensure that they are not sending conflicting messages to your people. A new firm of advisors can seem to your people like a new initiative, and this can lessen the impact of your culture work. Outsiders feed the fear your people have that this will just be another fad, because they tend to speak to your people as if theirs is the first time you have encountered this new approach. Because it is a new project for them, they find it harder to position their contribution in the context of the longer journey work you are on.

Your job is to provide this framework, both for your people and for the advisors themselves. Find business partners who fit with the culture you have targeted, and keep them with you for as long as you can in order to build consistency and trust. Demand that your advisors support the work of their predecessors and of others who are working with them. Shape their language and models. The contribution of these business partners needs to fit into your plan, not the other way around. But do not allow your team to blame consultants if things are not going as you wish. If they have taken over and are taking it in their own direction, this is a reflection of you, not them.

In broad terms, consultants should be used for two reasons:

- To offer specialist advice. You do not have the know-how inside your organisation
- To provide additional horsepower. You have the know-how, but not enough of it

In the cultural process, there are specific pieces of specialist advice and additional horsepower that are often best played by outsiders.

Specialist advice

Cultural Diagnostic. The first time you undertake a thorough and honest review of your culture, you need people to do this who can see clearly and are not a part of that culture themselves. Later, when you are measuring progress your need for outside help decreases.

Winning the top team over. Sometimes, the advice of an outsider and perceived authority in this field has more weight with senior line management than internal HR or enthusiastic middle management. This is an indictment on your current culture, and not a habit you wish to promote. However, to get you on your way, the ends may justify the means.

Holding up the mirror to individuals, and being their behavioural coach. Outsiders are not caught up in the hierarchy of the business, and can therefore more easily be honest in their feedback, and objective in their advice.

Input to your Cultural Development Plan. Specific advice on which levers to pull first in your plan, and the likely cultural return each will give. Consultants have the advantage of having seen more cultural changes than you, and thus can predict cause and effect more easily.

Shifting the level of awareness. Training programmes designed to enhance awareness are a specialised area, and you are unlikely to have this expertise in-house. Working with people at this level, and bypassing their defensive responses requires many years of experience.

Moving you to the next cultural wave. There comes a time when you feel you have broken the back of your cultural change work. You are no longer fixing something that is broken, but rather pursuing best practice. At this time you need access to cutting-edge thinking.

Additional horsepower

In addition to these specialist roles, you might use outsiders in an 'additional arms and legs' capacity for areas where you do not have enough resources and do not want to hire permanent employees. For example, running workshops or making changes to HR or planning systems.

SELECTING EXTERNAL ADVISORS

You need people who understand what goes on at the BE-level. This means being deeply immersed in what makes people tick. Many excellent consultancies understand what makes the mechanics of an organisation tick (processes, systems, finances, strategy) but this is work at the DO-level.

Assess their own self-awareness. Individuals and firms who themselves have not been through this journey will not be qualified to walk arm in arm with you through yours. If you perceive arrogance, avoidance, blame or silos in them, which they do not recognise or acknowledge, they will be unable to be congruent in their work with your people. This does not mean that you need perfection. But you need a good level of self awareness. Are these people sufficiently self-aware to be able to role-model that trait for your people? Are they walking your talk?

Culture is an emerging management discipline, and firms who provide services in this area have a wide range of backgrounds themselves. Those who have this as their area of speciality, are useful because they have the experience of having walked the path with a large number of clients.

Most firms have one of four heritages, and each has its strengths and weaknesses:

1. Large traditional consulting firms

The strategy, IT and accounting consulting firms have moved into human performance advice in recent years.

Advantages	Strength in large project planning and implementation
	Have the ear of senior management who are used to spending large sums of money with these firms, and listening to their advice
	Strong in designing new processes
Disadvantages	Focus on the DO dimension, easy to be lulled into believing real change is happening but over time benefits are often eroded because of lack of BE-level change
	Lack knowledge of emotions and their impact

2. HR Consultancies

Traditional partners of the HR communities, broadening focus on employee management to include culture.

Advantages	Understand employee motivation
	Have existing strengths in some of the cultural levers
	Accepted by the HR community

Disadvantages	Confuse climate with culture
	Tend to place this work too strongly in the HR bucket, which marginalises its impact as the business may see it as separate from the main game
	Focus on extrinsic motivators (remuneration, etc.), may lack know-how on the intrinsic side

3. Training providers

Behaviour, rather than skill-based training, has always had an influence on culture, and some have extended to offer advice and culture consulting.

Advantages	Know how to tap into the BE-level in the training environment.
	Some have strong backgrounds in personal development and work with people at the deeper levels of values and consciousness. Others are more skills, motivation and education
	Can provide trainers for rapid roll-out programmes
Disadvantages	Put too much emphasis on the training room, and work is not integrated into day-to-day work life
	Behaviour change not linked to symbols and systems

4. Advertising, communications, marketing

Have moved in recent years from focussing entirely on the external market, to a greater interest in employee communication. This has sprung in part from the recognition that employees form such a key part of the brand proposition.

Advantages	Both culture change and marketing seek to change people's behaviour. These people know what makes people tick and how to engage and work with emotions
	Using non-HR specialists is a break from tradition and gives a new perspective
Disadvantages	Sometimes superficial, just communication is not enough
	Not experienced in giving leaders feedback on their personal impact
	May not understand the special dynamics of the employee–employer relationship

All of these people can be useful to you if you recognise their core strengths and pick specialist advice when you need it, according to each advisor's core competency.

SUMMARY

In this chapter we have covered the formal structures you need to manage your culture, and the roles and people you need to place into those structures to maximise your chances of success. The leadership team, your culture champions, your directors and external advisors all have a role to play, and must all be prepared to walk the talk themselves.

By creating process of management that expects the culture work to deliver against the metrics selected as most appropriate, and provides a governance approach with the rigour of other large projects your organisation undertakes, you will enable everyone who plays a role to operate in the most effective manner. This will accelerate achieving the benefits in your business case.

SECTION 3

SPECIAL CIRCUMSTANCES

EVERY culture journey is unique, and this book is designed as a handbook to guide you through a typical path. You will have fathomed that no journey is typical, and yours certainly has some unique quirks about it. When you look back you will appear to have followed a reasonably logical path, but while you are walking forward it often does not seem that straightforward.

To build you a map for this path, I have used as my base a set of cultural circumstances. Our aim was to change a whole organisation which had become outdated, overtaken by rapidly changing market conditions with which the organisation struggled to catch up. The performance pressure these organisations were under forced an examination of the sacred cows of personal behaviour, organisational habits, unchecked egos and outdated value-systems.

Many of you will be familiar with these circumstances and will be in a position to influence culture in an organisation of this type. The framework I have laid out here will serve your needs.

There are a number of other scenarios where culture can be used as an asset, and I want to cover these in some detail during the next section of this book. This last section shows you how to:

• Change a small part of a larger organisation
• Decide whether to encourage different cultures within the whole

- Manage culture through mergers, acquisitions, joint ventures and partnerships
- Manage culture in a small business
- Manage the cultural changes of cultural growth
- Apply your knowledge of changing culture to circumstances outside of work

In each of these scenarios, there is an added dimension to be considered, on top of what is covered in the first two sections of this book.

Finally, included in this section is a description of one company's journey. This will help you to see how the process I have described can actually be introduced.

12

Managing Distinct Cultures
Within the Whole

MANY of you will not be in a position to implement an organisation-wide culture initiative. You are not the CEO, the head of HR or a member of the top team. But you believe passionately in this work, and want to implement change in your own area, as well as influencing the wider agenda. I encourage you to do this. But on one condition. If you are successful, you must be prepared to fold what you have been doing into a bigger initiative, if your organisation is attempting to pull off a larger scale cultural change, either now or in the future. Otherwise your cultural haven will become a silo.

For those who sit at the centre, the dilemma is to work out how important it is that you drive towards one common culture across the whole organisation. You probably have differences now, caused either by the past history, by the efforts of leaders in some parts of your business or by distinct customer or business needs. In future, do you want to drive a centralised or a decentralised approach, or some hybrid of both?

This chapter will cover the challenges faced both by those seeking to change from the middle, and those planning culture change across a diverse organisation.

CHANGING THE CULTURE OF A SMALLER GROUP
It is possible to change culture from the middle. You can create a

303

cultural haven within a more dysfunctional broader environment. I have seen many examples of this occurring, and have measured the differences using both culture surveys and performance outcomes. When I refer to a 'smaller group', I am describing everything from a single call-centre or factory, through to the country head of a global organisation, responsible for all operations within that geography.

There is a particular attitude required to pull off this kind of local transformation. It can be summed up by the wonderful prayer by Reinhold Niebuhr:

> God grant me the serenity to accept the things I cannot change, the courage to change the things I can, and the wisdom to know the difference.

Unfortunately, some people feel a victim to their lives. They focus their attention on those elements in their life which are completely out of their control, and drop themselves into a downward spiral of living *below the line* in blame and resentment.

Others feel masters of their lives. They focus their attention on those elements of their life which are within their control, and lift themselves into an upward spiral of living *above the line* in personal responsibility and choice. As they do this, they find that there is another big part of their life which, whilst not technically under their control, is certainly within their sphere of influence. This concept is described well in Stephen Covey's book *The Seven Leadership Habits of Highly Successful People*, and is summarised by this diagram:

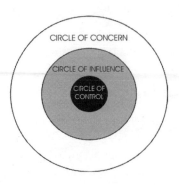

By living *above the line* in personal responsibility, people find that their ability to make a difference ranges further than might have been initially realised. They simply take responsibility for more and more, and gradually chip away at the areas not directly under their control.

This attitude is essential to changing from the middle. In fact it is central to changing culture from any position. I once met a CEO who told me he couldn't change his culture because the Board were so political in their approach that they completely dominated the culture. So don't believe that people at the top automatically believe that they make a difference.

Gavin was a member of an organisation acquired by another with a difficult culture. His colleagues found the transition challenging because the two organisations did things so differently. Some of his colleagues got worn down, went *below the line* and increasingly felt like victims to the situation. Gavin saw it as a big game. He got all of his team engaged, and created a whole language of game-playing. Each day was a new round. Some days they won and some days they lost. They revised tactics each evening. If they got stonewalled by the culture, they regrouped and found another way. Over a period of months, they got approval for significant investment which everyone had told them would 'never get through'. Their culture measured very well at a time when that of some of his colleagues was going backwards. Now the investments have paid off, and the rest of the organisation is becoming curious and asking questions about their approach to business and how he leads his team. He is influencing the bigger group, whilst still focussing on building the culture he wants from his position.

A great culture is a beacon for other groups. It is infectious, and others want to be a part of it. The main risk to this is arrogance. If your team becomes self-satisfied, this can be incredibly irritating for others!

The team as a mini-culture

Every team becomes a mini-culture in its own right. The team is the smallest organisational unit where the dynamics of a community exist. Every team that operates together for any length of time develops behavioural norms, habits, and unspoken agreements about the rules of 'engagement'. The stronger the team is, the more differentiated these may be from the broader community within which the team sits.

To exist as a mini-culture, the team needs to experience itself as an entity. People within it need to build a sense of identity (positive or negative), purpose and rituals. This is not an automatic outcome of a group of individuals reporting to one person. But if the team meets regularly, makes decisions together and has conversations about things that matter (not just social niceties), then a sense of identity will form.

Take care of these basic building blocks first. Define the purpose of the team, its goals, individual roles and accountabilities, team processes such as meetings. Then turn your attention to the behavioural norms which you can establish in the team. A tight team responds to these norms more quickly than a bigger organisation. The need to fit in is very strong, and consequently changing a team culture can occur fast if you follow the right steps.

- Start with the business case. What benefits exist if we transform the way this team operates?
- Describe the picture of what you want. Define the behaviours, values, principles and mind-sets you want for the team
- Hold up the mirror. Be honest about the current position. Use direct feedback and measurement tools
- Change yourself. Pursue the self-development paths I have described. Leadership has a direct and immediate impact on the team
- As the leader, help other team members to change, and hold to a set of expectations. Use the team to help you – peer pressure is very powerful

- Change every symbol and system you have the authority to touch
- Influence any others you can
- Talk about your aspirations together; hold sessions where you are working exclusively on the team dynamic

As you work through this, you will be surprised at the number of behaviours, symbols, and systems sources of cultural messages that exist within the control or influence of one team. This number is high enough to allow one team to build an extraordinary team dynamic, or mini-culture.

Dealing with broader cultural messages

The team has to agree not to use the dysfunctional culture of the broader organisation as an excuse for behaving that way themselves. As the leader you can direct this line of thinking through using *above and below the line* (see Chapter 8) to reinforce the difference between personal responsibility and victim mentality. Making the whole cultural dynamic transparent helps this process. By talking about the team's aspirations, and recognising how culture works, you lift the level of awareness in the team. It learns to recognise behaviours, symbols and systems, and to observe how these act to influence the behaviour of individuals within the group. This is 'standing on the balcony' thinking. Every time one of your team notices how behaviours, symbols and systems are influencing how they and others behave, they have the opportunity to choose a different behaviour.

Encourage conversations about these things in your team. Talk about the common behaviours in the broader culture, and about the standards in this team. Build their confidence to go against the flow. For example, if the broader cultural norm avoids conflict, show your team how to raise difficult issues in the team environment. If the broader organisation pushes decisions upwards, ask the members of your team to resolve issues between themselves instead of bringing them to you.

Discuss the specific culture-bearing symbols and systems which might lead your team to different behaviours. If you all sit in separate offices, and do not have the authority to pull the walls down, have your meetings in a different office each day. Sit on the floor.

Engage in conversations about the bonus system. Do they believe the bonus system encourages them to behave in ways which are not conductive to the team standards, you all want? What are the ways to get around this? How could we help each other to get great bonuses and meet our standards? There is a way around most of these if you work on it together.

However, there are some which are just damned disempowering. Many teams operate in some form of matrix environment in which demands come from sources outside of your team. Some of these demands require a behavioural response which goes against what your team has agreed to. For example, a hierarchical, command and control culture will demand attendance at certain meetings at short notice. Cuts to budget may occur without a process of engagement, and in contradiction to agreed targets and performance hurdles. You and your team cannot ignore these demands, and you need to stay on side with the broader organisation in whose hands your future career may lie.

Your team will expect you to fight some of these battles on its behalf. As the team leader, part of your role is to represent the interests of your team up the hierarchy. You will win some and lose some. Quiet, realistic but unwavering determination to build a great culture step-by-step seems to be the attitude that works best. Get too optimistic and you end up disillusioned. Give up and you spiral into feeling like a victim. Go at it with a battering ram and you end up utterly frustrated and get everyone offside. The process requires considerable finesse, but it can be done.

This is your starting point for building the culture you want. From the base of your team, you can extend down into your span of control using the techniques already described. Influencing the broader organisation is best achieved once your own backyard is in order. Select groups with which your team interacts. Suggest opportunities to meet and discuss how to work more effectively together. Seek to learn about them and what makes them tick, so that the process becomes one of mutual exchange. Invite them to your training programmes and communication forums. Let them experience the excitement of what is starting to happen for your people.

Engage individual colleagues in conversations about your aspirations. You will find large numbers of kindred spirits. Most people aspire to what you are aspiring to. Many have just lost hope or pushed it to the bottom of their list of priorities. Building alliances with others who want the same kind of organisation as you creates an informal marketing campaign. Gradually you will find the opportunities to influence upwards, and ideas will become actions. As your level of awareness heightens, you feel more confident and less fearful of telling the truth. When you speak from your heart about what you believe in backed with business rationale you'll find your influence increasing.

The key to changing a culture from the middle is to hold the right mind-set for long enough to make a difference.

THE ORGANISATIONAL RISKS OF MULTIPLE CULTURES

Most organisations believe that their culture is different across different parts of their business. The next section of this chapter addresses the issue of whether you want to encourage these differences or not. It is an issue that those who have a cross-business cultural role have to face. At the local level, it is right and proper that a local manager will do what they can to build the best culture to deliver the results for which they are accountable. But if you sit at the centre, planning or leading culture for the whole organisation, what are the implications of this?

How different do you want it to be?

'Oh, no, we're different.' This is the common response to the idea of building a new culture, expressed by each individual unit, geography or business. When I first heard this sentence I took it at face value. Over the years I started to look more deeply into the motives behind the sentiment and in some cases I changed my view.

Each unit within an organisation has been influenced over the years by a range of factors, which have created the behavioural norms – and their underpinning mind-sets. These influences include:

Geographic location	Small town, large city, remote location, the characteristics of the location influences the people who work there, their lifestyle and attitudes
	Country, national values and habits
	Close or far away from head office
	Physically co-located or spread across locations
Customer needs	One-on-one relationship management, mass consumer, financial bracket, attitudinal type, age
Profession	Tourism, medical, retail banking, investment banking, education, technology, manufacturing, mining, etc.
Employee type	Blue collar, white collar, level of pay, age range, large contractor/casual group
History	Growth, crisis, multiple mergers, privatised government unit, entrenched market dominance, etc.

Each organisation has combined all of these factors with a whole lot of their own making to become a unique entity. There are literally no two organisations which feel and behave the same, as anyone who has worked for several will confirm.

Within one organisation these factors, combined with others such as the nature of the work conducted, combine to make every unit different. The stereotypes do to some extent hold well. Sales will tend to be more pushy and extroverted, finance more cautious, technology less people-oriented. The nature of the work and the type of people attracted to this work naturally create different cultures. We know that certain mind-sets create certain behaviours and that if practised over time specific work routines will themselves influence the way people think.

It is true then, that every unit is different. Yet if these were the only influences on culture, then every bank culture in a particular country would be the same, and every hospital culture and every mine. Yet we know this is not the case. Those who move from one company to a competitor experience quite a different culture. When I have worked with organisations in the same industry I experience something similar to how I perceive my three children. I know they all come from the same family, and that their visible, physical, mental and emotional make up have a common tone. Yet they are completely different. The unit you work in will feel and behave differently from other parts of your organisation, and from the same unit in a competitor.

For all this, I have concluded that when building a great culture, in most circumstances you get the best outcomes if you work with the whole organisation, encouraging differences appropriate to needs, but working within one overall framework. Let me explain.

There is a universal nature to the aspirations most leaders have for their cultures:

- Customer-Centricity, the desire to understand and respond to those people who are buying your products or using your services is the same whether you are in Kuwait or Norway, in a remotely located quarry or a high-rise building
- Respecting and valuing people are universal traits. All the major religions in the world express it in some way
- The desire to learn is everywhere

- Teamwork can occur whenever people are working together, and will always produce a better result than a group of people working at odds with each other
- Someone who takes responsibility will perform better than someone who does not

When the cultural aspirations of most organisations are analysed, they apply across the board.

So what is it that makes different countries, professions and other groups so very different from each other? I have found two causes:

- The values hierarchy differs. The strength of one value relative to another differs from person to person, and groups of people have common hierarchies. This phenomenon in nations is explored by Fons Trompenaars in his book *Riding the Waves of Culture*
- The translation of a value into behaviours will differ from person to person and from group to group. Ethical behaviour is interpreted differently by different people, for example

Finally, and this is crucial to your cultural work, some people are more values-driven that others. This trait does not seem to be shared by any one national group, but is true of some peer-groups, and probably of certain professions.

When you are building a great culture, there are particular traits you want across your whole organisation. If you are embarking on a serious culture journey, you will have demonstrated to yourself that these traits produce the best business benefits. If this is so, then there is no argument for keeping certain units isolated from this push.

To be values-driven – to hold to a deeply held value rather than take the easy option
To stay 'above the line' – to operate from personal responsibility, rather than a victim mind-set

To have integrity – to hold the key beliefs and values which matter to your organisation.

To be on a path of personal growth – whatever field you are in, change is a given, circumstances demand that people continue to grow and learn

Your cultural path will be founded on these traits. I can see no argument for any division to opt out of this.

When people say they are different, they are referring to the detail of values-hierarchy and the meaning of value. These can be accentuated during implementation, and must be encouraged if you are to meet the differing needs of your customer groups, your geographies and your professions. The above list includes deeper traits, which cross all geographies, locations and industries, and it is these you want shared.

Why people love to think of themselves as different

In many cases, the motive behind the 'we're different' argument is an 'us/them' mentality. We're right, they're wrong. We're superior, they're inferior. In great cultures everyone is proud to be associated with the whole. It's when the culture is poor that everyone splits off and wants to do their own thing. Most of us are better team leaders than team members. Being a part of a dysfunctional whole, and working to make it great, is much more challenging than becoming a splinter group. The latter is a criticism of the whole, and a belief that we can do it better our way.

Divisions get concerned that the whole will drag them down. Often head office is seen as bureaucratic, and divisions feel they can make more progress turning their back on this and focussing on improving themselves. This, of course, is true. But not necessarily in the interests of the broader group in the long-term.

My advice is, be suspicious when people take this stance. It is fine when there is not cultural push taking place across the whole. But if the whole is on a cultural journey, you should be cautious when individual units choose not to participate, and go off by themselves. Of course there will be large parts of the culture development process which will be owned and implemented by individual units. But the broad thrust of the process is best led together, however hard this may be. Together builds momentum. Together produces a multiplier effect, because people start to get consistent messages from every part of the organisation. Together enables you to tackle the big difficult challenges like the budget process.

Exceptions

Some organisations have no connection between the different businesses within their portfolio. The business unit CEOs run independent businesses, this situation will never change through a restructure, there is no sharing of customers, people, products, services, knowledge, IT.

Others have a strong philosophy of devolution, and include culture in this definition. The centre simply does not want to become involved in anything that can be done by the units, culture included. Any disadvantages of the resulting differences are accepted as the price to pay for devolution. The only common value is, in fact, devolution.

On first reading, you may think of many organisations that fit these criteria. My experience is there are fewer than one might think. Even when these criteria do apply, there are still common financial reporting, common shareholder expectations and common requirements to meet certain standards such as safety, the environment and ethical behaviour.

Another consideration is whether there is any resource at the centre to act as the glue to do something together. Organisations with very independent businesses do not naturally collaborate unless there is a stimulus to cause this to occur. Getting this going is not going to be high on the priority list of anyone who works in one of the businesses.

Think of Europe. If you were going to design a European Union, starting 25 years ago, how would you go about doing it? Everyone in Europe has strong identification with his or her own country. The French will always love France, the Spanish Spain. The challenge for those wanting to build the EU has been to create some sense of allegiance to Europe. People will always resist efforts to build them into a bigger team. Small tribes are our natural instinct, probably dating from our time in caves. We are naturally programmed to identify most with those who are closest to us geographically, and this triggers our response to protect our kin. An important response for the survival of the species. Naturally people will resist efforts to make them European, even if it makes economic sense.

Similarly, people will resist attempts to make them one organisation, even if there is a strong economic driver to do so.

To overcome this instinctive local response you will need to build the sense of identity with the bigger whole, so it feels like my new tribe. In the European context, one could have done this through common language. Insistence 25 years ago that all children learnt one common language in schools would by now have produced a generation who could all talk to one another. There were efforts to do this, but local factions kicked in as to which language.

Opportunities to feel proud of being European would help. How about a single European soccer team which plays against a South American team. Golf, with the Ryder Cup, is the only sport where Europeans play as a team. (So strong is the tribal identification around soccer in Europe that inevitably when I tell this story to Europeans they roll in the aisles with laughter. I never said it would be easy, but it would be effective!)

Common flags, common music. Common currency. Removing immigration restrictions allowing people to live and work in different countries, increasing friendships, marriages and business relationships across the boundaries. Telecommunications making virtual relationships doable. Common rules and standards for agriculture, employment and health care.

How far down the road you travel depends on how strongly you see the benefits of a single entity. As the benefits outweigh the effort and pain of change, change does occur if the right plan is in place.

This analogy does apply to your organisation. Do you want your people to identify with being French, being European or being both? Where are the business benefits and how do they weigh up against the cost, including the effort of changing? These are great conversations to be had, and they stimulate heated debate. Remember that in the European journey, much of the early efforts were about controls and standards and rules. This is probably not the best place to start. Building identification with the bigger group, with Europe, must occur in parallel with the economically driven changes. As you shift the mind-sets, every other change becomes ten times easier. Whilst the mind-set is entirely French and Spanish, everything introduced will be seen as an imposition.

DESIGNING A 'LOOSE TIGHT' CULTURE DEVELOPMENT PLAN

If the dynamics of your organisation are suggesting that the issue of independence or shared approach will be an important one, then you will benefit from thinking this through carefully in your plan.

How did your culture work get started? In many cases, initial work will have been done in one or more units. The impetus to get going may well not have come from the top. Right now there could be half a dozen initiatives running in different parts of the business. Each may have a different set of values, a different leadership programme, and different conceptual framework, different processes and a different language. In the 1980s and early 1990s, it was possible to design a culture programme from scratch, treading virgin territory and providing clear, consistent messages. Today there are few organisations where this is possible. Most groups have had a go at parts of the journey covered in this book. You will find a range of feelings associated with this work. Some groups will be passionate about their own approach, and understandably reluctant to give anything up for the sake of a broader piece of work. Others will be completely cynical as a result of previous failed efforts.

If you sit at the centre and have culture responsibilities, your first task is to do a review of what culture initiatives are currently running. If you sit in one of the units, take the initiative yourself to team-up with other units who are doing similar work. Once you can see what currently exists, there are a number of decisions the top team needs to make.

What will be tight and shared across the group?
Here is my recommendation, in order of importance. How far down this list you drive a common approach depends on the approach you choose to take.

1. Values
People will have endless debates about their own list of values and why they should keep them. I have found that it always leads to tears. Over time, restructures occur, groupings change and sets of values get rewritten. The power of a culture journey lies in its longevity. Your success will be directly linked to the extent to which you can stick on one path for long enough to get real traction. Leaders with large egos love to start again and create something new which is their own. Every time you restructure or put a new leader in place you will find a new set of values and a new cultural direction appears. Values can act as the anchor. You may over time add one or change one, but they do stand a reasonable chance of being the common thread through your culture journey.

To some extent, having a common set of values will be a symbol, rather than a limiting factor to individual units tailoring their culture plans. They will also put their personal stamp on the values. You will notice a tendency to supplement them by other lists – called principles, credo and beliefs – which are their desire to create their own set of values by another name. I don't find this very useful as I think it confuses employees, but it is very hard to stop. If you sit in a separate unit, ask yourself what is your motive for creating a new list. Does this really add value to the process or is it the ego wanting to be special and different?

2. Measurement of culture

If you are serious about making culture a competitive advantage, you must hold everyone to account for improving in this area. This means a common way of measuring culture so that you can compare apples with apples across the divisions in your organisation. You cannot afford to have one part of the business opt out of culture, and your measurement system is the management tool to ensure this does not occur.

Pick one method, and stick with it. You need year-on-year results to be able to see improvements across the business.

The measurement will allow a group of senior leaders, to act as an overall management committee on the cultural agenda, and drive the business benefits that have been identified. It also allows the Board to see that culture is being managed.

3. Leadership development

A great organisation will have invested heavily in developing great leaders. Your leadership group will carry the culture torch. They are a key asset and as such belong to the whole organisation rather than a part. Building your leadership capability strengthens your culture. You want to build that capability consistently across the business so that your bench strength is strong and you can increasingly promote from within.

For these reasons I recommend that your core leadership programmes are common across the business. They become a platform for the emerging culture.

4. Improvement and collaboration processes and rituals

Rituals build identity. Common rituals enable people to work with others they do not know well, and quickly feel familiar with them and become productive together. Introducing common rituals is essential for One-Team Cultures, and useful in most others. Rituals could include:

- Problem solving techniques
- Quality improvement processes
- Meeting formats
- Feedback routines (including performance reviews)
- Safety routines
- Recognition schemes

5. *Values education/induction*

Over time, you want to achieve common mind-sets across your business. This means that the depth of values hierarchy and beliefs about what is important gradually becomes more aligned. A part of this process is the core programme you design to communicate what the organisation stands for culturally. Having all employees go through this programme sets a common standard across the group.

The counter argument to this is that the values programme provides the opportunity to tailor the core messages to each division. 'Customer-Centric' means something different to those who work in sales teams, compared to those who work in the technology division. Designing workshops where people have the chance to work this through builds local ownership to a group aspiration.

Localised values education also allows local leaders to marry their past cultural efforts with the emerging group view. This is essential to maintain the sense of continuity. Without this link, employees easily get the sense of uncoordinated change or 'flavour of the month'.

Ideally over time, your plan will contain both: a group-wide programme for all employees, and a localised one for each division.

6. *HR and financial systems*

There are many reasons for having these systems common which are not cultural. Management control and standards will usually drive the desire to build common HR and financial systems and processes. Independence in these areas has usually come about through historic circumstances such as acquisitions or divisional and geographic independence.

When HR and financial systems are common, they do play a part in creating a One-Team Culture. Whether they help other cultural drivers depends on their quality. The challenge with these systems is that it takes so much effort to bring them together and the cultural agenda is often not clearly voiced at the time, making it harder to influence their design to create a good cultural output.

If you want to create a single great culture MOVE PEOPLE AROUND. Put in place the HR processes to give as many people as possible exposure to the whole group. The sooner you do this, the sooner you have a set of global ambassadors who will take with them the common thread of your emerging culture.

7. *Communication*

Most communication is best conducted locally. The local leaders always have more credibility that someone unknown from a remote location. Local leadership designs the communication approach that works for them.

At a group level, some common communication material can be developed, such as newsletters. Common language is important if you are looking for cultural alignment over time.

SUMMARY

You will find the local versus global debate is much stronger during the early stages of your journey. As you succeed in making the global entity really attractive culturally, then people will be proud to be a part of it. The extent to which this occurs is a good yardstick of the progress you have made. Hold the line on some things early, and then build identity with the whole, through initiatives which make it an attractive place to be.

If you sit in a business unit or local group, stay in touch with what is happening culturally on the broader stage. Where you can, hook up with this, and use their programmes and initiatives. You know that it will be how you walk the talk that will matter most to your people. Focus on the behaviours and symbols locally, and use global pieces to link yourself to the whole. In this way you set your people up to benefit from both.

13

Mergers and Acquisitions

THE SUDDEN CULTURAL SHOCK

MERGERS are a unique situation culturally. During a merger or acquisition you have to manage culture in a different way. Mergers accentuate cultural issues which might have simmered along unnoticed in a 'business as usual' scenario. Anyone who has been holding lingering doubts about whether there really is such a thing as culture will have no doubt after living through the first few months of a merger. Culture will jump up and hit you in the face!

In the case of normal organic growth, an organisation's culture grows and changes as its value-set evolves naturally over time. In the case of a merger, two cultures, each an intact and working value-system in its own right, are pushed together. It is like an arranged marriage. The parents got together and worked out a deal, and suddenly the children find themselves lifting their veils to see a complete stranger. The underlying value-set of this new partner will not be immediately visible. What are apparent are the behaviours, symbols and systems.

These behaviours, symbols and systems will probably be very different from those you are accustomed to. In all of my years as a consultant, I have never come across a merger where the people involved saw the two cultures as the same. Even when on the surface the two organisations have similar backgrounds. The complexity of a cultural DNA makes finding two identical cultures almost as hard as finding two identical human beings.

If you are reading this before your organisation goes into a merger, then I will describe to you what you will experience and how to manage your own emotions and behaviours, as well as the broader organisational challenges. If you're already in the middle of one, then you will know the feelings, and I intend to provide some perspective which will help you feel more in control of the situation.

Much of what this chapter will cover applies to every situation where two different organisations are brought together. The business structures vary: merger, acquisition, joint venture, outsourcing deal, business partnership, and to a lesser extent, the amalgamation of two divisions within the same company. There are some important differences between each, which I will explain. Until then I will use the word 'merger' to apply to all.

We have found most people's early experiences of a merger are unfavourable. Most mergers bring out the worst features of tribalism. When one group sees the behaviours, symbols and systems of another, they judge them according to their own value-set. They make assumptions, usually negative ones, about the other group.

A very deliberate plan of action is required to build understanding, respect and eventually a new identity. Without this, the cost to the merged entity is very high:

- Large numbers of people leave as it becomes clear which tribe is top dog
- Decision-making is slow and integration synergies are delayed
- Individuals give up in their communication efforts, and start to withhold crucial information from each other, building silos and increasing cost through duplication of effort
- Customers suffer as internal battles rage

Understanding the emotional issues at play
Mergers are high-risk for those involved; large sums of money have been spent, reputations are at stake and the external market is

watching intently. There are rarely immediate benefits for customers. In most cases a great deal of planning occurs before merger-day to mitigate these risks and ensure the expected return on investment is delivered. It is common knowledge now that a large percentage of mergers – figures are often quoted at around 70 per cent – fail because of 'cultural issues'. However, the rigour associated with anticipating and managing the cultural issues is often considerably less than those associated with other elements, such as technology and product rationalisation. It is uncommon to have someone on an M&A team with cultural expertise, paralleling the contribution of the investment bankers. Mergers are undertaken for financial reasons, and those with financial expertise tend to outweigh those with cultural expertise both before and after the decision is made. Executives talk numbers before people, which is crazy especially in service industries.

A common mistake is to confuse culture with people, and to lump the cultural-planning in with the people-planning stream of an integration team. There are two sets of 'people' challenges afoot which come together during a merger, and each need outstanding leadership and emotional intelligence to navigate successfully. Whilst they overlap, they need to be considered separately as well as together, because the plans to address each will be different.

The first challenge concerns how people feel. The second, the differences in the two value-sets. The first impacts climate, the second culture. Only the second fits strictly into the framework of this book. But because the two tend to get muddled-up, both inside the minds and emotions of the people involved, and in those planning the integration, I will describe both. Many of the difficulties associated with merger situations emerge because all the normal cultural change challenges exist, but in a situation of heightened emotions and short time-frames.

How people feel after a merger

I would like to be really positive here, and tell you that people are filled with excitement at the time of a merger. It would be great if everyone saw the opportunities which were in the minds of the merger-designers, and embraced them with open arms. Unfortunately, these people are in the minority. Everyone knows there will be some rationalisation, and therefore people are competing with each other for jobs. Under these circumstances it is understandable that the other side is seen as the enemy. Most people feel one or more of the following during the first three months at least.

Insecure	Will I have a job? Will I have to move? Will I lose my friends, status, perks and opportunities? What will happen to my projects, plans, performance and customers?
Angry	Why did they do this? Why is no one consulting us? How come those people are being more advantaged than me? They're making a real mess of this
Undervalued	Doesn't anyone care about my customers, projects, plans and experience? Why is no one telling me anything? How come I'm not in the 'inner circle'?
Grieving	I don't want to lose our name, identity, team, rituals, friends
Arrogant	I'm better than them, we've come out on top here, we're invincible

Insecurity, anger, grief, feeling undervalued are emotions you will recognise. Arrogance you may not see as an emotion, but under these circumstances it most definitely is, and becomes a very important element you will have to manage going forward.

A merger will test the mettle of each person involved. Those with higher self-actualisation are inherently less insecure because they have higher confidence in themselves. This makes them less dependent on outside circumstances for their personal satisfaction and security, and consequently less fearful of change or loss. They are able to move *above the line* quicker, and take personal responsibility for their feelings and their future. This will bring out the best behaviour, and you will notice these people are constructive and productive in their day-to-day affairs. They waste less time complaining about management, blaming the other organisation for their problems, playing games of one-upmanship and holding on to the past. This has always been true of such people, but you really notice it at times of high emotional stress and threat. So any work you have previously done to raise your own self-awareness or that of your organisation, will pay big dividends at this time. (See Chapters 7 and 8.)

The people stream of a good integration team will address most of these emotions through change management planning. Involvement, frequent factual communication and speed are the basis of good change management during mergers. These all serve to reduce uncertainty and the emotions associated with being in the dark. Work on the vision and future will help to lift people out of their negative emotions and increase their excitement.

THE EARLY DAYS

The tone for the merger is established during the due diligence period. The first cultural battle is often centred on who will be the CEO and the Chairman. The role of the due diligence team is by its very nature invasive and implicitly critical. The target group feel on the back foot and defensive. Emotions can be cemented at this stage, unless the teams involved are trained to set up relationships and a working environment that will facilitate the future success.

MANAGING THE CULTURE

To effectively manage yourself and your organisation through a merger, you must be able to separate the management of these feelings from the management of the culture. The first is urgent, and important; the second can appear less urgent, but in the long-term is even more important.

Let's return to the analogy of the arranged marriage. The bride and groom may not like the fact that it occurred, or be angry about the manner in which it took place. However, it has happened. After a few months they are left with the reality of having to make a life together. At this point, it is their ability to understand and work with each other's values and beliefs about what is important that will make the real difference. Most relationships have their frustrations as a result of different personalities rubbing up against each other. But it is the values conflicts that are the most fierce. The reason some of the deepest arguments in relationships centre on money is because how an individual spends their money is an outward expression of what they value. Align around your values, and you become a strong partnership. The same is true in a merger.

During the first few months, emotions are high and most people are busy settling down to their own personal circumstances and re-establishing some kind of order in their lives. They are not thinking about values, they are thinking about personal security. Abraham Maslow's *Hierarchy of Needs* shows us that until the basic needs of security and survival are met, people do not tend to focus on other, deeper issues.

Your challenge, as a leader and a culture champion, is to find a way to focus on culture whilst simultaneously dealing with your own personal feelings, and those of others, about the merger. If you wait until things have settled down, you will find that a *de facto* culture has emerged which may not produce the best outcome for the future performance of the business. Most of the key decisions made in the first few months of integration have a cultural impact. Some of those made prior to the actual event have the most impact of all. For example, the choice of CEO and from which organisation this person comes. So the earlier culture gets on to the agenda in a meaningful way, the better chance you have of ending up with a culture that will support future plans and deliver the benefits laid out in the original merger proposition.

How culture operates in the first three months

Two organisations come together. The veils come up. Each group gets to see what the other looks like. Specifically what you see are the behaviours, symbols and systems of the other organisation. The DO level of the BE-DO-HAVE model. They may look like you, even talk like you. On the surface they may be in the same business, and therefore undertake the same activities. But very quickly you will notice that they are not the same as you. Of course you will have heard some information already about how the other tribe operates. Some of your members will have been involved in due diligence activities, or planning for the future merger. Others may have worked there previously in their career. Perhaps the other tribe was a past competitor or someone you met at industry functions. They might have been a customer or a supplier. You may share a parent, and be two divisions of the same group. They will have a reputation, and you will know what it is.

There is a large distinction between the observation of differences, and the formation of judgments about those differences. In one merger we worked on, one company had a strong verbal culture. Decisions were made in meetings, face-to-face, based on debate and presentations. The other had a written culture, based on extensive documentation. Decisions were made by individuals once all of the relevant information had been submitted. Both cultural systems worked. Both made mostly good decisions, and a few not so good ones. However, the judgments each made about the other were damning. 'They're so bureaucratic,' said the verbal tribe, describing their new colleagues. 'They take so long to make a decision most of the good opportunities pass them by. No wonder they're struggling in the marketplace.' 'They're cowboys,' retorted the others, 'they take insane risks and make subjective decisions.

We are fact-based and considered and this is best for business.'

Based on previous reputation, and rapidly cemented during the first few weeks of direct exposure, each tribe formed a view of the other which is primarily negative. You will notice that I have been using the word 'tribe' to describe each organisation. I have found mergers bring out tribal instincts in almost everyone involved. People's view of their own tribe is enhanced, whilst the other is seen in a negative light. They are the enemy, and we are the heroes. We the victor, they the vanquished. Or we have been taken over, the victims, but will fight to retain our true identity as the superior race. Why should this be? The merger is a threat, and therefore tends to bring out defensive feelings and behaviours. Attack is an effective form of defence. It is common to belittle those we feel threatened by, and to build up our own position. The other tribe is strange, they are different from us, and that makes them more of a threat because we don't understand them. The more defensive we become, the less clearly we see the others, and the more likely we are to describe what we see them DO in a negative light. We spend more time *below the line* blaming the others. At the same time you will find that people who were quite negative about your own organisation in the past, suddenly start to see it much more positively, and to consider it to be superior to the other one.

Many people are surprised by this irrational and emotional description of what happens during a merger. I myself found the behaviours surprising when I first started working alongside merging organisations. However they are so consistent from merger to merger, that I became convinced that we were not dealing with a rational situation, and therefore the emotions and the ego defence system had to be involved.

As a leader in a merger, your role is to help move yourself and your people past this stage as fast as possible, whilst simultaneously creating the culture you want.

There are five mind-sets that can potentially exist during a merger, and people have to go through at least the first four to reach the point where the culture becomes an asset.

1	My way is the only way	Ignorance about other organisations
2	My way is the best way	Arrogance, superiority
3	You have some good ways too	Understanding, objective observation, respect
4	Let me learn from your ways	Openness, benefits realisation
5	Let's build a new way together	New identity, best of both

My experience has been that almost EVERYONE involved starts at levels 1 or 2, even the most senior leaders whose jobs have been secured before the merger commenced. Some may only spend a few days at level 1 or 2. Others are still stuck at level 2 five years later. Many move up and down, jumping from 2 to 4 and back again as they come to terms with the new situation.

This seems to apply to all types of situations when two or more groups come together to work as one. The selection of a national football team, for example, involves bringing together players from several different cultures belonging to the local club teams where players spend most of their time. National coaches see the same attitudes as those described above, and have to undertake similar tactics as would be applied by the leader of a government department or a company in order to merge people into one culture. As an individual, you need to move through the levels as soon as you can if you are going to be a useful contributor in the merged organisation. As a cultural leader, it is your job to help others move through. Before I show you how to do this, there are a few more pieces of the jigsaw to put on the table.

Your cultural options

When two organisations merge, there are three cultural options available to you. It is important to make a conscious decision which option you are going to go with. If you don't, you will default to one or another, and may find later it was not the best option for your business strategy.

Option one: Build a new culture, incorporating the best of both cultures

Most organisations say this is the one they want, it sounds good and is what most people want to hear. It is actually the most difficult to achieve, and happens quite rarely. It almost never happens unless it is very carefully planned and implemented. It requires discipline and focus. By picking the best of both cultures, you create the opportunity to build a best practice culture, and use it as a true competitive advantage. This is what some dream of when planning an acquisition. However, the immediate challenges involved in mergers – the 'have to do's', such as extracting cost synergies, integrating technology platforms and product portfolios, implementing new structures and selecting people to fill them – tend to completely occupy the leadership teams. By the time you get through this, other cultural options will have asserted themselves.

This option is the most palatable for the 'underdog' organisation, for example the acquired organisation in an acquisition. It respects their heritage and strengths, and makes their people feel valued. They are therefore more likely to stay, and this is often key to capitalising on the value of the deal. It is the most challenging for the 'top dog' organisation, usually the acquirer, who will probably not have anticipated having to change themselves as a result of the merger, and may go in with a position of superiority.

Take this option if:

• Your strategy provides the opportunities for considerable cross-fertilisation between the two organisations. (Geographic, business integration)

- You are seriously committed to culture as a path for competitive advantage, and were before the merger occurred
- Neither culture is at best practice already
- You are prepared to work as hard at culture as at all the other urgent integration issues, from the first day of the merger
- Both organisations have very poor cultures

Option two: Use one culture as the basis for integration, and merge the other into it

This is the default position. Under most merger circumstances if no rigorous cultural plan is implemented, the dominant culture ('top dog') will gradually become the way of the whole. In the case of an acquisition, many will quickly put in place their own financial and risk-management processes, and this alone will strongly influence the other culture. Under many circumstances option two is the right one, but the key is to be straight about this to everyone concerned. The absolutely worst option is to give lip service to building a best of both culture, but in fact simply imposing that of the acquirer. That is the fastest way to lose the good people you have just acquired.

Option two is not available in joint ventures and partnerships or any circumstance where both parent organisations will be staying around. In these circumstances the on-going influence of both force the JV/partnership to navigate a path which incorporates elements of both parents.

Some organisations that acquire lots of smaller organisations use this option as standard operating procedure. It requires sharp, quick action and absolute clarity about 'how *we* do things'. Assuming the culture is a fairly attractive and effective one, and people are treated well on entry, a surprising number of acquired employees adjust and end up making a great contribution to their new organisation. It is a much easier option for the integration team, because when they are making decisions about factors which are levers for culture (remuneration, budgeting process, financial systems, office layout, leadership development, etc.) their default position will be to use that of the acquirer.

Take this option if:

- This merger is one of many for your organisation and you have, or intend to have, a formula for doing these integrations
- One culture is clearly best practice, and capitalising on this was a core reason for doing the merger (outsourcing contracts are a common example of this)
- The state of the business in one organisation is very poor, and will require extensive intervention (new management systems, importing managers from the other organisation) which will immediately impose new cultural norms
- You do not have the stomach for a major cultural intervention, and believe the rest of the integration challenges are enough to deal with. (In this case, be straight about your intentions from the start)
- You believe you can preserve the majority of the value embedded in the 'underdog' organisation if the culture is lost or changed (including the risk of losing people)

I had dinner recently with a man I have done work for over many years, who has been in charge of a number of very successful acquisitions undertaken by a global organisation, one of which was of an organisation considerably bigger than itself. These integrations have been internationally recognised as some of the most successful in recent years. Jim is a man of clear ideas. 'Our philosophy has been to identify the seven most highly paid executives and get rid of them all very early on. The acquired tribe, now leaderless, will re-align itself to its new leaders, those from our organisation.' Apparently this approach was used in the 14th and 15th centuries after the capture of towns. Jim and I have long arguments about the merits or otherwise of a more humanistic approach (he will smile when he reads this!). There is a part of me that would like it to be otherwise, but there are clearly circumstances where the directness of this approach leaves everyone knowing exactly where he or she stands, and moves the business forward quickly.

Option three: Keep both cultures separate

This option is often what the employees of both would like, but realistically is only possible under very specific circumstances. Keeping both cultures separate requires keeping both businesses separate, and this is not usually the intent of any of the merger options (acquisition, JV, partnership, integrating two divisions, etc.).

A more frequent occurrence is that pockets of the old cultures remain, and employees from both still identify with the past several years later. This results in a situation where the dominant culture is that of one organisation (whichever circumstances determined who was 'top dog') but there are little commando units running around trying to break away and thus creating silos. This leads to endless conflict and business outcomes as described in the section on the One-Team Culture in Chapter 5.

Option three is one which you would want to choose, if you want to satisfy employees who don't want to be a part of the new organisation. If you do choose it, it is the easiest, because you don't have to do all of the cultural integration work, and all employees get to keep the cultures they are used to. Your planning work needs to focus on keeping them separate, and not allowing one culture to gradually take over. Each organisation might then choose to undertake culture development work in its own right.

It is possible to train two different cultures from one organisation to learn to work together in, for example, a supplier/customer style relationship. This happens all the time, of course, between large suppliers (such as consulting firms) and their customers. It is a different type of relationship to a merger, and works best if both parties understand and respect each other.

Take this option if:

- You have a holding company structure and are making investments in separate businesses, the identity of the whole is not a strong brand in the minds of employees and customers, and you are happy for it to stay that way

- The power and authority lie in your business unit leaders, and you do not operate the top team as a real team, but more of a working group
- You have very few whole organisation policies, systems and procedures that will force the cultures to become similar
- Your two organisations are separate – geographically and/or in their business processes. If there is business relationship (such as supplier/customer) and the engagement principles between them are unambiguous
- You do not intend to move a lot of people around from one organisation to the other

Choosing your option

It is usually best to choose your option very early in the merger process, perhaps even before the final decision to proceed has occurred. This ensures that all decisions made, and communications put out to staff, will facilitate this cultural outcome. When this does not occur, you are in a process of trying to undo the negative influence of decisions and communications later found to be not aligned.

The CEO of an acquiring organisation wanted to show support for the employees of the newly acquired entity. Before the deal was done he assured the leadership team their culture would be valued and preserved. On merger day he stood and communicated the same message to large groups of employees. But he had not worked through what this would actually mean. He had a large corporate head office, and many procedures, policies and systems he had no intention of permitting the acquired organisation to circumvent. He did not tell the owners of those systems to tread carefully with regard to imposing them on the acquired entity. By day two, the gloss was coming off the deal in the eyes of the acquired people. There followed years of frustration as they saw what they valued, and felt they had been promised, gradually erode. Many left, taking with them the customer good-will. Much of the value disappeared. I spoke to many of these leaders one or two years after the acquisition. They told me it was almost impossible to recover from the promises made on that first day.

In another case, the HR director realised a few months in that there was real value in both cultures, and a best of both culture plan would provide an exceptional outcome for customers and staff. However, by the time this was decided, the top two levels of management positions had been filled. People from one organisation dominated these appointments, and everyone believed this culture would take over. The decisions and mind-set of this dominant group became much harder to shift than it would have been if the original selections had been made with the intent to merge the cultures firmly in mind.

CONSIDERING CULTURE AS A COMPONENT OF THE DUE DILIGENCE

Rigorous assessment of the cultural risks and opportunities often does not take place during the period when one or both organisations are doing their business case for an acquisition, merger, joint venture or outsourcing deal. I often hear the management teams and M&A teams talking culture, but not with the rigour applied to other business risks. People with cultural expertise often do not sit on the M&A team, and HR people, who may not have specialist culture know-how, are seconded in to deal with issues of remuneration and retention plans. From the outside, you may have a perception of the organisation's culture, but this may be based more on hearsay than on rigorous analysis.

It is possible to undertake cultural diagnostic on an organisation from the outside, though obviously more difficult if you do not have full access. Such an assessment is undertaken considering the elements of behaviour, symbols and systems that are available or visible, asking the question 'What are the messages this organisation will be receiving about the behaviour that is expected?'

You can also look at your own organisation in relation to its ability to manage a merger well from the cultural perspective. If you are intending to adopt option one, the best of both approach, one capability makes all the difference: the willingness to learn from others, sometimes displayed as curiosity, humility and respect. Leaders who display what Jim Collins calls Level 5 leaders in his book *Good to Great* have an instinctive ability to deal well with mergers. They are open to embracing the best of what they find in their new partner, to respecting difference and to changing and learning themselves. Level 4 leaders, who Collins describes as charismatic and egocentric, are less likely to display these characteristics.

Thus I have found an interesting parallel between a culture which has embraced diversity (of gender, nationality or race) and one which can embrace the different ways of a new partner, and use them for business advantage. The mind-sets are similar. Not 'my way is the best way' (Level 2 of the mind-sets on page 330) but 'you have a good way too' (Level 3) and 'let me learn from your way' (Level 4).

From this base you can look at the strengths of your culture and the strengths of the other, and consider the opportunities and challenges that a merger will produce. This analysis may sometimes cause you to reconsider whether doing the deal is a wise strategy. It will certainly prepare you for what you must do after it has occurred, and enable you to start planning your culture strategy from day one.

The different types of mergers

Every merger is unique. When working your way through your unique set of circumstances, and the cultural implications of these, consider the following questions. Your answer to each has a bearing on how you tackle the cultural issues:

- Who is the acquirer? Who is the biggest?
- Are the groups geographically separate?
- What cultural implications are contained in the structure of the deal?
- What are the business drivers of the merger?

- What relationship will the business strategy require that each organisation has to the other?
- What is the required speed of integration?
- Is the merger hostile or friendly? Are both groups keen? Who exactly was involved in the decision to go ahead?
- Which organisation will the CEO and other key appointments be from?
- What disciplines will the acquirer choose to impose from day one?
- To what extent are both cultures already homogenous versus diversified?
- How engaged / on board are the key players on day one?
- To what extent are all or parts of one organisation a mirror of the other?
- Are the synergies primarily costs or revenue?

This list is by no means exhaustive, but is a good starting point.

VARIATIONS ON THE MERGERS AND ACQUISITIONS THEME

So many of the challenges you will face apply equally to mergers, acquisitions, joint ventures, outsourcing and bringing together two internal divisions. But there are some things to be aware of when you are planning.

1. Acquisition by one large organisation of a smaller one

- The risk of swallowing the culture of the acquired organisation when it in fact contained the essence of the value acquired
- The risk of losing best people in the acquired organisation because both sides are not given support to work through the transition
- Allowing the smaller organisation room to breathe whilst still ensuring core management disciplines are met from the start

2. Merger of two organisations or groups of equal size

- Putting particular emphasis on building a new identity which is neither one nor the other
- Not allowing one culture to dominate unless you specifically decide this is the best strategy
- Being prepared to give equal weight to both in key decisions associated with cultural levels, such as management appointments, even if favouring one seems the best option for the short-term

3. Joint ventures

- Building a JV identity when staff still have ties back to their old parent company
- The impact of keeping both partners happy when they have different cultures and therefore different expectations regarding policies, performance, reporting, etc.
- The confusing messages received from staff being managed by leaders from first one and then the other JV partner

4. Outsourcing deals

- Helping outsourced staff to identify with their new employer when their relationships and often physical location is with their old one
- Building the right culture for the outsource company as a whole, when you/staff are acquired in large clumps from each new outsourcing contract
- Ensuring the outsource company's culture really is one that will deliver the synergies promised to the customer

5. Bringing together internal units through a restructure

- Focussing particularly on behaviours and symbols, since many systems will already be shared
- Distinguishing between groups which genuinely need to think and act as one, and those who simply share the convenience of reporting through to one person

- Managing the competing demands of a matrix-type structure where people belong to more than one team (for example a global technology group within a country-based organisational framework)

PUTTING IN PLACE THE CULTURE DEVELOPMENT PLAN

The Culture Development Plan of a merged organisation combines ingredients covered elsewhere in this book with those required for the special circumstances of a merger. It contains streams of work which are not entirely sequential, but rather will run alongside each other in a way which only you can determine. Its timing will depend on the timing of the rest of the integration. However, my advice is, start early!

Stream 1 Choose the model you want
- Option one, best of both
- Option two, one dominates
- Option three, keep the two separate

To do this you will need to:

- Look at the business strategy
- Review the rationale for the merger and where the value will lie
- Understand both cultures
- Consider the appetite for culture amongst the key leaders who will need to drive it (including a good look in the mirror)

Stream 2 Define the culture you want
Use the processes described in Chapter 4 to define values and behaviours for your intended culture. This is particularly important for option one, where you must define what 'best of both' actually means in your case.

If you are choosing option two, define the culture you want to dominate, in terms that the other organisation will understand. In particular, describe what will be different, what will be expected of them in terms of behaviour, values and mind-sets, and how to comply with the core business systems.

Stream 3 Help individuals move down the mind-set levels as far as is required by the option you have chosen

There are many interventions which will help this occur.

Objective feedback on two cultures
Use a method which removes the subjectivity and enables individuals to appreciate the strengths of each and how each works.

Grieving processes
There is a natural rhythm to moving on, and part of it requires permission to grieve and say good-bye to the past. Organise some good wakes, and respect people's need to go through this process. Encourage both groups to tell each other stories about their past.

New team-building
Accelerate the normal process you would use to build new teams. Give teams the opportunity to work together and get to understand how the other organisation thinks and behaves. Provide a new team start-up kit which covers the cultural dimension of both organisations. Pull teams together for special projects, like the integration planning.

Culture management education
Teach people what is in this book. Provide education on how to manage themselves and others in the unique dynamics of a merger – it is not something most people have to go through very often, and they need help understanding systems, symbols and behaviours.

Build identification with the new entity
The stronger people identify with the new entity, the more easily they can let go of the old. As the new starts to feel exciting, the old becomes less important. This can be achieved through new visions,

new branding, new business opportunities or problems to be tackled together, creating common enemies.

New leadership programme

Design and run a new leadership programme that defines and develops the mind-sets and behaviours. Your leaders – how they are at both the DO and the BE-level will define the culture you HAVE. Influence and develop them and you immediately build a common framework for the future.

Entry of new neutral people, and moving people around

Break up old cliques by moving people from a team dominated by one heritage, to one dominated by another. Bring in new people who have no association with either heritage organisation.

There is a point, and I suggest it comes about 6 months after the merger, where you really need all of your key leaders to be operating at the mind-set level 3, 4 or 5 (see page 330). After this it perhaps becomes time to suggest to some of them that they might be better off leaving and working somewhere else. You cannot have people holding on to past resentments when you are designing the future: they are too damaging. A simple litmus test is to listen to the language people use. I can always tell when someone is starting to make the shift when they begin using the word 'We' to describe the whole, new organisation, rather than their old one. The use of the word 'They' to describe the other group is also telling.

Monique runs a key division of her parent company. The division is made up of an acquired organisation, and a much smaller group who were part of the acquirer prior to the deal. Most of the leadership team come from the acquired organisation. About a year post-merger, they uncovered some serious deficiencies in relation to products delivered to customers several years ago which were very costly to rectify. These products had been delivered by the small unit of the acquiring organisation. It would have been easy for our client and her team to have disassociated themselves from the problem, and blame 'them'. Instead they made a decision to take complete ownership of the problem. No reference to 'them' was allowed. 'We' made the mistake, 'we' are responsible for fixing it, and 'we' will bear the performance implications (including bonuses) of the mistakes.

This position was very important both to the speed with which they acted on the problem, and on how the issue was viewed by employees from both heritage organisations. It sent strong beneficial signals about the expectations of behaviour in the new organisation. It was only possible because their mind-set shift had already occurred.

Stream 4 Select the symbols and systems

As you go through your integration planning, you will notice there are many opportunities to embed the culture you want through decisions that are being made in every stream of the integration work. Culture, of course, is not something that is created separately from the rest of the business, but rather by the decisions that are made every day in the business.

It is important that those making decisions associated with all of the symbols and systems described in Chapter 1, those who send cultural messages, understand this link. They will all need to be clear about the culture you are intending to create. One way to achieve this is to assign cultural champions to the teams making integration decisions, to act as the voice of culture. There will be other important criteria against which choices will be assessed, for example speed, complexity and cost, but it is important that the cultural voice is always heard. There will also be times when neither organisation have symbols or systems, such as the office layouts, the remuneration system or the planning process, which send the right cultural message. On these occasions you will find you have important debates about whether now is the time to design a new approach, or whether you just need to adopt one currently in use, and make a cultural compromise in the interests of time, simplicity and cost. One cannot be a cultural purist – there are always future opportunities for improvement. Your role is to ensure the right debate occurs, and that the risk of compromising culture is weighed up against other drivers – often in this environment culture is given a high priority.

Whether you need to implant cultural champions depends on the level of cultural awareness of your people. An approach with people who have reasonable cultural awareness already is to provide a crash course in culture-building, the role of symbols and systems, and the culture strategy you intend to adopt.

The selection of people is always a crucial symbol for the culture, and this is never truer than at merger time. If you define your desired culture early, you can use the selection process to build a team of leaders, from both organisations, whose values are aligned. This can provide a wonderful opportunity to lift standards. These leaders will set your new culture, and their mind-sets determine the extent to which the performance hurdles are met.

SUMMARY

The link between performance outcomes and culture is strongly highlighted during mergers. They offer the opportunity to do your best culture work, but also are the most challenging because of the pressures of the broader integration timetable. Start culture work early. If you don't have full interest, do what you can anyway. People will wake up a few months down the track and realise work has to be done. If you have done all the legwork already, you will be ready with the data and solutions when the broader leadership group is ready to listen.

Remember you are a part of this merger too, and will be going through some turmoil yourself. As always, work on your own mind-set first. The sooner you move down the mind-set levels, the more you will be able to support people from both organisations to build a winning culture together.

14

Growing Small and Medium Size Businesses

A CULTURE is created whenever a community of people come together over a period of time with shared purpose, interests and habits, and operate within a framework of rules. In larger communities, such as those found in large organisations, the culture feels as if it has a life of its own. People come into it, and find themselves being corralled into the behavioural norms of the group. The challenge for culture leaders is to grab hold of this nebulous entity, and actively manage it so that it can be developed in a way that will facilitate the achievement of strategy.

In a smaller organisation, leaders face these challenges, in addition to some others which are unique to their situation. My definition of 'small' here is one which is:

- Self-contained, and to a large degree in charge of its own destiny
- Has few enough employees for the leader to know everyone personally (normally 250 or less)

There are several business issues which are normally present in these smaller organisations which have an impact on the cultural challenges. Whilst your organisation may not contain all of these, it probably has most of them, and, as a group, they are different from the challenges being faced by larger organisations.

BUSINESS ISSUES FOR SMALLER ORGANISATIONS

As the leader of a small organisation, you are probably an expert in the technical side of the business. Whatever the business does to earn its keep, you personally probably know how to do it. If it's a sporting team, you were once a player; if it's a consultancy, you sell your own time to clients; if it's a medical practice, you are a doctor. You may well have been part of the team that started the organisation. You will tend therefore to dive in and out of doing the technical work as well as managing the business and its people. This phenomenon is described in an excellent fashion by Michael Gerber in his book *The E-Myth Revisited*. He distinguishes between working IN the business, and working ON the business. Working ON the business means managing, leading, planning, reviewing and would include culture work. Working IN the business means doing the work you were originally trained for, which is the work of the organisation: being a computer specialist, an architect, a client advisor, a doctor, etc. To grow, small business leaders need to spend more time ON the business, and less time IN it.

The founder of the business has a large influence on its whole operation

The drive, style, know-how and vision are often centred on one person, who may well have started the organisation. In slightly larger organisations, this may have spread to a small team who have known each other for a while and act as a tight knit group. In family businesses, the family members become the core. Delegation is often a problem. For the organisation to grow, this person or team needs to take a step up, move back from the day-to-day, and stop being the star. The risk you face is that the organisation will not survive if you leave – retire, get sick or want to do something different. Realising the value in the organisation, through growth or sale, will require this transition.

Because small organisations are leader-centric, these leaders can become somewhat stuck in the leadership style which created the business in the first place. I have found such people to be difficult to give feedback to. If you are a leader founder, you must read particularly carefully the section on receiving feedback in Chapter 7. It will be especially important for you to get advice from people who are outside of your small tribe. There are many excellent CEO clubs or forums, especially set up to provide objective peer support for the CEOs of small organisations. Join one.

Remember: 'For things to change first I must change.' For your organisation to grow, you will have to change your leadership style.

Rapid growth is a major business challenge

Bringing on lots of new people quickly takes tremendous effort, and creates a level of chaos. As the business grows the entrepreneurial spirit is at risk. The business needs more systems and organisation, but in the process, bureaucracy may creep in and the factors which created the success in the first place are threatened. It is at this point that you may first start to be aware of the importance of culture to your success – the risk of losing it through growth sharpens your awareness of its value. A good moment to be reading this chapter!

THE CULTURAL PRIORITIES FOR SMALLER ORGANISATIONS

Having a good culture – be it Customer-Centric, Achievement, One-Team, Innovative or People-First, or a combination of them all – is as important in smaller businesses as larger ones. The contribution to performance is the same. These are covered in Chapter 4 and what happens when they are not present in Chapter 5.

In addition to this, the following issues are common in smaller organisations:

- Through rapid growth you may lose the spirit which has made you unique in the eyes of your customers and your staff, and contributed to your success
- The strength of your own influence, as a leader/founder, may limit the organisation's ability to grow and change

The cultural contribution to the challenge of rapid growth

Let's assume that you love your organisation. It has a great spirit, great people and its culture is an asset. As a smaller organisation, you may not think of it as a culture, but having read parts of this book, you will now understand that this is in fact what you have. I have found smaller organisations tend to have less time and fewer resources for self-reflection, and therefore may be less familiar with the management-speak of the larger ones. There are advantages and disadvantages to this! Time spent on self-reflection (sometimes known as 'doing business with oneself') can make large organisations fat and costly. Certainly some of that self-absorption adds little value. However, the ability to observe oneself and then enact changes as a result is a requirement of successful growth and change. Without this ability to step back, you are too caught up in DO-ing to see the patterns and trends in what is occurring. Whilst your culture may be great, this may be due more to good luck than good planning. To ensure your success as you grow, you will have to become more aware of what you have achieved to date, in order to replicate it on a larger scale.

Whether you are the leader/founder, a partner or a member of the core team, there are ways to capture what you have and use it to help you grow, and this is your main cultural task.

Some smaller organisations work on culture and values from the start. Some do not consider them formally until they find themselves growing fast, and realise that what occurred in an intuitive manner in the earlier days, now requires more structure to be effective. Whichever situation you find yourself in, here is a guide to how to capitalise on your culture as a smaller business.

Define who you are

Smaller organisations are often happier with the culture they have than are larger ones. I have found most small business owners are proud of their culture, and consider that it is this that has been a major contributor to their success. You may feel you have a tight team, that loyalty is high, and that your staff are prepared to go beyond the call of duty to serve customers and ensure the business is successful. The 'can do' attitude is often a factor in smaller businesses. With reasonable leadership skill, it is easier to engage hearts and minds in a small business, where everyone knows each other and people feel that they are an important part of the whole.

Underneath these behaviours and approach to work, exists a set of values. It is important that you find a way to articulate these. Conduct a Cultural Diagnostic as described in Chapter 3. Ask people what they believe the organisation stands for. Put time aside, and structure activities where team members talk about what they see as valued in the organisation, and what they want to protect. Create links between these values and the business outcomes. If caring about the customer emerges as a theme, ask teams to identify when and how they believe business has been won and retained because of this value. If they know something about your competitors, get them to describe the difference between you and them.

During this process, your people may also talk about elements of the culture they are not happy with. You will certainly find that there is as much opportunity to build a better culture in a small organisation as there is in a larger one. But I have found that the values are easier to express in small organisations. They are closer to the surface, and most people will be able to articulate what your organisation stands for, and what, in terms of attitudes and behaviours, has contributed to your success. This heightened awareness and clarity comes from the smaller number of people, and the short link between the founder or leader, and all the people who play the values out every day. This produces greater consistency of message, because the sources of messages – behaviours, symbols, systems, are more concentrated.

In a *status quo* situation, this tightness of culture requires little conscious effort. It just happens. But by keeping it 'seat of the pants' you set yourself up for difficulties later on, because the whole thing is too dependent on one person. By articulating what you stand for, you enable others to take stewardship of it. The whole team can become the custodian of the values. This protects the asset as you grow, and gives it a life beyond the founder.

Explicitly link the behaviours, symbols and systems
A small company grows, and brings in a general manager to run the day-to-day operations. This manager comes from a larger organisation, and has been hired because she has the managerial disciplines required as the company grows. As she settles into the role, she introduces a performance management system, new disciplines of financial reporting, and changes the rules regarding authority to spend money. She uses an approach she has seen work successfully in her previous organisation. Unwittingly, she disrupts some of the drivers of the culture. During the next few months several scenarios may occur. The company rejects her. It becomes more and more difficult for her to be effective, and she ends up leaving, taking the management disciplines the company needed for its growth with her. Or, she introduces her new systems, but in the process kills some of the entrepreneurial spirit, which in turn causes several key people to leave the company.

Her intentions were good, her skill-set right, but her cultural savvy was weak, and the company did not set her up for success by helping her to understand the culture and how it was constructed.

To prevent this type of scenario happening to you, use the definitions you have created of your values and beliefs to provide a framework for the organisation. Build a document which shows how the values and beliefs play out in the organisation's behaviours, symbols and systems.

Here are some examples:

• Our bonus system is team-based, because we believe that no one in this organisation succeeds without everyone else's support
• We do not have a separate acquisitions group. If an individual team sees an opportunity in the market to buy something which will enhance their business, we would expect them to put up the proposal. We believe in full accountability, and this lies close to

the market, not in a head office group

- We spend big on annual conferences. They have become a ritual which reinforces that we believe in fun and valuing our people. Giving them a taste of luxury lifts their self-esteem
- Learning is our number one value. So we place very high priority on holding a meeting within a week of winning or losing a big sale, so we can lock in learning for next time

These principles and practices will not remain rigidly in place during your periods of growth. You must make the links specific between what you do and the values and beliefs that underpin this, to ensure that changes are made with a high awareness of their flow-on effects. When you change a symbol or system which has become a key plank of the culture, your people may conclude that you no longer hold the belief or value that underpinned it. You have to demonstrate that the substitute symbol or system also upholds the value. If you don't do this, and change a number of these in a short timeframe, they may well be right. Only you can calculate the flow-on business performance impact of weakening a particular value. What is the business cost of losing your reputation as being an organisation that really values its people? What will happen if people start to believe that playing as a star, rather than as a team, is the way to get ahead?

There will be many times when you will have to make changes, cut costs, and build in more processes. I am not advocating a no change situation here. In fact you need to watch very carefully for individuals who use culture as the excuse for no change. As leader, your role is to set the challenge of changing and holding true to those values and beliefs which you think are creating business benefits. By holding the line on this challenge, you force your people to find ways of doing both. These solutions always exist, but they are often not the easy option. You are seeking the 'and' solution. You will often hear people speaking in 'either/or' terms.

Introducing new people

Growth requires continually hiring new people. Over a five year time period, a successful smaller organisation can easily multiply the size of its workforce by ten, 100 or even 1000. In every organisation, the selection of new people is a strong cultural message. The type of person chosen sends messages to existing staff about the types of behaviours and mind-sets that the organisation values. Hire entrepreneurs and you are saying that you value originality of thought. Hire people who invest time in others and you are saying you value the people development. Your existing staff notice a pattern in the new hires.

Once these new hires come in, especially if they hold a leadership position, their behaviour will itself create cultural norms. Their decisions, use of time and quality of interactions send a new set of messages. Their personal value-set plays out within your organisation.

For a small and growing organisation, the selection and induction of new hires is the single most important capability you need to use your culture to business advantage. It will enable you to overcome the two threats to the future value of your business we identified earlier:

• The over-dependence on the founder
• The loss of culture as a competitive advantage

1. Have a clear description of what you want from a cultural perspective

Build a description of your values (including ideally the values hierarchy described in Chapter 1), beliefs and behaviours. You and everyone involved in hiring people need to have this picture very clearly in your mind. The more work you have done internally on culture, the easier this will be. Some people find it useful to think of individuals to role-model the values and behaviours that are important. The image of these people helps them with a yardstick to measure others.

2. Add to this description the characteristic of being willing to learn and change

If your organisation already has a leading-edge culture, you may find it difficult to find people with the skill-sets you require who also demonstrate the behaviours and values you want. If you are growing, many of the skill-sets you need are more likely to come from organisations larger than yours, and these will probably not be cultural icons. Most people have been rewarded over their whole career for displaying behaviours which are far from culturally enhancing. After all, the cultures of most organisations leave a lot to be desired, and organisational behaviour is full of politics, aggression, avoidance and all of the other human traits you are seeking to keep out of your organisation.

If you can isolate the 'willingness to learn and change' gene in your interview process, you will find people who, whilst they may have picked up habits from the past, will willingly embrace the values you have. This trait is found in people with a heightened level of awareness (see Chapter 6). Their ability to self-reflect and be aware of their own behaviour and thinking patterns places them on a continuous growth path, and if they can see the value of your cultural aspirations, they will have the capacity to change. They will be keen to join an organisation which supports a strong culture.

3. Train everyone who hires people to recognise values, beliefs, and level of awareness

The interview process and the reference-checking process need to be included here. Design questions which test these. Design values dilemmas which will show you an individual's values hierarchy. Use behavioural questioning to test whether an individual's past behaviour lines up with what they say are their values. With practice, you start to recognise an individual's values in what they say, how they describe past events and actions, what they have done with their life.

For example, in my organisation we value being *above the line* very highly. This means taking personal responsibility rather than blaming, justifying, denying, defending. We find it very useful to ask people to describe an occasion when something they were involved in failed. We listen for personal responsibility in their answers. Do they acknowledge their part in the situation; do they see the learning for next time? Or do they justify what happened, put it down to some external event, blame someone else and laugh it off?

4. Build a great induction process

During the early months, your new hires must be given every opportunity to understand your culture and what underpins it. You need to teach them what culture is and why it is adding value to your organisation – the specific links between culture and performance for you. New hires want to make a difference quickly, and if they do not see this link they may come in and change a whole lot of things to get quick performance enhancement. They may not see the importance of cultural alignment. Show them how you have built the culture, through rituals, behaviours, practices, policies. This explains why you do the things you do, and that their symbolic value is a part of your cultural heritage. Identify those elements which you feel are sacrosanct and why your beliefs and values form the core of the organisation's ethos. These may relate to how to treat employees and customers, ethics and integrity, discipline, risk, attitudes, relationships.

As you grow, this induction programme will probably become more formal. When you are very small it may consist of a series of informal discussions over lunch. You will find that teaching others what you stand for enhances its value. It is a great discipline for longer-standing employees to follow, and can be a lot of fun. Position it so that it is seen as an honour to be given the role of teaching a new employee what you stand for.

The induction process should take place over several weeks. Many organisations do this piece on the first day, which I have found is too early. On the first day people are focussed on understanding the basics of their job and the mechanics of how the place works.

ALLOWING YOUR CULTURE TO GROW

People I have met in fast growing organisations are very conscious of the risk of losing their culture as they grow. For those who have been around since the early days, this is often a real fear. On the one hand, you know that growth is what the organisation is all about and you are excited by the challenges and financial rewards growth will provide. On the other, the small organisation was fun, close and trusting. You knew you could depend on each other, and there was freedom to act and to make a difference. The very people who are attracted to working in small organisations in the first place, have a dislike of large, ponderous bureaucracies.

The motivation to build the business and keep what has been great about the culture is very strong. This is a key asset in your culture growth plan. If you are one of the 'old groups' you will be prepared to put effort into preserving what you love. However you must be vigilant that this love does not become an inappropriate attachment to the past. New people who come in may see you as a clique. Rigid, resistant to change, arrogant perhaps. Look at some of what is covered in the chapter on mergers, especially the chart on page 325. There is a very thin line between 'my way is the only way', a resistance to new ideas, and a genuine understanding of how your culture has helped create your success to date.

For new people coming in, this can be quite difficult. A small consulting organisation developed a good reputation and won increasingly large projects. As it grew, it started to hire people who had experience in managing larger, more complex pieces of work. These people brought with them management disciplines which were an essential part of such work. The old team saw them as lacking heart. They saw the processes they brought in as bureaucratic. Suddenly there were too many meetings and reports. The new people considered the original crew to be unprofessional and disorganised. At first, many of the new hires left, the organisation rejected them, made it too hard for them to perform.

This organisation needed to undertake substantial work on defining shared values and finding ways to reinterpret their culture in the context of a larger, more complex environment. The original group recognised that they had been confusing the form of their culture – the practices, habits, work style, the DO – with its substance – the values and beliefs, the BE. Practices and work style will have to change as an organisation grows. You cannot manage 500 people in the same way that you manage 20. But the values and beliefs can stay, and evolve and be enriched as new people come in.

What you DO will change. Who you choose to BE, as an organisation and as individuals, will evolve, but you do not need to lose the great values and feelings.

Understanding the difference between these two enables you to embrace the change required for growth. It is undoubtedly more difficult to hold true to shared values in a larger organisation, but it is absolutely achievable. The key is to work together on the BE-level. Your task as a leader in this type of organisation is threefold:

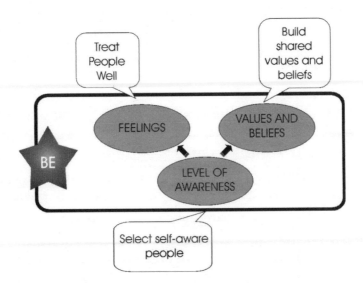

1. Build shared values and beliefs about what is important so that they will make decisions and behave in-line with your desired culture
2. Treat people well so they feel positive about being at work
3. Use level of awareness as criterion for hiring and promotion so that you have people who are self-aware and able to grow

Following these guidelines will enable you to realise the value you have created in your organisation over a sustained timeframe. You will reduce the dependence on the founder and capture the essence of what has made you strong. With this firmly embedded in your people, you can be confident that you can compete with larger players whose cultures may well be an impediment to their own performance. Culture is the hardest piece of an organisation to replicate. Your investment in ensuring you do not kill what you have through growth will pay dividends through this cultural advantage.

15

One Organisation's Journey

THIS book has been designed to show you how to build a culture for success. Every culture journey is unique, and in this book I have sought to provide you with a map to show you the choices you will need to make as you plan your own approach. I have worked alongside so many organisations as they move through this, and I am convinced now that there is no one right way to do it. As a leader, you run grave risks if you just follow a course of action which you have been told another organisation adopted successfully. You know now that this would be operating at the DO-level, without realigning yourself at the BE-level. Now that you understand this, I am going to devote this chapter to one organisation's journey. Not so that you will go out and copy what they have done, but rather to show you how all of this can actually come together to form an implemented plan of action which delivers substantial financial results.

Reading about other people's experiences doesn't automatically translate into an appropriate path for you, and the reason for this became very obvious to me as I interviewed people for this book.

> *At the end, looking back, your path looks like a straight line*
>
> *On the path, looking forward, you can hardly see more than one step ahead*

There is a lot of trial and error in developing the right culture. Humans are such complex beings, and when they come together as a community this complexity multiplies exponentially. In working with culture you are seeking to influence the workings of a group of minds, so that they behave in a different way and thus deliver a different outcome. However sophisticated your culture plan, you will never touch all of the messages that an individual receives about how to behave. But if you keep working at it, and consistently drive a few key messages, you will find the power of the group eventually starts working in your favour.

This is the moment when you can finally see the benefits of all the effort you have put in. When this occurs, you can look back and see how all the pieces of the culture plan that you put in place came together to produce a consistent and irresistible push which caused the change you wanted.

But at the time, on a day-to-day basis, as you work to influence your culture and the mind-sets and behaviours of your people, you will often wonder whether what you are doing is having any effect at all. You participate in one meeting where it really feels like habits are changing, and then hear about yet another example where someone has withheld information from a colleague in order to further their own cause. You need considerable stamina for this journey. It is actually the stamina, rather than the precise activities you undertake, that will ensure your success.

With that in mind, let me tell you the story of Lion Nathan. Lion is an organisation with which we have been associated for seven years. I observed and contributed to the organisation's cultural journey. And the change to their culture is spectacular. The performance benefits delivered undisputed. The experience, looking back now, has a clear step-by-step process. At the time, it did not feel like that. But there were a number of initiatives they undertook which turned out to be the ones that really made the difference. They took a stand on some issues that were crucial. Above all, they hung in there and kept at it. This is how they did it.

LION NATHAN

Lion is a drinks company with brewing, wine and spirits divisions across Australia, New Zealand and China. At the time of writing, 2004, they had a market capitalisation of around A$3.4 billion, revenue of A$1.8 billion, profits of A$180m and 5000 employees. In the seven years since they started their work on culture, their TSR has increased by 180 per cent (15.8 per cent annualised) compared to a TSR of 99.8 per cent (10.1 per cent annualised) for the ASX200 Index, which contains the top companies on the Australian stock exchange. TSR, Total Shareholder Return, is sum of the share price appreciation plus dividends, and generally considered a good measure of performance over a sustained period of time. In this period they have added A$42.2 billion to their market capitalisation. The growth in their performance closely parallels their improvement in culture.

I have worked with Lion Nathan since 1996 when the company started on this path, and our organisation introduced their staff to the mind-sets, methodologies and tools which started them on their way. As they built on those foundations, we have been brought back in to play other roles, or top up their learning. When I interviewed people for this chapter, I saw for the first time the whole picture of what they have done, and what have been the critical elements of their success. It was also apparent that this journey never ends – they have plans for the next stage which are as ambitious as those they developed in 1996.

CRITICAL TO LION NATHAN'S SUCCESS

I interviewed many people from Lion for this chapter. I have walked alongside the cultural journeys of many organisations. There are few who have moved so far, so fast. I looked for the factors that made the difference. What was it about this approach that gave it the edge on so many of the others? Four factors made the difference in Lion's journey:

- Consistency
- Focus on leadership behaviour
- Link with the strategy and product
- A mind-set of perpetual learning

1. Consistency

Consistency of cultural leadership. Two people led the drive for a great culture: Gordon Cairns the CEO and Bob Barbour the HR director. Both are very tenacious (some might even say stubborn!) and they simply did not give up. Culture was never bumped off the priority list, despite many other pressures. Many other key players changed, but the two key ones for culture – CEO and HR – remained the same during the crucial period of culture establishment.

Consistency of values. The values which drove the culture were defined at the start, two more have been added over time, but the core ones never changed. The team deepened their understanding of what each value meant, and the rationale to add one was thoroughly debated and understood. Over time, they became less accommodating of non-alignment to these values, and thus they gained potency.

Consistency of approach. There has only ever been one cultural journey, the Lion Nathan Way. Every part of the business was required to participate and the core levers for culture, such as leadership development, and remuneration were done one way for the whole. Each phase built on the one before. At no time did employees sense that a previous approach had just been abandoned – there was no flavour of the month. Ownership of this approach was always internal – external consultants were never allowed to take things off in a different direction. Lion dedicated a Learning & Development team to steer the journey.

Consistency of language. Key words which describe the Lion culture were not negotiable. Programmes which used other language were not allowed. Very tight control was kept over external influences such as consultants and new hires when it came to language.

Consistency of tools. Tools were selected to measure culture and behaviour, to evaluate people and define competencies. The company has stuck with these tools, so there has been no opportunity to avoid honest data on personal and organisational performance by changing the metrics. Leaders realised that this is not going to go away, and they had better work out what to do to improve their scores if they want to remain in the company.

Consistency of partners. Lion has developed long-term partnerships with suppliers of services that are cultural levers – consultants, trainers, recruitment and employee research. They have trained us in their expectations, and asked us to work with them to develop new services to meet emerging requirements. This has enabled them to be confident that external providers will reinforce their messages.

Consistency delivers a multiplier effect. Each part of the message is reinforced by another part, and the message just doesn't let up. An 80 per cent message (or tool, or word, or programme) delivered consistently over time will build the culture you want better than a series of 99 per cent perfect ones, changed consistently to get that last per cent of perfection. This does not exclude learning and continuous improvement. As you will see there has been lots of that at Lion. But this has taken place within a consistent framework of intent and of message.

2. Focus on leadership behaviour

Within behaviour, symbols, systems, behaviour has always been seen as the most important, and leadership behaviour above all else.

Standards set. Expectations of leaders were established early, and were linked to the desired culture. For the first few years, the cultural effort focussed almost entirely on lifting the standards of leadership.

Measurement. Leaders' behaviour was measured annually using the same tool over the seven years. The mirror was put up again and again, and leaders were expected to improve the image reflected back at them.

Competencies. Nine leadership competencies were developed for how leaders at Lion are expected to behave. One more was added over time as thinking evolved (Personal Awareness). The process for developing these was exhaustive and the top team were intimately involved in building them. This team came to know deeply what they were looking for, and to learn how to recognise it in others.

Remuneration. Three years into the journey, leaders were being evaluated and rewarded on a model of What + How. Results + Behaviour. The distribution of percentages within this matrix has evolved over time. At the time of writing, exceptional results with poor behaviour are rewarded less generously than acceptable results and exceptional behaviour. In fact exceptional results with poor behaviour have recently become not acceptable at all.

Leadership development programme. To date, three programmes have been developed and run through the management population. Starting from the top, each year another level was put through a programme, so there was a cascading effect. As more junior groups started the first programme, senior leaders were progressing to programme two. The content of the programme did not change substantially from level to level.

Mind-sets. All workers recognised that the way people think and feel (the BE-level) is the key to changing behaviour. Leaders and programme designers learnt how to impact this level.

Recruitment. The HR team recognised that new people can be a huge cultural risk, but also a great opportunity. Assessing new people against the leadership competencies and values is a crucial decision criterion. A lot of work has been done on this issue, yet still mistakes are made. But the team feels confident that they have honed their skill in this area, and that this prepared them to advise the Board on the ultimate new hire, a new CEO. In March

2004, Lion announced their new CEO in preparation for Gordon's retirement.

3. Link with strategy and product

There is a consistent logic and alignment between all of the pieces of the Lion picture.

Purpose. The Lion Nathan purpose is 'to make our world a more sociable place'. This links to their need to educate people in the sensible use of alcohol, and to reposition beer as a drink for both sexes, a social and fun experience in moderation.

Values. 'Sociability' and 'helping others' were added as values part way through this process, when it was realised that relationships with others were key to the industry, to their customer strategy and to their cost-effectiveness. Social skills are key criteria for hiring, at the end of interviews for key positions candidates are taken out to dinner to test this. The first and lasting impression of the company is that it is a social place run by a bunch of sociable people. Social is a natural fit for the company – it fits their product, their strategy and their people. The culture builds on a natural trait.

Performance drive. The business needed a grinding drive for performance to succeed – there were no easy wins. Developing an Achievement Culture was recognised as an opportunity for real competitive differentiation in a market where such positions are hard to find. Achievement was always the driver, and was a natural fit with CEO Gordon Cairn's style. He has always had a reputation for driving performance relentlessly. The original work on culture sprung from an analysis of the business which concluded that internal efficiency would only be achieved through substantial changes to behaviour and mind-set.

Tiered approach. To date, the journey has had three phases: first, change workshops focussed on building one business (the One-Team approach from Chapter 4), next leadership for growth, then Achievement. Now the HR team are working on the next phase, Customer-Centricity, even as the third phase is rolling out. Each responded to the business requirement at the time, and each built on the previous stage. The business drivers in each instance created the burning platform. Leaders' thinking expanded over time.

4. A mind-set of perpetual learning

I am often asked what I believe to be the key mind-set for succeeding in achieving culture goals. I have concluded it is the curiosity and openness that leads to perpetual learning. The Lion leaders of this cultural journey have this in spades.

Desire to learn about self. These key leaders all had, or developed early on, a passion for personal growth that went beyond just a business imperative. The journey itself became a part of their personal purpose. They moved past the defensiveness associated with the discomfort. They knew that 'for things to change first I must change'

Above the line. The personal responsibility model on page 198 we introduced to Lion very early. They took it deeply to heart. That mind-set is the pre-requisite to learning because it allowed them to see their part in any situation, and correct it for next time.

Desire to learn from best practice. The turning point was a trip to visit best practice companies in the US. The 20 senior leaders went together for two weeks. The HR team scoured the world for the best models and the best input to bring into their learning. The team are very open about the sources of their influence, but they always remain at the centre of the hub; everything is repackaged to fit their messages.

Continuous journey. Lion leaders do not express a belief that they are anywhere close to having arrived at the end of their cultural work. Every year they map out the next stage. This year they will focus on the brewery technicians, and on building a much more external focus amongst leaders, which they call market connectivity.

These are the factors that made a difference at Lion. Individual elements of these exist in the work of most organisations tackling culture, but it is rare to see them all packaged together and stuck to over a seven year period. If your organisation's cultural work is already underway, compare it to the one described here. This may help you to strengthen areas where you are weak.

THE JOURNEY ITSELF

Looking back, you may have the impression the journey is a straight line. It doesn't feel that way when you're at the beginning. I want to describe the Lion experience because I think it will encourage you. From where you sit right now it may feel that you are not making much progress. As you will see, just taking one step and then another, coupled with the attributes I have just described, will get you there.

First stage 1996–97 – Out of a business need

The Lion team pinpoint 1996 as their starting point. At this time, the company had been through a number of strategic moves, led by its founder Douglas Myers. Lion Nathan, which commenced as a New Zealand brewer, had grown to become a drinks company with large operations in Australia and a small foothold in China.

Its culture was aggressive – the recently departed COO had seen too much complacency and deliberately shaken things up with his controversial style and tendency to fire people on the spot. It was a take-no-prisoners, ready, fire, aim place, where you certainly knew you were alive, but there was little sense of direction. Douglas Myers describes it like this: 'When Gordon Cairns came in the major strategic moves had been made, we'd changed industries, merged with others to get big enough to do something significant in Australia without being muscled out. The next step was about grinding out the performance.'

Prior to Gordon's appointment as CEO, The Lion performance team was set up as an elite team to review the whole business and work out to how to deliver the required performance short, medium and long term. The team, headed up by Jim O'Mahony and supported by global consulting firm McKinsey & Co., reviewed brands, channel strategy and best-cost operations. It became clear

to Jim and Joe McCollum, the then HR director, that the answers
lay in a complete transformation of how they did business, and that
this would involve a change in how people operated.

My organisation was brought in to help this process, and it was
at this point that we first met the Lion Nathan team. Our first step
was a workshop with the top team at which they defined values for
the company, as well as holding the mirror up to their own
behaviour.

The three values:

- Act with integrity
- Face reality
- Passion for the business

still stand today.

We helped Lion Nathan design and run a series of Change
Workshops, part of the Lion Nathan way for change. This
leadership programme introduced the company to the mind-sets
and behaviours leaders would need to take this change forward.
The programme included:

- Personal responsibility (above and below the line)
- For things to change first I must change
- A 360-degree leadership feedback tool which distinguishes
  between constructive and defensive styles of behaviour

In addition to change leadership, the programme emphasised that
Lion was moving to being One-Team, not a number of small
fiefdoms centred on local brands and breweries, the result of the
previous acquisition strategy. The Lion performance team work
had demonstrated that the big opportunities for enhanced
performance lay in economies of scale, sharing best practice, and
doing some activities once for the whole company. The intent
(which has been realised) was to achieve a 5 per cent efficiency gain
every year, which with the predicted revenue growth meant that

costs would have to stay flat at a minimum. The key message was: 'The sum of the parts is greater than the whole.' The business rationale for Lion was similar to that described under One-Team in Chapter 4, and this was their challenge.

Kate Peterson was working in the Queensland operation in Australia at the time: 'We were not taking learnings from one business and applying them in others, we never even told others, we were always reinventing, it was our business, not the dreaded Lion Nathan. Every business had their own infrastructure, own reporting mechanisms, own terms and conditions.

'When Lion Nathan entered the Australian market, it decided not to build brand equity in the Lion Nathan name because of the strength of the local beer brands. The challenge was how to create identification with Lion Nathan as an employer, and a willingness to look at the world through eyes which saw the benefits for the whole. When this process started, people didn't talk about Lion, they resented being owned by a New Zealand company with a head office in Sydney.'

The Lion Nathan performance team was hugely symbolic. 'Here was this team, resourced by top employees [important symbol], special, bright, talented and arriving in the regions with ideas and workshops and folders headed up 'Lion Nathan Way for Change'. For the first time we became conscious that the same thing was happening across the whole business.' Attendance was mandated across the company – otherwise it would not have happened. Resources were built at head office to look at the business as a whole.

Key points from the first stage
- Driver for change was totally business needs driven, strategy provided direction for cultural direction and never seen as separate
- Top team were bought in from the start, although perhaps did not quite understand the nature of the journey to which they were signing up
- Key cultural interventions were mandatory, not voluntary

- First building blocks (values, readership feedback tool, language) were established and still used today
- Culture was not used at all as a term at this point, even the HR team did not have a clear view of where they were heading

Second stage 1998–2000 – Leadership

The next stage of the Lion journey was marked by the elevation of Gordon to CEO, and his elevation of Bob Barbour as his HR director. Gordon continued to drive performance, accelerating the push to become one business and extracting the value from this opportunity. Bob took hold of the cultural agenda, and named it as such.

In 1998, culture was not a word widely used in the business community. Some organisations had started this type of work, but to be an expert on culture was not something a CEO expected of his or her HR director. Bob had known that our organisation specialised in culture, and he knew there was a sister tool to the leadership one they had been using, one which measured culture. What convinced him to tackle culture was what he saw happening with the leaders who had attended the change workshops.

Nicolette Wood had come into the HR team at that time: 'People wobbled after the change workshops. They found the real world cold, and worried that they would not survive if they tried to adopt the behaviours they had been taught. In the HR team we started to ask the question, "What environment would we need to create to help people make that change?"' From there, they moved to, 'How do leaders need to be, to help people change?' Their answer was, 'Caring'. People would not change if they felt threatened, bullied or ignored. Whilst these aggressive traits might have worked for the business in the past, they would not facilitate change, and change was what the business strategy required. This was a major insight in a business with a seriously aggressive, gung-ho and macho culture.

The process to have this insight shared by the business, and embedded as a core belief that would drive decision-making and behaviour, was a monumental one. This stage of Lion's journey is a wonderful example of how culture change can be driven by a committed HR team, rather than by the CEO or a business leader. Bob and his team got hold of this idea and just did not let go of it.

They measured their culture on a large scale for the first time, and have done so every two years since. They built leadership competencies based on the Lominger Competency model, assessed everyone against these, lined-up their recruitment processes, and introduced a Competencies + Results model for performance evaluation and remuneration. (Later renamed What x How.) (The team started with What + How, but changed it to What x How when they realised that 10 x 0 = zero, and this was the message they wanted to convey). Each one of these steps can be described within one sentence but took significant amounts of time and effort to achieve.

The leadership competencies they selected, following three workshops where the top team debated and agreed what leadership was, remain today.

Lead courageously

Champion change

Partner others

Coach and develop others

Achieve results

Provide vision and direction

Develop solutions

Foster teamwork

Functional/technical excellence

Personal awareness

Each was fleshed out with a more detailed description.

They prepared presentations and continually spoke about what they were doing and why. They ran workshops to deepen everyone's understanding of the values. They started to understand, and to teach, what values really were and how they drive every element of behaviour once they become deeply embedded. They encouraged arguments about how values should best be applied to the many business challenges managers were facing.

They designed a leadership programme, being intimately involved in the design, and running two different pilots of content which were rejected. One because it did not exactly deliver the message they wanted, the second because it was 'old style' training which did not shift people at the BE-level of values, feelings and level of awareness. The final programme covered:

- Lion's leadership model (competencies + results)
- 360° leadership feedback tool
- Sense of purpose (core purpose, vision and values)
- Lion Nathan competencies (introduction, setting standard)
- Personal awareness

'Helping others' was added as a fourth value, reflecting the increasing understanding that caring for others was a key attribute the company wanted. Gordon and his team articulated a core purpose for Lion at this time: 'To make our world a more sociable place.'

Within this environment, probably the most significant achievement of this period was the way in which Gordon faced what this change meant to him personally. He embraced his own personal development needs, and thus was able to face the organisation with integrity, with the most powerful message of all: 'I know how my behaviour is holding this organisation back, and I intend to change, just as I am asking you to. I want your feedback to help me to this. Help me walk the talk.'

Gordon always believed in leadership, but his style up until this point had been fairly aggressive. Charismatic and persuasive, but defensive and arrogant too. He had a long-standing reputation for driving performance hard, and still does. So Gordon's transformation, visible to all who knew him, and measured (and published) through his changes to his leadership feedback scores, was a wonderful role-model for everyone.

The relationship between Gordon and HR director Bob Barbour, and the coaching role Bob played with Gordon, was key to Lion's cultural success. Their relationship had been stormy in the past – in fact a particular incident in 1995 resulted in a very poor relationship between the two. This could have easily led to Bob's departure from the business when Gordon became leader of the Australian beer business in 1996. But instead they worked through their differences and built tremendous trust in each other. Jim O'Mahony, who led the original Lion Nathan performance team and remains close to both men although he has since left the company, saw this moment as significant in the future power of their cultural alliance: 'The partnership was forged on forgiveness and compassion on both sides. That they were able to move through what had been a huge rift and form such a good working relationship sent powerful signals to all of the senior players who had known what had occurred.' This was not the traditional Lion Nathan style.

Bob himself went through a deep internal transformation when he saw his early 360° feedback results. He is a deep thinker, and took himself away on holiday to think through the impact he wanted to make having been hit between the eyes, through the Lion Nathan way for change, about the potential of this work to impact performance. The result was a document called 'Bob Barbour: The Next 90 Days', which pulled together a potential culture process, including Bob's own personal behavioural challenges, in a way that would be compelling to the top team.

The hook for Gordon was the performance one. All of Bob's thinking and presentations demonstrate over and over again the opportunity this work offered to deliver on Lion's aspirations. Bob's style is low key but utterly determined. He just kept talking with Gordon, giving him feedback at the end of each meeting, and chewing things over at the end of the day over a beer. As Gordon became more confident of the power of the work, he took on a coach, and his personal style gradually changed.

Quarterly sessions with the top 100 were conducted, some of which I had the pleasure of facilitating, where Gordon spoke about their values and what they meant, and the team was encouraged to challenge his interpretation and refine the gap between walk and talk for everyone. The link to performance was very explicit – each session updated on business performance and strategy and then discussed the contribution each person could make.

Bob's HR team was particularly good at learning. Members of the team were assigned the task of scouring the world for the best thinking on this topic, and key ideas and models that fitted were introduced into the mix.

Dave Ulrich's work on the role of the HR team had a big influence, and was used to recast the HR team's focus towards business partnership. Collins and Porras' book *Built to Last* contributed the 'Genius of the "And"' which Lion applied to thinking about what *and* how, as well as the importance of vision *and* values.

'To make our world a more sociable place' was crystallised as the purpose, and 'Be sociable' was added as the fifth value. 'Our intent to edge the world we touch towards being a more sociable place has guided our actions in a whole range of areas,' Gordon told me when I interviewed him for this book. 'It has shaped how we work, how we treat women and the environment and our policy towards the arts.' As a part of Lion Nathan's sponsorship of the Sydney Opera Company, 300–400 employees have had the opportunity to go to the opera for the first time. For many brewery technicians and their partners, this has opened an appreciation of the beauty and fun of the arts which they had not previously encountered. 'The sociable piece shaped both our culture and our role in society, as well as reflecting how we want people to enjoy our product. Our common characteristic has been that we are sociable people, providing a sociable product.'

Daniel Goldman's work on emotional intelligence brought in the emotional dimension, as well as the importance of self-awareness and social skills. Interestingly Lion's use of this is an important example of consistency of language. Sean Bowman, head of HR for Australia and an important driver for the later years of the cultural journey, explained: 'We use the word "engagement". We don't use "emotional intelligence". Any programme that someone in the business brings in from outside and wants to run, we vet for language. If people cannot tailor their programme so it reflects this language, we do not allow it to be used. Consistency is more important than one part of the business meeting a need by introducing an emotional intelligence programme.'

At the end of 1999, when all senior leaders had completed the leadership programme, the leadership competencies were hardwired into the pay systems. This was a breakthrough moment. From this point, a stable senior management team stayed together for the next 2–3 years who were completely aligned to what Lion was trying to achieve, and it was during this next period that the real leap in performance benefits and cultural results was seen.

Key points from the Second Stage
- CEO clearly positioned himself as needing to participate in a personal change journey – active leadership of process and walking the talk
- Leaders knew what was expected of them, and these competencies were linked to financial reward
- Culture was linked to strategy and product through 'sociable' theme

Third stage 2001–03 – Achievement Culture
A feature of Lion's journey has been the waves of thinking, each one giving the process a new focus, but always building on the previous one so it is seen by the business as a continuous process. These waves reflect the learning that occurred along the way, and the increased confidence that culture could be targeted to help every aspect of Lion's performance challenges.

The trigger for the next breakthrough lay in the work of David McClelland on the achievement motivation. We had been doing a lot of development work based on his research, which identified the characteristics of people whose primary drive is to experience the buzz of achieving, and introduced Lion to our thinking.

The challenge in a large organisation is how to create a culture that fulfils the achievement need that most employees have, in a way which aligns with organisational outcomes and supersedes many of the other human drives which cause such chaos. Examples include to look good and to beat other people. These traits were very strong at Lion, which has roots in a duopoly and thus has highly competitive environment. Beating CUB, the competitor in Australia, was the name of the game. A number of business decisions had been made which only made sense if your goal was to beat them above everything else. Some of these had not been successful. The company had been late into the game regarding the shift of drinking patterns from beer to other alcoholic beverages, because they saw their mission as beating a beer competitor. The subtle, but crucial shift from competitiveness (the need to win) to achievement (the need to succeed) was at the core of the next phase, and it required significant cultural development.

For an organisation that prided itself on its performance orien-tation, it was a confronting exercise to acknowledge that it did not yet have an Achievement Culture. There was still room to hide if you looked good and played the game. The HR team swung into gear again.

A US tour of best practice companies was organised for Lion by the consulting firm Accenture. The top 20 people in the business travelled together for two weeks, visiting 17 companies and sitting together at night in hotel rooms drinking beer debriefing their experiences, and working out what they wanted to apply and how. One of the companies they visited was Enron, and the team realised how far they had come when they saw elements of that culture which absolutely did not align with the Lion values. Through their work to date they learnt to see values in action by watching behaviour, symbols and systems, and they could smell things they did not want in the other companies, particularly an internally competitive culture.

The US tour was a very important trigger for the next phase. The symbolism of taking the top 20 people out of the business for two weeks for the purpose of learning was unparalleled. As a team-building exercise it was outstanding – by debating each evening what they had seen and what it meant, the team was aligning themselves at the BE-level – they were developing shared beliefs and values about what was important. This alignment influenced so much of their future decision-making, and made them appear as one coherent team singing from the same hymn sheet to the business on their return. To sing from the same hymn sheet, as the expression goes, one has to have all studied the same sheet, and this is what the trip allowed the team to do.

On their return they set to work. The next iteration of leadership development, the achievement programme, was designed to teach achievement mind-sets and skills, and was rolled through the senior ranks as the middle and junior managers completed the leadership programme from the previous stage.

The goal-setting process became more participative, with much higher ownership of goals being achieved up front, resulting in more rigour about what the goals should be, and greater risk-anticipation and contingency-planning.

The What + How assessment of people was refined so that greater weighting was given to the How. It was no longer OK just to deliver the What, no matter how brilliant a 'What' it was.

A lot of work was done at systems level, introducing discipline into the target-setting processes, and understanding how to cause behaviour change through more rigorous measurement. For example, a measured call cycle was introduced for sales people to ensure they were four-and-a-half days a week on the road. There was a lot of push back, but the team forced it through. As a result appointments were booked rigorously with customers, whereas previously, sales people had been more casual in their approach to turning up at customers' premises. The feedback from customers has been very favourable – knowing for certain the sales person will be there at a fixed time has meant that the most senior person at the hotel will appear, whereas previously Lion sales reps did not often meet this individual. The team believes there is more potential to unlock value here.

The Board became more closely involved with the culture work, and standards of behaviour were agreed. The Board considered how they could best be sure their practices line-up with the principles of an Achievement Culture. They recognise their impact on the organisation, and the value of Lion's culture. One of the key accountabilities of the Board, defined in their charter, is 'to ensure a high integrity Achievement Culture is developed and maintained in the company'. The Board is about to apply the leadership feedback tool used in the company to each of the directors.

Realising the importance of recruitment in sustaining a culture which was starting to get real traction, Lion formed a partnership with executive search firm Egon Zender, and together they worked to really understand how they could improve the recruitment process so that they could find people who fitted the values, mindsets, behaviours and leadership competencies Lion had now established. As the journey progressed, this task became more difficult because the organisations from which their recruitment pool was drawn, especially at senior levels, did not have cultures which encouraged these behaviours. Those who had the technical skills Lion wanted, had spent a career being rewarded for a different approach to leadership. They had often been successful despite their leadership style, not because of it. It became important to be able to assess potential to change to the new expectations, as much as having demonstrated them already.

The company began to take a much stronger stand for what it believed in and what it expected from its people. Because results were now coming through on the culture measurement tool, they had more confidence to go public with what they had achieved. A

PR campaign placed a number of articles in the press about the Lion's focus on culture, and Gordon and Bob started carefully choosing speaking engagements. During this period they were one of three organisations to appear every year in the top ten of the Best Employer Survey carried out by Hewitt & Associates, well-recognised in Australia, which used an independent evaluation committee to assess companies. Finally, the market had caught up. Having a great culture not only delivered performance outcomes, but was a well-known and very important factor in the employ-ment market.

Bob Barbour cites that in the cases of the last two senior appoint-ments Lion made, both successful candidates came from much bigger jobs: 'It was the culture that attracted them, they were simply unhappy in their previous organisations, and being in a positive environment has become an important criteria for success-ful senior executives.'

As the value of the culture became more apparent and the leadership standards more explicit, it became more obvious who did not fit. Several key and very senior leaders left the company during this period. It became clear to both the individuals themselves and Gordon that they just did not belong under the 'What x How' criterion.

These conversations were the most difficult moments of Gordon's cultural journey. He put it like this: 'The socialising ethos made it particularly hard. We were all friends outside work as well as inside the company. I put it off – I wouldn't be human if I hadn't. What I realised was that as we moved up the league ladder, we needed different people. The people who got us from third division to bottom of the first division were not the same ones who could necessarily take us to the very top. This was very difficult for them to accept. They had helped take us to where we had come, and it was heartbreaking to bring them to the realisation that they were not right for the next stage. There are no textbooks to tell you how to do that.' Gordon's clarity about the strategic direction and the requirement for this to be supported by an exceptional culture, gave him the courage to act. It was not a step he was ready to make earlier. In the end, he owed it to the rest of the business to support the path forward. When I asked him what he would do differently if he had his time over, his answer was that he would 'make changes to people who didn't fit sooner. Every time I acted, the organisation said "Why didn't you act sooner? We couldn't understand why you couldn't see it." If we had asked for a list of who didn't fit the values, we would have always received the same names. Not acting jeopardised the clarity of our cultural message. We were saying one thing, but my non-action sent a different message.'

There was a time during this period when the culture was placed at serious risk in one division for quite a long period. Looking back, it seems it was a combination of a new divisional leader and a new HR manager, both hired before the company was as clear as it now is about its recruitment criteria. People in the business believe the culture could have survived one or the other being out of alignment, but not both. This testifies to the strength of the HR role in this particular cultural journey. Fortunately changes were made in time.

Key points in the third stage
- New focus added, achievement, layered on top of existing work, as understanding of the performance benefits culture could deliver increased
- US trip moved the top team up to another level in terms of expectations
- Employment brand strengthened as a means to win the war for talent

Fourth stage 2004 – Market connectivity
That brings us to today, the time of writing.

At a top team workshop I facilitated recently, in a review of the previous few years and the next challenges, the team identified their culture, and Gordon's rigour on performance, as the two most significant contributors to their success. They identified an insufficient focus on customers and the external market as their greatest weakness. The next focus for the Lion Nathan journey is emerging, and it will probably be called market connectivity.

Sean Bowman told me: 'As we have identified market connectedness as the next key organisational capability to develop, we defined what HR's role in that will be. We intend to bring key external signals into the business in a way that everyone will respond to. We have been arrogant in the past. The signals were there, but we did not hear them. HR will play a key role in making the organisation hear them.' Whilst others in the business may be more heavily involved in designing the responses to those signals, HR, because of its understanding and influence of the mind-sets, can ensure the shift happens at the BE-level. This initiative was kicked off at a leaders conference where a range of customers, suppliers and investors were invited to talk to the top 150 leaders about their view of Lion Nathan.

In addition to this, there will be a strong focus on the front line in the next years. For a long time, the culture design team have focussed on the leadership population, and admit that they did not think the work being done there would work for their front line, who are primarily brewery technicians, a blue collar and unionised workforce. In 2003, they took pilots of the achievement programme to this group and received a fantastic response.

Sean Bowman told me: 'We had the view that brewery technicians were different, that they were not ambitious. That view was arrogant. We forgot they are just people like the rest of us, and just as important, they are also leaders. In the same way that other leaders became engaged, the brewery teams are becoming engaged too.'

March 2004 saw the announcement of the new CEO, in a selection process heavily influenced by the leadership competencies work done over previous years.

Gordon's rationale for retiring from the chief executive position, after seven years and aged 54, lines up with the beliefs which underpin the Lion journey. 'I am not the right person to take the next step for Lion Nathan. I believe a CEO's best work is done in the first years. My primary role is to hold up the mirror and make bold decisions. After seven years I have a built a reputation I now want to protect. This is likely to make me risk-averse.'

The team are confident the selection of Rob Murray will build on the cultural achievements. Rob had been spotted a while back through the process of constant market scanning undertaken by the HR team. At the time he was running the local branch of another multinational company. Lion did not have an obvious position for him, and Rob did not want to leave his company except to move into a CEO position. So Lion offered Rob a position on their Board. In this way, they were able to watch him in action for 18 months, and ensure that he fitted in with the culture. They were always aware that an external hire could represent a cultural risk, because despite the best efforts in reference-checking and interviewing, the fit with the culture is never as clear as with an internal candidate. Rob's position on the Board bolstered an already strong internal line-up of candidates for Gordon's position.

Eventually he emerged as the chosen successor.

The timing of the change of CEO enabled the culture journey to reach a point where the values were so strongly embedded, from the Board downwards, that the selection of a CEO became one more activity carried out against the decision-making criteria set by the Achievement Culture. From such a point, the risk many of you may feel, that your culture progress could easily be derailed, is dramatically reduced.

THE PERFORMANCE BENEFITS
Lion Nathan's performance over the past few years speaks for itself. They have outperformed both the Australian stock exchange top 200 and other global brewers.

Core Earnings per Share Compound Annual Growth 2000-2003

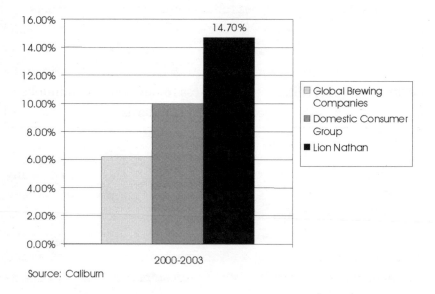

Source: Caliburn

They have admitted to making some important strategic errors, particularly in the years prior to establishing a real achievement drive in their culture. Despite these errors, they have been able to build strong outcomes from the circumstances in which they found themselves, and continue to deliver for their shareholders.

They have become an unquestionable employer of choice, important at a time when the alcohol industry has been under scrutiny in the media because of the damage of alcohol misuse. They have been able to build pride in the company and an understanding of social responsibility that has guided their decision-making. People want to work for this company – job applications are prolific.

They have successfully managed the selection of a new CEO which has ensured support for the in-coming appointment, and in the process are confident their culture and performance success will continue.

They have a culture now which delivers wide business benefits:

Rigour, discipline	Better goal-setting, risk-mitigation, higher confidence in the numbers
One business, teamwork	Best practice sharing, cost efficiencies, improved service
Innovation, learning	Openness to new ideas, continuous lifting of standards
Coaching, encouraging	Improved working environment, 80 per cent internal hires, reduced employee churn

THE PERSONAL BENEFITS

I want to end my description of the Lion Nathan journey by quoting out-going CEO Gordon Cairns:

> I realised that there were right ways to behave in the manner I conducted my life and that I believed I had to do it at work, because work is such a big part of my life. Through this journey I have come to believe that the purpose of life is to find spiritual awakening, to find meaning and to improve as an individual. It has not been about the money. It has been about the opportunity to do something meaningful. What I have learnt about myself on this journey has been much more important than the money. It has been the gift of this process. What I have learnt I can summarise in three ways:
>
> • **'There is value in suffering.'** Parts of the experience have been very painful, parting with friends, looking in the mirror
> • **'The acceptance of responsibility.'** I did not really understand what this meant, and I see many of my peers in the business community seek to avoid it. This process helped me to know

what it really means. I have come to believe that, no matter how big the problem, we can solve it

- **'Dedication to the truth.'** When a mirror was held up and I saw myself from another person's perspective, I came to accept that was the truth. My quest became to change the behaviour that has caused another person to see me that way. How others see me became important to me. I have become a better father, husband and friend because of what I learnt about myself on this journey

His words will echo the sentiments of most people who achieve great things through culture.

16

The Onward Journey

I ANTICIPATE that between 2000 and 2020 there will be tremendous lift in the profile that culture holds. The gap will have widened between those with great cultures and those with cultures that limit their performance and are frustrating and depressing places to work. Those who failed to tackle their cultures soon enough will find themselves falling further and further behind. As the good cultures attract the best people and the best profiles, the poor cultures lose the war for talent and for investment, and thus spiral further into poor performance because their growth capability is limited.

There are many reasons for this conclusion.

COMPARATIVE CULTURE DATA

There is more access now to comparative data regarding good and poor cultures. Global surveys measure many organisations using the same questions, and this data, whilst currently kept confidential, will eventually move into the public domain. In the same way as the consumer movement in the 1960s and '70s provided us with objective comparisons between products, objective comparisons between cultures will be freely available. To date, the media has not comprehensively made these comparisons, and does not compare employee data in the same way as it does financial data or executive salaries. Right now, if I wanted to work for an oil company, for example, I may not have a full range of objective data to tell me which of the top ten companies has the best culture, and will therefore be the most stimulating, fun, empowering and satisfying to work for. That will change.

Imagine if it was public knowledge that people in your organisation were not valued, their opinions not sought, their contribution not valued. Or that 70 per cent of the projects you start, quietly die a death without having delivered their business case benefits. Or that it is standard practice for people in other divisions to undermine the efforts of their colleagues. Or that there are endless meetings, and when people leave the room they go off and do what they want anyway. Who would choose to work there when there is another organisation down the road where the opposite occurs?

MOBILITY OF WORKFORCE

People are moving from organisation to organisation far more than they ever have before. As they move, they compare the experience of working in one organisation to that of another. Those who have marketable talents will refine their choice to include best culture. Those who find themselves in a culture which is frustrating, disempowering and depressing, will up and move to an even greater extent than they do now.

As people move around more, organisations will need to become experts at bringing new people in and helping them to be effective very quickly. In the case of contractors, whole teams of people move in and need to almost instantly be operating at their peak within your environment.

Good, strong, effective cultures send messages the day people arrive about the behaviours they expect. These behaviours are of a very high standard. Good cultures eject people who cannot meet these standards very quickly. They have such momentum that they cannot afford to have this held back by new entrants whose behaviour is defensive, selfish or not based on sound values. Three months is usually about as long as a person like this, who is unable to change, survives in a great culture.

QUALITY OF LIFE WILL INCREASE AS A PRIORITY

Poor cultures take more time to produce the same outcomes. They encourage the macho form of one-upmanship which requires everyone to stay at work later and later to demonstrate that they are committed and performing. They thrive on last-minute changes, on large amounts of effort being put into looking good: beautiful presentations, long documents. They are demanding and insensitive in a way that does not actually contribute to performance, but is rather the response of individuals seeking to fulfil their own needs at the expense of others, without a strong values-based framework within which to behave.

It does amaze me how much people put up with. It is easy to get sucked into this routine, and wake up 20 years later and realise you have dedicated a large chunk of your life to supporting an organisation of this type. I know many leaders stay because they think they can make a difference, and I hope this book will give them some strategies to do this. Others stay because they are concerned they will not find another job. Or because they believe all organisations are the same.

However, there is an emerging trend of people who are deciding this is not good enough. If this trend picks up, then great cultures will be more highly-valued by employees. Those organisations which support an approach to work that enables a higher quality of life both at work and outside of it will be the ones people choose.

INCREASED CULTURAL AWARENESS IN THE BROADER BUSINESS COMMUNITY

There have been some high-profile corporate disasters of late. Media and analysts have been asking questions about how these examples of fraud, high risk-taking, and deception of customers, investors and community can occur within what from the outside look like respectable organisations. Culture is being referenced in post-disaster audit reviews as being the cause of behaviours which have cost large amounts of money, and in some cases brought down the entire organisation.

As this continues, the Boards, analysts and governments will seek to reassure themselves that management is actively managing culture. Whilst current levels of expertise to assess this are not high, this will change. A larger number of specialists will emerge who can assess a culture from the outside, and know the questions to ask to determine whether it is a risk to the company.

There is some debate as to whether when individuals, or teams, within a large organisation behave appallingly, is this an isolated incident, or indicative of a broader cultural defect? I believe over time the business community will become better-educated on culture, and come to the conclusion that good cultures stack the odds very strongly in their favour that such an incident will not occur. That it did happen is a very strong indicator that something similar could occur in another part of the organisation.

A better-educated investment community will conclude that good cultures have a higher probability of delivering a good return, and a lower risk of an unmitigated disaster, than their poor culture cousins. Once this realisation occurs, and is backed by the ability to objectively assess culture from the outside, then organisations with good cultures will be favoured with investment which enables them to grow beyond their competitors.

HEIGHTENED CUSTOMER AWARENESS

Customers have always been on the receiving end of poor cultures. It is almost impossible to consistently deliver good products and services from a poor culture. But most customers would not necessarily make the link between their experience of your organisation, and the culture that sits behind what you deliver to them. As culture becomes high-profile customers will make this link. Particularly in business-to-business relationships, customers will anticipate the experience they will have from those organisations with poor culture brands, and will choose not to take that risk.

Conversely, they will understand better that when they are dealing with an organisation with a great culture, that organisation will be in a better position to anticipate and meet their future needs, whatever they may be, as well as fulfil their promises today.

THE CULTURAL IMPERATIVE

You need to accelerate your culture journey if you want to avoid being branded as having a poor culture in the employment, investment and customer community. It will take you three years to make a real shift, and by that time, public awareness will be much higher than it is right now. The lift in cultural profile will probably result in unrealistic expectations about how quickly a culture can be changed. Unfortunately the way people tick means that there is a rhythm to their changing, as has been described in this book, and that rhythm is remarkably stubborn. What I hope will occur is that leaders will gain more courage to act on culture, and in particular to act on those individuals whose behaviours are holding back progress.

So my message is, get moving and get moving fast!

THE BROADER COMMUNITY BENEFIT

The possibility exists that this push towards better organisational cultures will provide broader community benefits. When people change at the BE-level, described in full in Chapter 7, this change affects the whole of their life. For example if I start to value people more at work, I am likely to take this value into the rest of my life, and value them more at home and in my community as well.

Achievements with culture produce a large group of people who operate from a values-base, and who have learnt how to hold to values at times of pressure when the temptation exists to revert to selfish needs, or to settle for an expedient option. There is tremendous personal satisfaction that comes from doing this. Once experienced, many do not want to revert. In this sense, it is a transformational experience, one from which there is no return.

It is my hope that enough organisations start to operate in this way that their employees make a difference to the level of awareness of the community at large. Values-based leadership is needed in every sphere of life. People who have undertaken a journey of personal development at work, through cultural initiatives, do become more cognisant. They are aware of the behavioural choices they have, and, as their values become stronger, more frequently choose an option which takes into account the good of the whole, not just their own personal needs. Such people make fine leaders.

The techniques that I have described to change an organisational culture can be applied to changing the culture of any group. Every community has a culture which leads those people in it to behave in certain ways. Members of a nation, a group of teenagers, a prison community, a sporting team, a profession, a family, a religious group, all receive messages about how to behave in that group. These messages come from behaviours, symbols and systems. In each case the behavioural role-models will be different, the important symbols different and the systemic levers unique. However, the principles are the same: planning and implementing ways to change the sources of those messages so that new behavioural norms dominate. In every case, it requires a group of leaders who are prepared to walk the talk and invest, in a co-ordinated fashion, in implementing such a plan. So use these techniques in every community in which you play a leadership role.

YOUR OWN JOURNEY

Above all, you will find this to be an experience that changes you. This is the most exciting part. Once you are able to take personal responsibility, live *above the line* and operate both on the balcony and on the dance floor, you will wonder how you were able to function without these skills. You will be able to cause change in the circumstances and the people around you, by changing how you operate. Gandhi called this:

> *Be the change you want to see*

That is walking the talk.

It starts with you. Good luck. If you need assistance, email me at carolyn@axialent.com and I will put you in touch with people who can help.

Further Reading

Collins, J.C., *Good to Great: Why some companies make the leap and others don't*, Random House Business Books, London, 2001.

Collins, J.C. & Porras, J.I., *Built to Last: Successful habits of visionary companies*, Random House Business Books, London, 2000.

Covey, S.R., *Seven Habits of Highly Effective People: Powerful lessons in personal change*, Simon & Schuster, New York, 1989.

Emerson, R.W., *Letters and Social Aims*, University Press of the Pacific, US, 2001.

Gerber, M.E., *The E-Myth Revisited: Why most small businesses don't work and what to do about it*, HarperCollins, London, 1995.

Goleman, D., *Emotional Intelligence*, Bloomsbury, London, 1996.

Heifetz, R.A. & Linsky, M., *Leadership on the Line: Staying alive through the dangers of leading*, Harvard Business School Press, Boston, MA, 2002.

Heskitt, J.L., Sasser Jnr, W.E. & Schlesinger, L.A., *The Service Profit Chain: How leading companies link profit and growth to loyalty, satisfaction and value*, Simon & Schuster Inc., New York, 1997.

Kasser, T., *The High Price of Materialism*, The MIT Press, Cambridge, MA, 2002.

Kotter, J.P. & Heskett, J.L., *Corporate Culture and Performance*, The Free Press, London, 1992

Lombardo, M.M. & Eichinger, R.W., *The Leadership Machine: Architecture to develop leaders for any future*, Lominger Ltd Inc., Minneapolis, MA, 2000.

Longstaff, S., *Hard Cases, Tough Choices*, Pan Macmillan, Sydney, 1997.

Maslow, A. H., *Motivation and Personality*, Harper & Row, New York, 1970.

McClelland, D.C., *The Achieving Society*, The Free Press, London, 1961.

Moss Kanter, R., *The Change Masters: Innovation & Entrepreneurship in the American Corporation*, Simon & Schuster Inc., New York, 1983.

Parks, T., *An Italian Education*, Vintage, London, 2001.

Semler, R., *Maverick: The success story behind the world's most unusual workplace*, Century, London, 1995.

Tichy, N.M. & Sherman S., *Control Your Destiny or Someone Else Will: How Jack Welch is turning General Electric into the world's most competitive organisation*, Bantam Dell Pub Group, New York, 1993

Trompenaars, F., *Riding the Waves of Culture: Understanding cultural diversity in business*, Nicolas Brealey Publishing, London, 1993.

Ulrich, D., *Human Resource Champions: The next agenda for adding value and delivering results*, Harvard Business School Press, Boston, MA, 1997.